Language and Literacy Development in Early Childhood

Language and Literacy Development in Early Childhood provides educators with an integrated approach to language and literacy learning in early childhood. Written by a team of leading academics in the field, it explores how children learn to talk, play using language, become literate and make meaning – from birth through to preschool and the early school years.

Emphasising the importance of imagination, play and the creative arts in language learning, the authors address a wide range of contemporary issues, including digital literacies and Aboriginal and Torres Strait Islander perspectives. Taking a broad and inclusive world view, the book highlights the impact of diverse socioeconomic, language and cultural backgrounds on young children's language and literacy development, and shows how early childhood teachers can effectively partner with parents and caregivers to help children learn through and about language.

The book connects theory and current research to practice by providing case studies, interviews, reflective questions, clear links to the *Early Years Learning Framework* and the *Australian Curriculum*, and a rich array of practical and creative activities for use in early childhood environments. Illuminating and accessible, this is an invaluable resource for pre-service and practising early childhood teachers alike.

Additional resources are available online at www.cambridge.edu.au/academic/ECliteracy.

Robyn Ewing is Professor of Teacher Education and the Arts, Faculty of Education and Social Work at the University of Sydney.

Jon Callow is Senior Lecturer and Director of MTeach Primary, Faculty of Education and Social Work at the University of Sydney.

Kathleen Rushton is Director of Professional Experiences, Faculty of Education and Social Work at the University of Sydney.

Language
& Literacy
Development
in Early
Childhood

Robyn Ewing
Jon Callow &
Kathleen Rushton

CAMBRIDGE
UNIVERSITY PRESS

CAMBRIDGE
UNIVERSITY PRESS

University Printing House, Cambridge CB2 8BS, United Kingdom

One Liberty Plaza, 20th Floor, New York, NY 10006, USA

477 Williamstown Road, Port Melbourne, VIC 3207, Australia

314–321, 3rd Floor, Plot 3, Splendor Forum, Jasola District Centre, New Delhi – 110025, India

79 Anson Road, #06–04/06, Singapore 079906

Cambridge University Press is part of the University of Cambridge.

It furthers the University's mission by disseminating knowledge in the pursuit of education, learning and research at the highest international levels of excellence.

www.cambridge.org
Information on this title: www.cambridge.org/9781107578623

First published 2016 (version 3, October 2018)

Cover designed by Tanya De Silva-McKay
Typeset by Newgen Publishing and Data Services
Printed in Singapore by Markono Print Media Pte Ltd, August 2018

A catalogue record for this publication is available from the British Library

A Cataloguing-in-Publication entry is available from the catalogue of the National Library of Australia at www.nla.gov.au

ISBN 978-1-107-57862-3 Paperback

Additional resources for this publication at www.cambridge.edu.au/academic/ecliteracy

Contents

Contributors

Dr Jon Callow is a Senior Lecturer in the Faculty of Education and Social Work at the University of Sydney and Director of the Master's degree of Teaching Primary Program. Jon is an experienced primary school teacher, academic and literacy educator, having worked in schools, universities and in professional development for teachers in Australia and internationally. His research interests include visual and multimodal literacy, children's literature, student engagement and digital media.

Dr Robyn Ewing is Professor of Teacher Education and the Arts in the Faculty of Education and Social Work at the University of Sydney. She teaches in the areas of curriculum, English, language, literacy and drama, and works with both early childhood and primary undergraduate and postgraduate students. Robyn has worked in partnership with Sydney Theatre Company on the School Drama™ professional learning program since 2009 and is immediate past president of the Australian Literacy Educators' Association.

Dr Kathleen Rushton is Co-Director of Professional Experiences in the Faculty of Education and Social Work at the University of Sydney. She has worked as an English-as-an-additional language teacher and as a literacy consultant for the NSW Department of Education and Training. Her interests include all aspects of language and literacy development, especially engaging with Aboriginal students and students learning English as an additional language.

Chapter contributors

Dr Lisa Kervin (co-author, Chapter 3) is Associate Professor in Language and Literacy in the Faculty of Social Sciences at the University of Wollongong. She is currently involved in research projects funded by the Australian Research Council focused on young children and writing, digital play and the development and implementation of the Australian English Curriculum. Previously She was the NSW State Director of the Australian Literacy Educators' Association from 2008–2015.

Dr Victoria Campbell (co-author, Chapter 9) is Lecturer in Drama and the Creative Arts in the Faculty of Education and Social Work at the University of Sydney. For the past five years she has been a teaching artist for the Sydney Theatre Company's School Drama™ program.

Acknowledgements

We are deeply appreciative of the early childhood teachers and educators who have shared their expertise and insights during our various research projects.

In particular, many thanks to Helen Empacher, Amenah Mourad, Genevieve Lempriere, Lisa Mumm, the Yuin Elders and community and the Little Yuin preschool for sharing their language. Special thanks to the Buultjens, Cusworth, Coffey-Smith and Billett families.

And to all the children who are part of our lives and have taught us so much about language and literacy learning.

The authors and Cambridge University Press would like to thank the following for permission to reproduce material in this book.

Figures 2.1, 2.2, 3.2, 7.1, 7.2, 7.3, 9.1, 12.1, 12.2, 12.3, 12.4: Courtesy Sarah Buultjens; **3.1, 3.3**: Courtesy Lisa Kervin; **4.1**: Courtesy Kathleen Rushton; **4.3, 4.6**: Courtesy Genevieve Lempriere; **4.4**: Courtesy Lisa Mumm; **5.1**: Courtesy Amenah Mourad; **6.1**: *Our Little Yuin* published 2015 by Little Yuin Aboriginal Preschool. Text, design and topography © Little Yuin Aboriginal Preschool Corporation 2015. Images © the children of Little Yuin Preschool, as indicated, 2015; **Pages 86–7**: (water) © Shutterstock.com/Maksym Sokolov, (grass, sea) © Shutterstock.com/Sergej Razvodovskij, (trees) © Shutterstock.com/Hu Hu, (sky) © Shutterstock.com/Episcons, (Bush) © Shutterstock.com/Lucciana; Figures **6.2, 6.3**: Courtesy Helen Emphacher; **8.1, 11.1, 11.2, 11.4**: Designed by Freepik.com; **10.1**: F. Watts and D. Legge (2007) *Parsley Rabbit's Book about Books*. (Sydney: ABC Books for the Australian Broadcasting Corporation. Reproduced with permission from HarperCollins Publishers Australia Pty Ltd; **10.3**: Excerpt from *Fossil* by Bill Thompson, reprinted under a licence arrangement originating with Amazon Publishing, www.apub.com; **10.4**: A. Blabey, *Pearl Barley and Charlie Parsley*, Melbourne: Puffin, 2009. Reproduced with permission by Penguin Australia Pty Ltd.

Every effort has been made to trace and acknowledge copyright. The publisher apologises for any accidental infringement and welcomes information that would redress this situation.

CHAPTER 1

Introduction: The importance of language in our lives

> The surest sign of whether our nation has a soul is whether it cherishes *all* of its children . . . Unless there is serious commitment to upholding *every child's birthright to acquire the educational and personal foundations for a full and satisfying life*, we fail the first test of any civilised community. That involves doing justice by the most vulnerable among us, our children. (Vinson, 2010, p. 73, *our emphasis*).

The central importance of quality early childhood education in a child's first eight years in shaping his or her future chances in life has not always been given the attention it deserves in western societies. This book aims to develop our understanding, knowledge and skills about the language and literacy development of young children. As Ruqaiya Hasan (1991) so eloquently reminded us almost three decades ago, our language and literacy is integral to who we are and how we make our way in the world. There is no question that all children have the right to be cherished and supported as they learn to make sense of their worlds and communicate with others. It is of great concern to us that it is often the children who are in the most vulnerable circumstances who are deprived of rich and educative language and literacy experiences and opportunities.

Grounded in current language and literacy research and practice, this book represents our serious commitment to the need for every child to have the best opportunities to develop rich language and literacy skills to equip them for the complexities of 21st-century living. The book begins with an exploration of how children learn how to make sense of their world, how to mean and, in doing so, how they learn to talk as a precursor to learning to be literate. The impact of diverse socioeconomic, ethnic, language and cultural backgrounds on young children's identity, language and literacy learning is also highlighted. As *Belonging, Being and Becoming: The Early Years Learning Framework* (2009, p. 13) reminds us:

> There are many ways of living, being and knowing. Children are born *belonging* to a culture, which is not only influenced by traditional practices, heritage and ancestral

knowledge, but by the experiences, values and beliefs of individual families and communities. Respecting diversity means within the curriculum valuing and reflecting the practices, values and beliefs of families.

This book honours the many and often complex histories, cultures and languages of families reflected in their different stories, traditions and lifestyles. It acknowledges the diverse ways of knowing, being and becoming in the world today and at the same time the uniqueness of every child.

A number of principles, premises and themes that we believe are critical to language development and learning underpin this book. These include:

- enabling children to learn and develop their language(s) and literacy skills which should be a partnership with parents and caregivers wherever possible – trusting relationships are central!
- enhancing and encouraging the ongoing development of children's already rich imaginations, inherent creativity and problem-solving skills
- embedding creative arts processes (including drawing, painting, designing, dancing, dramatising, singing and making music) will enhance language and literacy learning
- providing access to children's literature and authentic informative texts in all their forms should be a cornerstone of every early childhood context/setting (and indeed across every level of education)
- offering adequate time and resources to play represents 'serious work' for young children and is essential for language development and literacy learning
- giving children multiple opportunities to explore a broad and inclusive world view will help them reflect on how the diversity of cultures and approaches enrich our lives
- developing dispositions such as empathy, flexibility, confidence and resilience will help children flourish in a world of ever-accelerating change, conflicts and dilemmas
- applying productive learning methods where children are engaged and motivated and having fun
- liberating literacy methods from the idea that it is a single global skill acquired once in a lifetime using a 'one size fits all' instructional recipe. ALL children must be able to engage in, understand and analyse an ever-increasing range of ways to apply multiple communication modes.

We have written this book explicitly for early childhood teachers and caregivers as well as interested parents and family members. It includes a range of scenarios and vignettes drawn from our research and based on authentic individual or composite experiences. The included language experiences, strategies and activities focus on the needs of children ranging from birth to eight years of age in a diverse range of early childhood (home, long daycare, preschool, playgroup, family daycare and Foundation to Year 2 – F–2 – school) contexts and settings. The book closely aligns with Australia's first national early years framework for early childhood educators – the *Early Years Learning Framework* (EYLF, 2009; available at www.education.gov.au/early-years-learning-framework) and the *Australian Curriculum* (available at www.australiancurriculum.edu.au). The EYLF particularly emphasises play-based learning and the importance of communication and language. It aims to provide a framework that will ensure all children can be assured of the best start in life. *The Shape of the Australian Curriculum* (Australian Curriculum, Assessment and Reporting Authority, 2010, p. 16) states that the general capability of literacy involves: 'listening to, reading, viewing, speaking, writing and creating oral, print, visual and digital texts, and using and modifying language for different purposes in a range of contexts.' Literacy therefore is critical across all key learning areas and must be understood and developed alongside the other curriculum capabilities (numeracy, information and communication technology, critical and creative thinking, personal and social capability, ethical understanding and intercultural understanding) and the cross-cultural priorities of Aboriginal and Torres Strait Islander histories and cultures, Asia and Australia's engagement with Asia and sustainability.

The chapters are sequenced so that the book intentionally starts with language learning in the earliest years. They explore key theoretical ideas about how young children begin to make meaning from the moment they are born as they learn to talk, listen and interact with those around them. Subsequent chapters present the pedagogical knowledge required to guide young children's learning of language and literacy practices. These chapters explore a number of important areas, including Aboriginal perspectives, the role of quality literature in teaching reading, understanding words and images in picture books, the value of storytelling and writing as well as digital literacies for young children. Within each chapter, informal, scaffolded and more formal experiences appropriate for early years contexts are included together with helpful resources for the early literacy classroom.

We have particularly focused on examples from the Australian context but have referenced pertinent international research and we believe the book is certainly relevant for international audiences. Where possible the book briefly considers some of the relevant histories and controversies that have dominated language and literacy learning over our years in the field. All chapters, however, provide educators with easy access to a range of experiences, materials, media, as well as places to question and reflect. Key concepts are defined and are supported by suggested further reading and references. It is not necessary to read the book in a linear fashion: the reader is invited to read particular chapters that are of interest to them in whatever order. Many of the theoretical principles are relevant more broadly, and suggested experiences and activities can be easily adapted for older age groups.

Enabling young children to have the time, resources and, where appropriate, the scaffolding (explained in Chapter 2) and explicit teaching, to engage in imaginative play, exploration, storying, creating, questioning, reflecting as they come to understand multiple ways of meaning-making is one of the most important gifts adults can provide. We hope this book contributes to providing that gift for children.

Further reading

Australian Curriculum, Assessment and Reporting Authority, ACARA, (2010). *The Shape of the Australian Curriculum*. (Version 2.0). Retrieved from: www.acara.edu.au/verve/_resources/shape_of_the_Australian _Curriculum.pdf.

Australian Curriculum, Assessment and Reporting Authority, (2015). *The Australian Curriculum*. Retrieved from: www.acara.edu.au/curriculum/ curriculum.html.

Australian Government, Department of Education, Employment and Workplace Relations for the Council of Australian Governments, (2009). *Belonging, Being and Becoming: The Early Years Learning Framework for Australia (EYLF)* Canberra: Commonwealth of Australia. Retrieved from: www.mychild.gov.au.

EYLF (2009)—see Australian Government Department of Education, Employment and Workplace Relations for the Council of Australian Governments (2009).

Hasan, R. (1991). Questions as a mode of learning in everyday talk. In T. Le & M. McCausland (eds), *Language Development: Interaction and Development*. Launceston: University of Tasmania, pp. 70–115.

Vinson, T. (2010). The social context of literacy acquisition. In F. Christie & A. Simpson (eds), *Literacy and Social Responsibility*. New York: Equinox.

CHAPTER 2

Learning how to mean: Dimensions of early language development

This chapter explores the wonderful way that young children start to make meaning of their worlds, understand their environment and communicate with others from the very moment they are born. It initially and briefly discusses the nonverbal ways that babies and toddlers use to communicate their feelings and needs before they learn to talk and then explores the early development of language in those critical three years. It provides a snapshot of several theories about language learning and explains why a sociocultural approach can help us understand how children learn their mother tongue and the implications for parents, caregivers and educators. It also reflects on how learning the mother tongue helps children learn how to become part of a particular culture and community.

Anticipated outcomes for the chapter

After working through this chapter you should be able to:

- discuss the way young children begin to make meaning of their world from birth
- recognise that learning language means learning about culture and community
- understand how babies and toddlers begin to communicate their feelings nonverbally
- appreciate the importance of the first three yeas of life in the early development of a child's language
- explain the implications of a sociocultural approach to language learning for parents, caregivers and teachers.

SCENARIO: A NEW BABY

The birth of a child is a wondrous occasion and there are many different cultural and religious traditions and rituals associated with welcoming a baby into the world.

New baby Samuel has arrived safely and is warmly welcomed by his proud parents and extended family. From the very moment of Samuel's birth, his parents and all of those who meet him talk to him as if he understands everything they say. Samuel is already a meaning-maker: he is immediately part of the conversations as if he can respond to each comment. This seems to be a common practice in many cultures. In Australia the initial conversation might include the following kinds of comments:

Welcome little one!

I can see ten tiny fingers and ten tiny toes.

Aren't you a beautiful boy?

Look you have your father's dimple on your chin and your mother's tiny ears . . .

Let's wrap you up so you're nice and warm.

Are you ready for a bath?

Samuel is on a lifelong journey to make sense of who he is in the world around him although his first three years will be critical for his *language* development. Whether there will be a naming ceremony, a baptism, christening or blessing, a circumcision, a feast or whether he will be confined to home for the first 40 days of his life, Samuel's parents have already begun to share the power of words with him.

Figure 2.1 A first-time grandmother and her new grandson communicate with each other just hours after his birth

Introduction

Last year there were nearly 300,000 babies born in Australia, which is one of the most diverse nations in the world. According to the 2011 census almost 75% of Australian families also identify with an ancestry other than Australian and 2.5% of the Australian population identify as indigenous (Australian Bureau of Statistics, 2015). Since the end of World War II nearly 750,000 refugees have been resettled from Eastern Europe, Asia, Central America and the Middle East and Africa. Today Australians speak over 200 languages and nearly 61,000 Australians speak one of 50 indigenous languages. The most popular languages other than English include Chinese, Italian, Greek and Arabic.

Have you ever wondered what your life would be like without language? As humans we use language to organise, describe and represent ourselves and our worlds. Words become an integral part of who we are. We use language to ask for what we need, to think about and make sense of events that happen to us and to others, to speculate and ask questions and to dream about new possibilities. Once we learn to talk it seems that words are always with us. Language shapes our thought just as our thoughts rely on language. Whether thought precedes language or language comes first is an age-old debate – a 'chicken or egg' issue!

Babies are born as curious and creative beings, intuitively sociable and immediately 'seeking affectionate relations with companions' (Trevarthen & Delafield-Butt, 2014, p. 3). From the outset they are ready to experiment and are keen to make sense of the world around them. They begin to communicate with their parents, caregivers and extended families as soon as they arrive in the world. Most babies, toddlers and young children who grow up in a language-rich and stimulating interactive environment seem to learn to talk effortlessly. And, despite being the most complex learning a child will do, learning to talk seems to happen naturally for most children, without any formal teaching.

This chapter introduces some key features of language learning in the first few years of life. Many of these features are elaborated in subsequent chapters. It also discusses how learning language is at the same time about learning to be in any culture. Three aspects of learning language are embedded in this discussion: learning our first language (or mother tongue) as distinct from learning another language; learning *through* language; and learning *about* language. The importance of the way we talk to babies and young children and treat them as meaning makers using rich language is also explored.

What enables learning of our first language?

There are physical, environmental and social dimensions of learning to talk as the child's brain and body develop at a rapid pace in those first months and years. It is important to note from the outset that the child is innately social with the capacity and desire to engage with and learn from interaction with others.

SCENARIO: ROSINA

First-time mother Rosina underlines this immediate shared communication when she speaks of the eye contact and exchange of meaning she remembers as her baby daughter was delivered:

> When my doctor put her on my stomach, her beautiful blue eyes looked directly into my eyes. They were quite piercing actually and seemed to say 'I'm here! We have a lifetime ahead of us.' And I remember feeling that we had just shared a very powerful moment. I will never forget it.

Rosina's assertion is controversial. While there are more research studies that demonstrate that a fetus can recognise his or her mother's voice (Nagy, 2011) and that newborns can respond to the expressions of others and imitate these within minutes of their birth (such as Meltzoff & Moore, 1997; Trevarthen & Delafield-Butt, 2014), these findings conflict with older and more established beliefs that infants cannot be so aware of others at such an early age.

Neuroscientific research regularly and frequently helps develop more understanding of how the brain works. The detailed timed observations made possible by increasingly sensitive recording technology have also been extremely important in developing our understanding of language learning both in utero and in that first year after birth. Trevarthen and Delafield-Butt (2014), however, trace our understanding of the making of shared meaning to the work of psychologist James Baldwin in the 1890s. Baldwin observed what he described as the repetitive or circular movements that babies made. Babies repeat movements of their arms and legs, head and eyes many times. Similarly they touch things over and over again and vocalise the same sounds repeatedly (1894). A Russian neurophysiologist, Nikolai Bernstein theorised that the brain assembles or synthesises the different components of an action into a mental image or pattern. These repetitive, circular motor actions or 'embodied movements' (Trevarthen & Delafield-Butt, 2014, p. 1) develop into repetitive cognitive processes or **schema** as the child grows and develops. A movement or a thought tends to be repeated and, when successful, is retained and further developed with variations over time.

Schema A pattern of thinking or cognitive structure that helps us represent or organise an idea or relationship or way of doing something.

Close study of video recordings of newborns have demonstrated that they try to imitate simple vocal sounds in those early hours of being in the world. They may even repeat their imitation to provoke another response from the adult (Nagy & Molnar, 2004). Babies quickly grow adept at signalling their feelings and needs and, soon after, their intentions to their family and caregivers and, later, to the growing community they move within. Their desire to engage through movement to respond to the playful attentions of others is called 'languaging' (Maturana et al., 1995). They will soon smile when spoken to and make cooing noises to indicate pleasure. Some parents are able to discern different ways their child cries to communicate their different needs. Right from the beginning then, young children will listen and respond to talk, to changes in tone and rhythm and any expressive accompanying facial expressions or hand movements. The caregiver should take every opportunity to respond through expressive gestures, words, singing and play. Such shared exchanges or **protoconversations** 'nourish the infant's vitality and imagination' (Trevarthen & Delafield-Butt, 2013) and are an early foundation for a child's future self-confidence.

> **Protoconversations** An interaction or exchange between a baby and a parent, caregiver or older child where meaning is communicated before the baby starts talking. It will be comprised of gestures, sounds and words.

Learning to talk

Just as blind and deaf Helen Keller coined this phrase when learning the sign for water for the first time in 1936, young children discover with delight that 'everything has a name'. They very quickly learn thousands of words and their meanings and, as Cassirer (1944) suggested, this marks their desire to understand and make sense of their world. It seems miraculous to those of us who observe their insatiable enthusiasm for learning. Parents and caregivers thus have an enormous responsibility to nurture this curiosity.

Interestingly, despite their place of birth, most babies develop language in a similar way. The process moves from recognising that crying will attract attention to stringing sounds together (babbling—'nannannannan') from about three or four months old. At about the same time they will laugh and show enjoyment in ritual fingerplays, action songs and dances (for example, 'Round and Round the Garden Like a Teddy Bear'; 'Liangzhi Laohu' (Mandarin, 'Two Big Tigers'); 'All the Children Sing'; 'San Ttoki' (Korean, Mountain Rabbit); 'Open Shut Them, Open Shut Them'; 'Hokey Pokey'; 'Punchinello'). They will be able to follow the instructions for these games, clap their hands on demand and ask questions through gestures. Games like peekaboo will also be fun with the child gradually taking more initiative and responsibility for the playing of the game.

Renowned linguist Michael Halliday's work on children's development of **protolanguage** shows clearly that children are very deliberate meaning makers at this time in their development. He closely studied the development of his own child, Nigel, and demonstrated that by about nine months he had developed protolanguage, a set of simple gestures with sounds

> **Protolanguage** A set of sounds that are usually accompanied by a gesture that a young child puts together to represent the beginning of learning to talk.

to help him make meaning with close family members. Because a child's parents, siblings and caregivers know the child so well, the tones used in these sound-and-gesture combinations make sense and they can discern whether the child is asking for something, interacting with them socially, questioning, imagining or informing. Halliday's book *Learning How to Mean* (1975) is an important landmark for our understanding of how young children learn the 'meaning-potential' of words.

Protolanguage is discussed further in Chapter 4. Many children are beginning to learn individual words alongside their protolanguage, usually 'mumma' and 'dadda' (interestingly there are lots of similarities in these words across many languages but sounds not featured in a particular language tend to fade away in the child's repertoire). By about 18 months of age, two- and three-word sentences are frequent (such as 'Ronnie Donald!' as the child points to the well known symbolic 'golden arches' or 'More ice-cream, Mummy?' as the child holds up their bowl.)

During the second year, a child will learn and understand the meaning of lots of words. They will be able to name and demonstrate parts of the body and everyday things like 'shoes' and 'juice'. From about thirty months onward, there seems to be what has been described as an explosion of words. Many of these words become questions about what, why and how things work. They begin to have conversational exchanges, mastering the idea of turn-taking in these interactions. With growing confidence some children will provide a running commentary of what they are seeing and doing at every moment: 'Look at me! I'm flying!' 'There's a ment-mixer'. By three years of age, most children can tell a story, especially if it is co-narrated with another person supporting them.

There are a number of useful websites that provide helpful sequences that can be a guide for the **speech** and language milestones progress that most young children will make in learning their mother tongue over the first three to five years. See The Australian Parenting Website as an example. It is important, however, to remember that the approximate age assigned to every set of milestones is only indicative and that each child is unique. Each journey into language brings its own experiences. Each language itself has its own nuances.

Speech Talking through the coordination of our tongues, lips, jaw, lungs and voice box to produce recognisable sounds.

Similarly, young children also come to terms with how **grammar** works in their mother tongue almost effortlessly. They seem to absorb word order and how to string words together. The next section will discuss this in more detail.

Grammar A set of rules about a particular language.

The relationship between meaning and language structure

Developing an understanding of how a language is structured, its rules or grammar, also seems to happen easily for most children from about the age of two. Grammatical principles in some languages are very complex yet children grasp things like word order and the use of different kinds of clauses quite quickly. Often children will apply a grammatical rule logically to find there is an exception ('We goed to the zoo'; 'I bringed my teddy'). They also demonstrate their creativity in inventing new constructions ('I'm all by my own'). There is much discussion about how quickly children learn the lexico-grammatical complexities of their mother tongue). Theories of language learning derive from behaviourist, innatist and social constructivist foundations and are briefly defined below.

In his book *Verbal Behaviour* (1957) well-known behaviourist B. F. Skinner, theorised that children's language development could be explained by environmental learning. He believed that using the behaviourist principles of modelling and reinforcement, a child would gradually build a vocabulary. For example, when a child correctly pronounced a word or sentence he or she would be positively reinforced with a parent or caregiver's approval.

In stark contrast, Noam Chomsky's cognitive view published in 1959 asserted that all humans are born with an innate mechanism to enable them to learn language. This became known as a Language Acquisition Device (LAD). Chomsky argued that this device is activated by the child when they are listening to others talk. He asserts that this is why children's understanding of grammar develops so quickly.

In 1970 a thirteen-year-old girl later known as 'Genie' was found after her mother sought help. She had been confined to a room for most of her life, often tied to a potty chair and was malnourished. She had been isolated and abused by her parents for her whole life. Researchers keen to test the nature-versus-nurture dilemma worked with her over several years but found that while Genie initially was able to learn a number of isolated words, she did not progress with learning grammar beyond three word sentences. Genie's experience, and other examples of children raised in isolation, has led to a belief that there are critical phases for learning language and that interaction between the environment and the child's cognitive capacity is central to the development of language.

While both behaviourist and cognitive theories of language development can explain some aspects of the process, neither can adequately explain the sophistication that young children display with the learning of the language rules or grammar in such a short time. Children do not only repeat what they hear or imitate what is modelled in their home, childcare centre or playgroup. They experiment and play with language and create their own words. Other theorists including Jean Piaget and Lev Vygotsky describe an interactive language-development process that involves both social and cognitive processes. Vygotsky explained that children internalise what they have enacted externally: 'Every function in the child's cultural development appears twice, first on the social level and then on the individual level, first between people (interpsychological) and then inside the child (intrapsychological)' (1978, p. 57). He also proposed that children move from self-talk, or speaking to themselves, to guide and direct their actions. Initially this happens aloud and later is internalised as they become more proficient in a particular area.

The importance of social interaction in language development

Vygotsky (1978, 1962) viewed a child's external speech as the precursor to self-talk or private speech and then thought. He postulated a Zone of Proximal Development

(ZPD) which emphasised the importance of parent–child communication. In Vygotsky's own words:

> What we call the Zone of Proximal Development . . . is a distance between the actual developmental level determined by individual problem solving and the level of development as determined through problem solving under guidance or in collaboration with more capable peers. (1978, p. 86)

Vygotsky's notion of a ZPD was extended by other researchers including Wood, Bruner and Ross (1976) and Bruner (1990). They used the term 'scaffolding' as a metaphor for the temporary role played by a parent or a more experienced peer or educator in providing intellectual support. Just as a building under construction needs the help of scaffolding, a child who is learning to talk is scaffolded by an adult or older child. Moll and Whitmore (1993) stress that it is the *quality* of cooperation between the child and the adult (our emphasis), requiring a mutual trust and active involvement that is central to the scaffolding process. The ZPD should be conceived of as being mutually and actively created by the child and the adult, and the ensuing collaborative dialogue can be seen as joint problem solving. We would go further and suggest that it is an opportunity for all involved to build knowledge and understanding (Swain, 2000, p. 113).

Scenario 3 illustrates this collaborative dialogue between a grandfather and his four-year-old grandson and demonstrates the grandfather's gentle scaffolding.

SCENARIO: WHAT IS 'REAL'?

Xerxes, aged 4, had listened to the longtime favourite story of *The Velveteen Rabbit* (Williams, first published in 1922 and still in print) where the concept of what is 'real' was introduced to him. The following conversation is based on how Granpa retold it later.

Xerxes and Granpa were watching the television program *Bananas in Pyjamas*.

Xerxes (indicating the cartoon B1 and B2 characters on the TV): Granpa, are the Bananas real?

Granpa: Well, do you think they're real?

Xerxes: I don't know.

Granpa: No, they're not real. They're cartoon characters on the television.

Silence

Xerxes (indicating his Gruffalo toy): Is Gruffalo real?

Granpa: Can you hold Gruffalo? Can you throw him on the floor?

Xerxes: Yes.

Granpa: Yes, Gruffalo is real . . . but he's not alive.

Silence

Xerxes: Granpa, what's 'alive'?

Granpa: Well, you can hold Gruffalo? He's real.

Xerxes: Yes.

Granpa: Can he talk? Eat? Wee and poo?

Xerxes: No.

Granpa: Can you talk and eat and wee?

Xerxes (emphatically): Yeah!!

Granpa: Is Gruffalo alive like you?

Xerxes (laughing): NO!!

Granpa: Gruffalo is real but he's not alive.

REFLECTION

In this conversation, Granpa does not immediately give Xerxes all the answers. Instead he asks him both closed and open-ended questions to ascertain what he knows. He helps Xerxes develop an understanding of the difficult concepts of 'real' and 'alive' using his own experiences. He then scaffolds the discussion to help Xerxes build his own knowledge and understanding about being real and alive. After that discussion Granpa and Xerxes had further 'real' and 'alive' conversations. It soon became a game in which Xerxes would laughingly hold up various items and ask Granpa whether they were real or alive.

In *The Meaning Makers* (2009) Gordon Wells published his findings from a large study conducted in Bristol in the early 1980s. Many children's conversations with adults and peers were recorded in their everyday contexts. His findings emphasise the importance of such close listening and responding by adults to children's questions in helping them extend their development of reasoning and reflective capacities.

Think about other questions Granpa could have used to help Xerxes answer his question.

It will be extremely valuable to engage in extended conversations with young children in your early learning centre or preschool. You could record your conversation and listen to the way you responded to the child and extended their understandings.

Learning language: Learning culture

Language A set of shared rules allowing the expression of ideas that make sense orally or through writing, signing or gesture. It comprises vocabulary, grammar and discourse.

Vocabulary The words a person has stored in long-term memory.

It is clear, however, that listening and responding to young children, asking questions, wondering together and sharing experiences enriches their **language** and is critical for their future life chances. A number of studies have shown that ignoring the young child's constant questions or putting children in front of the television and hoping that the presenter will engage them does not build their **vocabulary** or conversation skills. In fact some studies (such as Hart & Risley, 2003) have demonstrated the huge numerical differences in language experiences that children from different educational and socioeconomic contexts would typically have and how that impacts on their future learning. Linguists and educators have drawn on many other disciplines including anthropology, sociology and psychology to understand the intricate and complex relationship between language and culture. The anthropologist Bronisław Malinowski researched traditional cultures in the Trobriand Islands off the coast of New Guinea during World War I, and demonstrated how different cultures using different kinds of language systems and structures actually envisage reality differently (1922).

Restricted codes Ways of speaking that are highly specific to a particular context.

Elaborated codes Use of more formal language so that the meaning is less dependent on a particular context.

Discourse When using spoken or written language to exchange ideas, literacy researcher James Gee talks about it as 'discourse' (small 'd') (1996). He uses Discourse (with a capital 'D') to refer to the combination of language and other social practices like behaviour, dress and customs within a specific group as a way of being in that particular world. We may belong to a number of different Discourses.

Sociologist Basil Bernstein's work on **restricted** and **elaborated** codes (1970s–1990s) is central to understanding the different kinds of language **discourses** that all children need to access and understand so that they can interact meaningfully across many different contexts and situations. He suggests that we all need to be able to use language appropriately for different purposes. Most families and small communities develop highly context-specific ways of knowing, understanding and speaking that are special to that family or group. They often include specific vocabulary and references that are sometimes not easily translatable outside the family or small community. Children's early attempts at particular words and phrases (for example, *here I is*) may become absorbed into the family's everyday vernacular. Slang or colloquialisms are also examples of, in Bernstein's words, these kinds of 'restricted codes' or ways of speaking that are highly specific (and appropriate) to one family or sub-cultural group's particular context. Children who are exposed to a wide variety of codes and discourses grow to understand the different purposes for which language is used. They become adept at using these codes appropriately and often without thinking about them. Children who have not experienced this range of discourses may use words inappropriately. Over time, children need to learn that the highly contextualised codes of families and peer groups may not always be appropriate in more formal contexts and their talk needs to be more elaborated in broader contexts. School can be one example of a more 'elaborated code'.

Similarly, Shirley Brice Heath's landmark ethnographic study *Ways with Words* (1983) powerfully illustrates the different cultural expectations that young children bring to school due to their different orientations to language and literacy, despite living in the same geographical area in one North Carolina town. Her stories about families from three different cultural groups (Trackton, Roadville and Maintown) and their language practices demonstrate that some children start school with a broader understanding of literacies and their many purposes in the wider community. Each group of parents had loved and nurtured their children, and shared their cultural experiences. They all wanted their children to do well at school. Some of the children's backgrounds, and orientations to story, language and literacy had already given them a privilege by better preparing them for the challenges and expectations of schooling.

In Australia, Geoff Williams' (1998) research on mothers reading with their four year olds across ten different socioeconomic groups in Sydney during the early 1990s resonates strongly with Heath's findings. In Williams' study, transcripts of mothers from differently advantaged areas across Sydney reading with their four-year-old preschoolers were analysed. Those mothers from well-educated, highly advantaged backgrounds prepared their children more effectively for the reading experiences that would be part of their schooling. They linked the child's own life experiences with those in the story being shared. They asked the child pertinent, often open-ended, questions and encouraged the child to display their own knowledge and understandings about the story. Less educated and advantaged mothers often read more to 'settle' the child before bedtime or because they knew it was a valuable thing to do. Reading sessions were less interactive and more often characterised by the child being read to. There was little questioning or explanations evident in these reading experiences. These children were less prepared for the school reading sessions they would experience the following year. This was not because they were less able or that the bedtime stories read to them were not valuable; rather, it was due to the type of social behaviours expected in our middle-class schooling that value and build upon particular reading and literacy practices not experienced by all children.

SCENARIO: WELLBEING STUDIES AND LEARNING

Growing up in Australia: The Longitudinal Study of Australian Children is a large and ambitious study following 10,000 Australian children (some from birth; some from four or five years old) and their families. It investigates the contribution children's social, economic and cultural environments make to their adjustment and wellbeing (Australian Institute of Family Studies, 2015). Alongside the study, The Australian Broadcasting Commission (ABC) has produced the television program, *Life Series*, that documents the stories of eleven of these families and it looks at issues such as personality, resilience, school readiness, creativity and stress. It draws marked contrasts between the different needs, interests, personality traits and abilities of these children. It would be valuable to watch this series of documentaries and reflect on the different orientations to learning that are developing for children from different backgrounds.

In your view, which children will be more comfortable and successful with the language and practices of the school? It is important not to think of any of these children's experiences as deficit: they represent different experiences and understandings, and the early childhood educator must be aware of these differences.

Supporting children's language development in the early years

In 1988 well-known Australian literacy researcher Brian Cambourne suggested eight conditions that parents, caregivers and teachers often unconsciously provide to enable children's oral language development. He later offered them as a model that should be used in other literacy learning situations – and more generally as a model for learning (Cambourne et al., 1988). We have extended them below as a summary of how children's language development needs to be supported in their early years. Subsequent chapters build on and extend these principles.

1. *Immerse* children in a *playful* and *language-rich* environment to surround children with talk, story, song, dance and interesting books to encourage them to develop a love of language.

Figure 2.2 Immersing children in a language-rich environment

2. *Model* active listening techniques and engage in talking, reading and writing activities for authentic purposes. For example, ask questions you genuinely want to know about, read a story that you really enjoy; make a shopping list

together so you don't forget what you need; check the ingredients and method for your favourite recipe.

3. *Engage* children actively in experimenting with language in a risk-free environment where they feel comfortable to make mistakes.

4. *Provide* children with opportunities to succeed and have high expectations for success.

5. *Give* children choices about stories to tell and books to read. Set up the environment to promote self-direction. Provide easy access to books and literacy materials on low shelves and in baskets, and show children how to take care of them.

6. *Accept* children's approximations (Play *wego; we have ouch other; my lellow raincoat*) when they are learning to talk, read and write. Congratulate them on their accomplishments. Guide them gently into accuracy and soon they will begin to self-correct.

7. *Create* a climate for functional and meaningful uses of oral and written language. Encourage children to read along with you, help you write notes, letters, and lists, and engage in lots of conversations.

8. *Listen* and *respond* to children, welcome their comments and questions, and extend their use of oral and written language. Celebrate the enormous language and literacy learning that is occurring daily!

REFLECTION

What implications for home, early learning and childcare centres, and preschools can you draw from these conditions for effective language learning?

Drawing it all together

Children from all language backgrounds and cultural groups are born with the capacity and desire to communicate with others. From birth most children actively seek to make meaning in the world around them. The role of the trusted adult or older child is critical in the child's development of language. The majority of children will learn to talk with seeming effortleslness if they are provided with rich and interactive language experiences with others. Many of the principles underpinning the creation of such a rich environment have been discussed briefly in this chapter and will be explored in more depth in subsequent chapters.

Questions for further discussion

- There are many ways of celebrating the arrival of a baby into the world. What cultural rituals do you think are particularly important?

- What do you think about the age-old debate regarding the relationship between thought and language?
- What do you find most interesting about the way children develop language?
- You suspect a child's language may be delayed. What steps might you take to investigate this concern?

Further reading

Halliday, M. (1975). *Learning How to Mean*. London: Edward Arnold.

Trevarthen, C. & Delafield-Butt, J. (2014). The infant's creative vitality, in projects of self-discovery and shared meaning: how they anticipate school and make it fruitful. In S. Robson & S. Flannery Quinn (eds), *Routledge International Handbook of Young Children's Thinking and Understanding*. Oxford: Routledge, pp. 3–18.

Vygotsky, L. (1978). *Mind in Society: The Development of Higher Psychological Processes*. (Trans. M. Cole). Cambridge, MA: Harvard University Press.

Useful websites

Australian Parenting Website, Raising Children Network.
http://raisingchildren.net.au/articles/language_development.html

Learning English through rhymes.
https://learnenglishkids.britishcouncil.org/en/parents/articles/learning-english-through-sharing-rhymes

References

Australian Bureau of Statistics (2015). Retrieved at: www.abs.gov.au/websitebs/censushome.nsf/home/data, viewed 1 August 2015.

Australian Institute of Family Studies (n.d.) Growing Up in Australia: The Australian Longitudinal Study. Retrieved at: www.growingupinaustralia.gov.au, viewed 1 July 2015.

Baldwin, J. (1894). *Mental Development of the Child and the Race*. New York: Macmillan.

Bernstein, B. (1990). *Class, Codes and Control: Volume 4 – The Structuring of Pedagogic Discourse*. London: Routledge.

Bruner, J. (1990). *Acts of Meaning.* Cambridge, MA: Harvard University Press.

Cambourne, B., Handy, L. & Scown, P. (1988). *The Whole Story: Natural Learning and the Acquisition of Literacy in the Classroom.* Auckland: Ashton Scholastic.

Cassirer, E. (1944). The concept of group and the theory of perception. *Philosophy and Phemonological Research* (1), pp. 1–36.

Chomsky N. (1959). Review of Skinner's *Verbal Behavior. Language,* 1959, 35, pp. 26–58.

Gee, J. P. (1996). *Social linguistics and literacies: Ideology in discourses* (2nd edn). London: Taylor & Francis.

Halliday, M. (1979). One child's protolanguage. In M. Bullowa (ed.) *Before Speech: The Beginning of Human Communication.* London: Cambridge University Press, pp. 171–90.

Hart, B. & Risley, T. (2003). The early catastrophe: The 30 million word gap by age 3. *American Educator,* Spring.

Heath, S. B. (1983). *Ways With Words: Language, Life, and Work in Communities and Classrooms.* New York: Cambridge University Press.

Malinowski, B. (1922). *Argonauts of the Western Pacific: An Account of Native Enterprise and Adventure in the Archipelagoes of Melanesian New Guinea.* London: Routledge and Kegan Paul.

Maturana, H., Mpodozis, J. & Letelier, J. (1995). Brain, language and the origin of human mental functions. *Biological Research,* 28, pp. 15–26.

Meltzoff A. N. & Moore M. K. (1997). Explaining facial imitation: a theoretical model. *Early Development and Parenting,* 6, pp. 179–92.

Moll, L. & Whitmore, K. (1993). Vygotsky in classroom practice: Moving from individual transmission to social transaction. In E. A. Forman, N. Minick & C. Stone (eds), *Contexts for Learning: Sociocultural Dynamics in Children's Development.* New York: Oxford University Press.

Nagy, E. (2011). The newborn infant: A missing stage in developmental psychology. *Infant and Child Development,* 20(1), pp. 3–19.

Nagy, E. & Molnar, P. (2004). *Homo imitans* or *Homo provocansi?* The phenomenon of neonatal initiation. *Infant Behaviour and Development,* 27, pp. 57–63.

Piaget, J. (1962). *Play, Dreams and Imitation in Childhood.* London: Routledge & Kagan Paul.

Skinner, B. F. (1957). *Verbal behaviour.* Acton, MA: Copley Publishing Group.

Swain, M. (2000). The output hypothesis and beyond: Mediating acquisition through collaborative dialogue. In J. P. Lantolf (ed.), *Sociocultural Theory and Second Language Learning.* Oxford: Oxford University Press, pp. 99–116.

Trevarthen, C. & Delafield-Butt, J. (2013). Biology of shared meaning and language development: Regulating the life of narratives. In M. Legerstee, D. Haley and M. Bornstein (eds), *The Infant Mind: Origins of the Social Brain*. New York: Guildford Press, pp. 167–99.

—— (2014). The infant's creative vitality, in projects of self-discovery and shared meaning: how they anticipate school, and make it fruitful. In S. Robson and S. Quinn (eds), *International Handbook of Young Children's Thinking and Understanding*. Oxford: Routledge, pp. 3–18.

Vygotsky, L. S. (1962). *Thought and Language*. Cambridge MA: MIT Press.

—— (1978). *Mind in Society: The Development of Higher Psychological Processes*. Cambridge, MA: Harvard University Press.

Wells, G. (2009). *The Meaning Makers: Learning to Talk and Talking to Learn* (2nd edn). Bristol: Multilingual Press.

Williams, G. (1998). Children entering literate worlds. Perspectives from the study of textual practices. In F. Christie and R. Misson (eds) *Literacy and Schooling*. London: Routledge, pp. 18–46.

Williams, M. (1922). *The Velveteen Rabbit*. New York: HarperCollins.

Wood, D., Bruner, J. & Ross, G. (1976). The role of tutoring in problem-solving. *Journal of Child Psychology and Psychiatry* 79(2), pp. 89–100.

CHAPTER 3

Playing with language: Imaginative play, language development and technology

This chapter has been co-authored with Lisa Kervin, University of Wollongong. It considers the importance of building on children's innate creativity and imagination. This aspect will be discussed alongside the role of imaginative play in language and literacy development. The relationship between traditional play and digital play as a new way of playing with language is also explored.

Anticipated outcomes for the chapter

After working through this chapter you should be able to:

- discuss the importance of creativity and imagination in the lives of all young children
- understand the critical role that imaginative play can and should play in language and literacy development
- consider the relationship between traditional forms of imaginative play and digital play
- begin to understand the role of digital play in fostering creativity and language development
- reflect on popular culture's effect on imaginative play and language learning.

SCENARIO: ALIENS

Two eight-year-old boys with a collection of sticks are in the playground. They are on their hands and knees, sorting the sticks and arranging them on the concrete. On closer inspection, it is apparent that the sticks are being used to compose a message: 'aliens are coming tomorrow'. After conversing with the children it is revealed that 'aliens' is a game the children have invented. It isn't a game that is played daily; the stick message on the playground serves as an advertisement to other children that the game will be played the following day. The children share that they don't really know what will happen in the game, it will depend on who comes to play, how much time they have and the part of the playground where they are able to play.

Creativity There are many definitions of creativity and you may like to do some research around the concept. As a beginning, you might think about creativity as being able to act on an idea that is new to you. Dimensions of creativity include not only the imaginative idea or process – they also include the ability to persevere to see something through, to collaborate with others and to problem solve.

Play A universal definition is elusive but we suggest it transcends the concept of recreation. It involves moving spontaneously outside constraints or boundaries to explore an object or concept more flexibly or creatively so the object or concept can be understood and enjoyed in new ways.

Imaginative play Building on the experience for children to explore, experiment, act out, role play engage, represent and make sense of their worlds.

Figure 3.1 Announcing 'Aliens coming tomorrow'

This scenario reveals how complex creativity and collaborative young children's play can be. It also underlines that they should be given playful spaces and places to make their own decisions about imaginative play. It is important to be aware of children's rhythms of play and respect their control of this rhythm, and how the design of physical spaces and the manipulation of artefacts within this can affect the development of play.

Introduction

Chapter 2 began the discussion about the interrelationship of play, imagination and language development and it also referred to the importance of the arts in children's learning (see Ewing, 2010). Chapter 9 particularly focuses on the role of story and storytelling in language learning. As discussed in the book's Introduction, Australia's *Early Years Learning Framework* (EYLF, 2009) places a strong emphasis on play-based learning and the importance of imaginative play:

> Play provides opportunities for children to learn as they discover, create, improvise and imagine. When children play with other children they create social groups, test out ideas, challenge each other's thinking and build new understandings. (p. 5)

We firmly believe that play should be an integral part of both children's and adults' lives. Children use play to make sense of their world, their relationships and those of adults and older children around them. Play is a universal experience: children in every cultural group engage in playful activities (Gosso, 2010). At the same time, play is culture-specific (Brown, 2012). Young children playing with tiny worry dolls in Guatemala to help put their worries aside and sleep more easily, the incorporation of singing, music and clapping in some children's playtimes, imitating adult spear throwing by young Papua New Guinean boys are broad examples of how children incorporate their culture's relationships and adult world of work in their play. At the same time the increasing saturation of many children's lives with electronic and digital technologies has also led to a 'shared world of popular media culture' (Arthur, Beecher & Diaz, 2013, p. 68). Given the frequency of English in some popular media culture they are also becoming what Saltmarsh (2009) suggests is a 'communicative currency,' even for bilingual children.

As Fox (1993) has long argued, serious work happens when we play. Some theorists have classified play (for example, Hughes, 1996) into different types although, in our view, they are often interrelated. This chapter focuses on imaginative play and considers its importance in building on children's innate creativity and imagination when developing language and literacies. It also considers the role and responsibilities of early childhood educators in scaffolding children's playful activities.

Creativity is a word used to mean many different things. We include in our concept of creativity: the openness and inventiveness typical of the children described in the scenarios in this chapter; receptivity to new ideas or new ways of doing things, imagination, and expressiveness (Hoyt, 2002, p. 3). It is closely related to being able to relate to, collaborate and communicate with others. Vygotsky challenged more conservative opinions of creativity being restricted to an elite view. He argued that 'whenever a person imagines, combines, alters, and creates something new' a creative act occurs (Vygotsky, 1978, p. 10).

This chapter also explores the newest kind of play: **digital play**. It particularly highlights the interrelationships between embodied and digital play and the real world through a number of scenarios and reflections.

Digital play The playful use of digital technologies.

Play

Children have the right to play. The United Nations Convention on the Rights of the Child (1989) is a legally-binding international agreement that sets out the civil, political, economic, social and cultural rights of every child, regardless of their race, religion or abilities. Article 31 of this convention states that:

- Every child has the right to rest and leisure, to engage in play and recreational activities appropriate to the age of the child and to participate freely in cultural life and the arts.
- Member governments shall respect and promote the right of the child to participate fully in cultural and artistic life and shall encourage the provision of appropriate and equal opportunities for cultural, artistic, recreational and leisure activity.

We believe the rights embodied in Article 31 are central to childhood itself. The opportunity for children to play contributes to the pleasure of exploring the world and making sense of the important people in their lives and, ultimately, of growing up. Furthermore, play contributes to children's development, not only as individuals, but also as caring members of their community as they become aware of the perspectives of others, and develop capabilities in cooperation and conflict management.

Not all children are given the time and opportunity to play. Sadly child labour is still alive and well in some parts of the world. A number of debates about the purpose of play in early childhood also continue. For example, Wardle (1996) claims that some bureaucrats, parents and politicians have viewed play as a waste of time while others regard it as the very important 'work' children need to do (Sutton-Smith, 2009). An organisation called the Childhood Alliance (www.allianceforchildhood.eu) argues that play must be restored to early years education (for example, Miller & Almon, 2009). Over time, a body of research evidence unequivocally demonstrates that play is indeed integral to the development of a child both affectively and intellectually. Children want to play, and they are endlessly resourceful in finding opportunities to do so (Genishi & Dyson, 2009). As such, 'play spills into the processes of learning language and literacy and becomes the inevitable ingredient of child-worthy curriculum' (Genishi & Dyson, 2009, p. 145).

For example, through play, children experience and make connections with their environment. Imagine a child at a park who comes across something they have not seen before – perhaps it is ants busily moving on a patch of concrete, or some bark that has come off a tree. They stop and look, they smell and poke, sometimes taste. Before long the bark has become a hat or the child has begun to move like an ant while simultaneously talking to the tiny creatures. Children are able to make observations, activate their senses, manipulate and explore **artefacts** they find and bring these into their play contexts. This play often moves into the subsequent interests of the child; for example, they might enjoy books about ants, seek out popular culture representations of ants and may even express an aspiration of becoming an entomologist. When children play, they do not follow a script. At first, they will play on their own and later engage in parallel play where they will play alongside another child but not together. Over time they may sometimes take an interest in what the other child is doing. Later this will develop into group play.

Artefact A handmade object or artwork.

Corsaro (2003), a childhood sociologist, identifies play as a socially complex communicative act as children determine how they can use and manipulate objects, how they can play with others, how they can experiment with their voices and their bodies. Their language abilities develop remarkably quickly as they play independently and with adults or each other to create a representation of their understanding of the world.

Imaginative play is a major influence for cognitive growth. Theorists such as Piaget and Vygotsky stress the importance of imaginative play. Piaget (1962) identified imaginative play as one of the purest forms of symbolic thought available to a young child. Vygotsky (1978) recognised that when children are free to experiment and explore new possibilities they are working in their zone of proximal development; that is, they are operating at a little above or beyond their usual capabilities. Consider a scenario where an educator has just shared a fairytale with a group of children. These children excitedly begin playing at being princes and princesses. They might move to the dress-up box to find a shiny cloak to wear or something that can be worn as a crown. The children imagine a situation worthy of princes and princesses and create rules around the royal play as it emerges. While they may be influenced by what they heard in the fairytale, the children work out how they are going to play princes and princesses while playing the roles. They make decisions about who the characters will be, who will take on those roles, what will happen and how the characters will respond to this event. They interact with each other and negotiate for how long they will play the game. The children actively create the play scenario as it emerges.

In this example, the children have conceived an imaginative play situation and through this activity they have invented roles. By acting out these roles, opportunities for the children to engage in problem solving present themselves. These children are demonstrating what they know about the scenario and, in the process, they are operating at a higher level by demonstrating more complex knowledge than they might have done by discussing the fairytale alone.

Play can also enhance children's social development. Playful social interchange can begin from birth (as in the scenario capturing Rosina's interactions with her baby daughter and the early protoconversations described in Chapter 2). Imaginative play enables children to take on roles they observe within their community. These roles may represent important people in their lives (for example, a parent, grandparent or older sibling), in the community (for example, a firefighter or doctor), a character from a book or from popular culture (for example, characters from a television program). Regardless of the role, children who are putting themselves in someone else's place are developing feelings of empathy and learning to consider others. Play teaches children about the social world. It provides opportunities to explore different contexts, rehearse social skills and learn about acceptable peer behaviour firsthand. With age and experience, children's awareness of peers playing around them increases. This leads to more interactions between children and collaborative play.

The artefacts or toys that children choose to play with are important. We define these as contextual materials and resources available to a child. It is through toys and artefacts that children make sense of their world, which is critical to their development. Dyson (1997) examined the stories children created, focusing in particular on how they used superheroes and characters drawn from the media. This research found that children can use these characters to help them translate images of power and gender into their own worlds. The choices children made in relation to toys and the ways they chose to interact with these toys, revealed how complex this decision making is, but also how these interactions can help children deal with the contradictory pressures of growing up in contemporary society.

When children are in environments where they are encouraged to follow their interests, experiment and feel valued, amazing things can happen.

REFLECTION

Observe a child immersed in imaginative play. What artefacts are they using? Listen to the conversation. What kinds of understandings is the child developing in this instance? Is there a way you could get involved to extend the conversation? How could you support the scenario being developed?

Fostering language development through imaginative play

SCENARIO: ANASTASIA

Three-year-old Anastasia has, like countless other children, male and female, very much enjoyed the movie *Frozen*, a film based very loosely on Hans Christian Anderson's *Snow Queen*. She frequently engages in sustained dramatic play around the events in the story, improvising and enjoying being Elsa. Well ahead of her fourth birthday she requested a *Frozen* party and her likeminded guests enthusiastically joined her in dressing up as one of the characters, re-enacting and innovating on some of their favourite moments including singing the theme song 'Let it go'.

REFLECTION

This scenario could attract criticism for reinforcing stereotypes and dominant gender discourses. While it may reflect many children's current and longstanding fascination with both traditional and contemporary stories, the constant advertising of related merchandise may further reinforce this particular popular rendition of the traditional narrative. It is important to think about whether popular culture should be integrated into the curriculum in early childhood contexts. Including such texts in the early childhood centre and classroom acknowledges its presence in children's worlds. At the same time it enables teachers and caregivers to discuss these texts with children, encourage dramatic play and alternative story and character constructions. Suggesting other possibilities and ways of looking at the world can help children develop a critical perspective and respect their agency and decision-making (Arthur, Beecher & Diaz, 2013; Vasquez, 2014). Can you think of some questions you might ask Anastasia about Princess Elsa or the story itself?

Popular culture Mainstream cultural ideas, attitudes and images that are often influenced by mass media.

Children's language development is stimulated through imaginative play with words. Children enjoy playing with their voices and manipulating individual words, names, rhymes, songs, nonsense syllables and jingles while telling stories and reading together. Sometimes they will invent their own words and phrases. For example, when five-year-old Timmy and three-year-old Jordy are rumbling or tickling each other, they have invented the word *treeytree* when ready to start and *babjeebanj* as code for 'stop'. Other times they adapt words they already know to make sense of new terms *gentle froth* for dental floss; *verandah* flowers for ranunculus. They will delight in repeating favourite words and phrases or using words in a different way: *We've got our eyes peeled for yellow cement mixers nannie.*

Many well-known picture books are built on children's love for rhythm and rhyme. Consider Father Bear's refrain *I can't stand this!* in Jill Murphy's *Peace at Last* or 'Cooee' in Libby Gleeson's *Amy and Louis*. The critical role quality literature can play is discussed in detail in Chapter 5. As children interact with different play contexts, they adopt the language of what it is that they are doing. For example, a child who has a favourite picture book often brings the language of that book into their play. A class of kindergarten children who had enjoyed *Farmer Duck* (Waddell and Oxenbury, 1991) would quack in different ways to indicate their enjoyment or fatigue or boredom when their teacher asked them: *How goes the work?* They were mirroring the language of this picture book but applying it to their own classroom activities.

From a young age, many children have a favourite story (or even a collection of stories). These texts play an important role in language skill development and are often brought into play scenarios. Reading these books provides children with the opportunity for frequent, sensitively tuned, language-rich interactions that draw them into conversations about books, the world, language and concepts (Dickinson et al., 2012). Reading and talking about books helps to foster language and literacy as it requires children to be active and respond interactively about the meanings of the text and the connections they make to it.

Imaginative play fosters the development of language skills (for example, Vygotsky, 1978, Meek, 1982; Hill, 2011; Gussin Paley, 2004). There is extensive research about the role of dramatic play in the lives of young children (for example, Dunn & Stinson, 2011; Ewing, 2012). Imaginative play encourages language development as children

Figure 3.2 Dressing up can be an important part of dramatic play

set up the play context, negotiate roles and interact in their respective roles. Adults support language by joining in the play ('May I have a ride in your new car please?'), encouraging and commenting on children's play ('I see you are driving that car', 'That's a big blue painting you're making!'). Such comments reinforce concepts and build on the play context. Such verbal interactions from significant others provide a language-rich environment that encourages play while at the same time honouring children's agency and actions.

Play is a vehicle for expressing feelings. Language is tied to emotions, which are expressed and explored through imaginative play. The opportunity to 'pretend' gives children the freedom to address feelings, anxieties and fears. Through imaginative play, children recreate and modify experiences to their liking. They foster a sense of comprehension, control, and mastery (Schaefer, 1999). After reading *Storm Boy* Timmy and Jordy re-enacted Thiele's ending before creating two alternative endings they preferred to Mr Percival's death. When their mother commented that the pelican's death may have been too sad, Jordy commented that this was his favourite part of the story, which was not because of his death; it was because of its exploration. Timmy reminded her of some of the final words of the book: *Birds like Mr Percival never really die.*

Introducing a new kind of play: Digital play

SCENARIO: AIDAN

Five-year-old Aidan was enjoying his first season of playing cricket. The focus of his cricket program was on learning the skills of batting, bowling and fielding. Aidan spent the summer in front of the television during test matches and one-day games with his cricket bat in hand. He watched the movements of the batsmen and during the replays he simulated their movements in front of the screen using the bat to mimic the angles, the swipes and the elated jumping as a sign of success! As he engaged in these movements, he began to use the language of the commentary — he talked about the need to transfer weight between his feet, while swinging the bat through the line of delivery, following through with the swing, and keeping his head still in the line of the ball. For Aidan, this experience brought him closer to his dream – to represent Australia in cricket!

| Aidan prepares to bat | Aidan rehearses his swing, mimicking a successful play | Aidan supports the partnership with the run count | Aidan celebrates with his team mates |

Figure 3.3 Mimicking cricketers' moves while watching television

REFLECTION

Early childhood has been concerned with issues of 'screen time' for some time. While technology (computers, mobile devices and game consoles) are rapidly becoming available in many children's homes, ongoing debate continues about how (and whether) digital technologies can fit in the lives of young children (Verenikina & Kervin, 2011). The arguments for and against young people's use of digital technologies in education and entertainment appear to be concerned with the quality of children's experiences with digital technologies and the value of such experiences for their physical, cognitive and socioemotional development (Plowman, McPake & Stephen, 2010). Referring back to the the Aidan scenario, Owen and others who are cricket fans know the hours it takes to view a cricket match (those who are not fans would also know the hours it takes for a match to finish and regular television programming to resume!).

Did the hours Aidan spent in front of the television with his cricket bat become a sedentary activity? Or did this time serve as a playful opportunity for Aidan to creatively use technology to help him get closer to his dream of becoming an elite cricketer? What were the language opportunities that emerged from this experience?

In 2007 early education researcher and author Lisa Guernsey presented us with the 'Three Cs' to consider when thinking about children and screen-viewing time. They are also relevant considerations in the provision of other playful opportunities for children:

1. Content
    Any digital media should expand children's access to new information, experiences and areas of interest to them. It is important that adults scaffold the different skill levels, knowledge development, and opportunities for playful learning and creativity.
2. Context
    Digital play should not happen in isolation. A child will have a more meaningful experience when using digital devices when they engage with the device while interacting with significant others (both adults and peers). Children should not be passive consumers; it is better when they can interact in a way that allows them to create new content.
3. The Child
    When making decisions about having access to digital play, the age, developmental level, needs, interests and abilities of each child need to be carefully considered. The opportunity for digital play should provide the child with a valuable and worthwhile experience.

Play has assumed new guises, structures and contexts with the expansion of technology. The distinctions among forms of technology, and what these mean for the content and the user, has been blurred by multi-touch screens and movement-activated technologies that detect and respond to the child's movements. While we agree that we need to be wary of time children spend on passive, non-interactive technologies and screen media, we would also like to propose that parents and early childhood educators need to be open to a reconceptualisation of screen time when considering the multiple kinds of devices available (such as mobile devices) to young children, and also the playful opportunities they offer.

The interrelationship between digital and more traditional forms of play

There appears to be disjunction between warnings of the toxic effects of technology and the uptake of technologies in the lives of young children (Plowman et al., 2010). This then requires us to rethink an either/or approach for digital play and more traditional forms of play as we move the conversation to consider how it is that these can work together. Play involving digital technologies is becoming more complex as children at play are finding synergies between online/offline and digital/non-digital activities (Burke & Marsh, 2013; Marsh & Bishop, 2014; Kervin et al., 2015). An increasing number of young children have access to technology and are using it for leisure from a very young age. Davies (2009) identified 'many new technologies provide routes to playful activities' (p. 31). Children's access to mobile media devices (such as tablets) continues to increase. The label 'Net Generation' is sometimes used to describe children of this time – a distinct generation with inherent and spontaneous ability to navigate the digital world, who learn to communicate, work, shop and play in profoundly new ways, are incredibly technically aware and leave their parents far behind in the adoption and use of new technology. While we may agree or disagree with this label, the reality is that this 'digital play' is playing a considerable role in the lives of many young children.

This is the first time, in a very long time, that children have had such a different kind of play to engage with. Participation in onscreen and offscreen spaces provides opportunity for children to communicate their ideas and understandings in new, interesting and different ways (Vasquez & Felderman, 2014). As children negotiate digital play, they negotiate a range of technological literacies (for example, the device and how to interact with it, what application or software program to use) and a range of content and activities (for example, specific applications) that all compete for their attention. When talking about computer play, Salonius-Pasternak and Gelfond (2005) said that this is potentially 'the first qualitatively different form of play that has been introduced in at least several hundred years,' and 'it merits an especially careful examination of its role in the lives of children' (p. 6). A decade later and we see the increased access many young children have to mobile devices (such as tablets and iPads), and we need to continue to examine the role of digital play in the lives of young children. Applications (apps) for these devices are often more affordable for families, they have the capacity to be frequently and easily updated and devices often house a range of different apps that have been downloaded. This means that decisions need to be made about which apps children play with, how long they spend with that app and other issues about managing children's access to the complex digital environment. Marsh and colleagues (Marsh et al., 2015) found that 'apps can promote play and creativity in a wide range of ways, subject to the design of the app and the individual child's preferences' (p. 31). What is critical though, is considered and judicious choice and use around the apps children use. All screen interactions are not created equal (Kervin, 2016).

SCENARIO: OWEN

Four-year-old Owen was enjoying the Toca app 'Hair Salon Me'. In this app he was able to run a hair salon as he cut, coloured and styled the hair of the six clients built into the app. Alternatively he was able to take and use photographs to create new clients. His parents described to us that he photographed himself and family members, and was observed to frequently spend time 'doing' their hair. His father shared the story where he was to take Owen and his brothers to the hairdresser to get their hair cut. Owen asked if he could take the iPad with them. His father thought this was to occupy him while he was waiting for his turn, and he agreed. Imagine Owen's father's surprise (and that of the hairdresser) when Owen produced the iPad to demonstrate to his hairdresser how it was that he wanted his hair done!

There is an increasing body of research depicting children as active rather than passive users of technology (eg. Plowman et al., 2010; Verenikina & Kervin, 2011). In this example, we see the connections that Owen was able to make between his digital play and a real-world activity that his family were participating in. He took on a powerful agentive role through his digital play, as he enacted the processes of the hairdressing profession. This empowered him to be able to enter into the professional discourse as he asserted his own needs and desires.

The technological world and all that it offers to play can support children's development. Fine motor skills, language skills and social skills can be supported through digital play. Merchant (2014) identified the gestures that are needed to interact with apps, including taps, swipes, drag and drop, tilting and occasional blowing.

SCENARIO: ANITA

This scenario builds on the earlier conversation in this chapter about imaginative picture books. Eight-year-old Anita uses the Aurasma app to catalogue much-loved picture books in her home. Aurasma is an augmented reality app that uses image-recognition technology to recognise real-world images and then overlay rich media on top of them in the form of animations, videos, 3D models and web pages. Using the book covers as the real-world images, she held the iPad over the book to activate the rich media she had collected for the books. This media included a video excerpt of her reading a sample of the text aloud connected to the front cover. The back cover was connected to an audio book review where she interviewed a family member about the book. An interview Anita conducted with three-year-old Iris about the picture book *Pete the Cat* follows.

Anita: What's the story about?

Iris: Pete the Cat was walking down the street in his brand new white shoes and he stepped in lots of different things.

Anita: What was your favourite part?

Iris: Blueberries. And I like to eat them.

Anita: What is your favourite colour?

Iris: Green.

Anita: How could you change the story so Pete the Cat gets green shoes?

Iris: He could step in avocado? Or green grapes?

Anita: Is this a book you would like other children to read?

Iris: [Nods] Because some people like it and I like it too.

This transcript shows how Iris was able to summarise a large amount of information to retell the story. She was able to make connections for herself by identifying her own favourite colour and innovate on the text by providing another scenario to contribute to the story. Iris was also able to evaluate the story with her recommendation for others to read the book too. Anita used the digital catalogues she created to transform the family's picture book collection into a library. The family could use the iPad to activate the rich media she had collected to help them select a book to read.

The social interaction inherent in Iris and Anita's activities has enriched their language and literacy development. These two children established a play context focused on a text and then collaborated to create a response to the text. While Anita took the lead, there was the need to negotiate roles and coordinate actions. The opportunity to take on roles and negotiate the activity within these, provided opportunity for the children to engage in social play where Iris in particular practised more advanced linguistic forms that she likely used in other interactions. This provides an example of the insight that children are more likely to use more complex language when they play than when they do not. Play with adults and peers enhances language development because it encourages greater and more complex language uses (Hart & Risley, 1995).

Play, technology and social interaction

Opportunities for play provide contexts for social interactions for young children. Marsh and colleagues (Marsh et al., 2015) reported that parents actively engage with their children's use of the tablet, although the extent to which they did this differed in terms of the time of day and the child's purpose for using the tablet. Interactions appeared to be most prevalent when children were learning to use new apps or engaging in educational uses of the tablet. Through social interactions children begin to establish a sense of who they are and ways to communicate with others. Drawing upon established work (for example, Borke, 1971) we know that children from a young age communicate with significant others (such as through gestures and vocal sounds). There is typically a sequence of interactions, as an action or gesture is continually modelled and as the child takes control of these interactions he needs less modelling and support. For young children, these interactions occur primarily within the family.

Hart and Risley's (1995) important work showed the benefit of conversational partners. Our understanding of 'talk' has changed. It is not simply a matter of some children being showered with vocabulary and others not: it is the opportunity to engage in conversation with significant others that matters. We know too that certain speech activities have internal structure or predictable routines. From an early age children show awareness of the framework of a telephone conversation – for example, giving a greeting, exchange or farewell.

Videotelephony technologies through apps such as Skype or FaceTime allow for spoken interaction without being physically face-to-face. These apps redefine the contact young children have with 'significant others' and expands the availability of conversational partners. Using a broadband connection and a device with a microphone and a camera facility, these apps allow for inexpensive local and international interactions between individuals or groups.

SCENARIO: THE MUKHERJEE FAMILY

The Mukherjee family, who recently emigrated to Australia from England with their three children (aged eight, seven and five) shared with us the importance of these communication apps for the children to remain in regular contact with extended family, particularly their grandparents. Using the FaceTime app, these children were able to share stories about life in Australia as they moved the iPad so their relatives could see the view from what the children focused the camera on. This view from the iPad included specific items for conversation including beach scenes, sporting activities, demonstrations of proficiency with reading aloud and glimpses of the weather from the window. Likewise, the children were able to reconnect with familiar English experiences as their grandparents showed them favourite meals being cooked, photographs in the local newspaper, and the development of garden beds the children had helped plant.

This example shows how technology became the mediator for playful social interaction. In this case, a family was separated by physical distance but felt the presence of each other through their interaction with the technology, and sharing of experiences and artefacts. The ability to control images shared across devices enables individuals to interact with others who are outside the immediate environment. Being able to show and see artefacts visually while explaining them in conversation connects those within the experience to places, times and reciprocal relationships. The talk that emerges from these interactions can become richer and more extended (Pahl & Rowsell, 2010) as children's social skills develop. With increasing confidence they demonstrate greater willingness to interact with their environment.

REFLECTION

Consider the role of non-passive digital technologies for social interaction. Is it making a big difference that children can Skype/FaceTime with significant others? What are the speech structures that exist in these exchanges? What is the role of artefacts in these exchanges?

Play-based pedagogy for language learning

Play is certainly complex with multifaceted dimensions. Throughout this chapter, we have argued the importance of imaginative play and the need to ensure children have opportunities to engage with a range of play contexts. When children engage in imaginative play they make decisions about their actions and negotiate interactions with others. For example, they decide what to do first, and then they carry out their intentional actions while at the same time monitoring how others are participating in the situation. Young children often say what is happening, thereby demonstrating their developing language skills as they listen and use instructions, and explore new vocabulary associated with the play context. Through these processes, children actively build their vocabulary by transferring what they hear and observe in their environment in creative ways.

In ensuring that imaginative play is an important part of the children's daily experiences, we need to acknowledge play as a valuable way to learn language, but also to teach language and literacy. In doing so, a 'pedagogy of play' may be employed in everyday practice. Through such an approach, we are able to articulate the purposes and nature of play in the various contexts young children engage with. We are able to explore the role of adults in planning for play and taking part in playfulness in child-initiated or teacher-directed activities to support children's language development.

To do this, we draw upon research from Siraj-Blatchford (2009) who shared a model of pedagogic progression in play (p. 82) and through this identified different playful activities that support major developmental phases for children. Emphasised in these playful activities, is the role of playful collaborations between peers and adults (the 'significant others'). In what follows we identify two playful activities we believe are critical for imaginative play as we examine the play context and opportunities for language and literacy learning.

Playful activity

Communication with significant others

Earlier in this chapter we examined the importance of social interactions and conversational partners with significant others. It is through communication with significant others that children become confident and competent language users as they develop their understanding of text, image and symbols in a range of real-world contexts. Aidan demonstrated the important communication the cricket commentators gave him in terms of learning technique. Talking about a play activity enables many levels of relating between the players – from taking on a role, to providing a model, scaffold or extension to the experience. Throughout this chapter we have provided examples of communication in digital and non-digital contexts.

Shared experiences with significant others are powerful communicative acts which can lead to language learning. Many of the scenarios we pose in this chapter demonstrate the importance and value of interactions with others. Think back to the scenario shared about the Mukherjee family; these interactions provided valuable opportunities for the children to engage in conversation with their grandparents. Anita and Iris showed us the conversations that can happen in relation to text. Opportunities for children to engage in play contexts where talking, reading and creating text feature, support language development. Quality literature, music, rhymes, puppets and digital applications are powerful resources that can encourage communication with significant others.

Artefact-centred joint activity

Throughout this chapter we have shown how engagement with different artefacts can stimulate and promote children's language use. Children's interactions with artefacts in pretend play, and object substitution demonstrate their understanding of their perceived and actual properties. These understandings determine their possible uses, including how they are understood and used by the child, what challenges they present and how they might be used (Carr, 2000). The artefacts that are available are therefore important, as is how children use them and the ways children use existing knowledge, expertise and skills in these interactions. Play resources and activities have different affordances and potential for flexibility, especially where children have the freedom to make their own novel combinations and transformations. By affordances, we mean human–computer interaction to indicate possible actions of a particular object. Digital technologies have brought additional dimensions and affordance to familiar objects and activities such as learning familiar trades (such as hairdressing), practising specific skills (such as in cricket) and communicating with significant others from a distance, to name a few. There is an exchange between peers when interacting with shared artefacts as children move from parallel play to increasingly acknowledge (and accept) the perspectives of others.

As children engage in play activities, they are able to transform ideas, artefacts, textural resources, actions and behaviour from one thing into something else, thereby creating new knowledge, different meanings and unique interpretations.

Educators play a powerful role in using playful pedagogical approaches in adult- and child-initiated play contexts. In doing this, educators empower children as they are engaged on their terms while respecting their interests and world views. Opportunities to engage with playful activities create an environment where intended learning outcomes are combined with the possible outcomes that emerge from children's interests, engagement and participation.

REFLECTION

There are complex relationships between different kinds of play and children's learning. Early childhood educators need to carefully consider their role in play: it is not a matter of simply providing the space and resources, and observing what young children do at play. How should we conceptualise play-based curriculum? What role can pedagogy play in extending children's thinking?

Drawing it all together

Given the importance of imaginative play in the lives of young children, parents, caregivers and early childhood educators must be proactive in respectfully nurturing and scaffolding imaginative play opportunities. This chapter also illustrates that how we understand space, time and imaginative play have been altered by technology. Digital play can foster creativity, spontaneity and enormous potential for learning. New technologies provide new opportunities for children to play through the devices but also the range of content (through software and applications) that are available to them. Technology can extend play rather than usurp play and can provide opportunities that facilitate children developing new ways of being, playing, communicating, thinking and knowing.

Questions for further discussion

Spend some time perusing the range of digital apps that are available for young children (perhaps you might do a search for recommended apps or look at an app store). Choose an app designed for young children (four- to eight-year-olds) that encourages playful literate activities.

- Can you describe the literate activities promoted in this app? (Consider whether there are opportunities for talking, listening, reading/viewing, writing/composing.)
- Are there opportunities for children to explore, imagine and problem solve? Will it maintain their interest? How?
- Does the app reflect and build on what the children already know?
- Does the app involve many senses and include sound, music and voice?
- Is the app open-ended, with the child in control of the pace and the path?
- What opportunities for interaction does the app promote?

Further reading

Arthur, L., Beecher, B. & Diaz, C. (2013). Utilising popular culture to extend children's literacy. In L. Arthur, J. Aston, B. Beecher (eds), *Diverse Literacies in Early Childhood: A Social Justice Approach*. Melbourne: ACER, pp. 65–85.

Ewing, R. (2010). *The Arts and Australian Education: Realising Potential*. AER 58. Melbourne: ACER.

—— (2012). Imaginative play in the lives of young children. In R. Ewing (ed.), *The Creative Arts in the Lives of Young Children: Play, Imagination, Learning*. Melbourne: ACER.

Gussin Paley, V. (2004). *A Child's Work. The Importance of Imaginary Play*. Chicago: University of Chicago Press.

Kervin, L. (to be published February 2016). Powerful and playful literacy learning with digital technologies. *Australian Journal of Language and Literacy*.

References

Alliance for Childhood (n.d.) www.allianceforchildhood.eu

Australian Government Department of Education, Employment and Workplace Relations for the Council of Australian Governments, (2009). *Belonging, Being and Becoming: The Early Years Learning Framework for Australia (EYLF)*. Canberra: Commonwealth of Australia. Retrieved at: www.mychild.gov.au/agenda/early-years-framework.

Borke, H. (1971). Interpersonal perception of young children: Egocentrism or empathy? *Developmental psychology*, 5(2), p. 263.

Brown, F. (2012). The play behaviours of Roma children in Transylvania. *International Journal of Play*, 1, pp. 64–74.

Burke, A. & Marsh, J. (eds) (2013). *Children's Virtual Play Worlds: Culture, Learning and Participation*. New York: Peter Lang.

Carr, M. (2000). Technological affordance, social practice and learning narratives in an early childhood setting. *International Journal of Technology and Design Education*, 10(1), pp. 61–80.

Corsaro, W. A. (2003). *We're Friends, Right?: Inside Kids' Culture*. Washington, DC: Joseph Henry Press.

Davies, J. (2009). A space for play: crossing boundaries and learning onscreen. In V. Carrington & M. Robinson (eds), *Digital Literacies: Social Learning and Classroom practices*. LA: SAGE, pp. 27–42.

Dickinson, D. K., Griffith, J. A., Golinkoff, R. M. & Hirsh-Pasek, K. (2012). How reading books fosters language development around the world. *Child Development Research*, 2012.

Dunn, J. & Stinson, M. (2011). Dramatic play and drama in the early years: Reimagining the approach. In S. Wright (ed.), *Children, Meaning-Making and the Arts* (2nd edn). Sydney: Pearson/Prentice-Hall, pp. 115–34.

Dyson, A. H. (1997). *Writing Superheroes: Contemporary Childhood, Popular Culture, and Classroom Literacy*. New York: Teachers College Press.

EYLF (2009) – see Australian Government Department of Education, Employment and Workplace Relations for the Council of Australian Governments, (2009).

Fox, C. (1993). *At the Very Edge of the Forest. The Influence of Literature on Storytelling by Children*. London: Cassell.

Genishi, C. & Dyson, A. H. (2009). *Children, Language, and Literacy: Diverse Learners in Diverse Times*. New York: Teachers College Press.

Gosso, Y. (2010). Play in different cultures. In P. Smith (ed.), *Children at Play*. West Sussex, UK: Wiley Blackwell, pp. 80–98.

Guernsey, L. (2007). *Into the Minds of Babes: How Screen Time Affects Children from Birth to Age Five*. New York: Basic Books.

Hart, B. & Risley, T. R. (1995). *Meaningful Differences in the Everyday Experience of Young American Children*. Baltimore, MD: Paul H Brookes Publishing.

Hill, S. (2011). *Developing Early Literacy: Assessment and Teaching* (2nd edn). Melbourne: Eleanor Curtain.

Hoyt, D. (2002). *Some Thoughts on Selecting IDEA Objectives*. Manhattan, KS: The IDEA Center. Accessed at: Some Thoughts on Selecting IDEA Objectives. Retrieved at: https://txwes.edu and search for title, viewed 1 September 2015.

Hughes, B. (1996). *A Playworker's Taxonomy of Play Types*. London: Playlink.

Kervin, L., Verenikina, L. & Rivera, M. C. (2015). Collaborative onscreen and offscreen play: examining meaning-making complexities. *Digital Culture & Education*, 7(2), pp. 227–8. Retrieved at: www .digitalcultureandeducation.com/uncategorized/kervin-html.

Marsh, J. & Bishop, J. C. (2014). *Changing Play: Play, Media and Commercial Culture from the 1950s to the Present Day*. Berkshire, UK: Open University Press, McGraw-Hill.

Marsh, J., Plowman, L., Yamada-Rice, D. et al. (2015) Exploring play and creativity in pre-schoolers' use of apps: Final project report. Retrieved at: www.techandplay.org.

Meek, M. (1982). *Learning to Read*. London: The Bodley Head.

Merchant, G. (2014). Young children and interactive story-apps. In C. Burnett, J. Davies, G. Merchant & J. Rowsell (eds), *New Literacies Around the Globe: Policy and Pedagogy*. New York: Routledge, p. 121.

Miller, E. & Almon, J. (2009). Crisis in the kindergarten. Why children need to play in school. College Park, MD: Alliance for Childhood. Retrieved at: http://files.eric.ed.gov/fulltext/ED504839.pdf, viewed 9 August 2015.

Pahl, K. & Rowsell, J. (2010). *Artifactual Literacies: Every Object Tells a Story*. New York: Teachers College Press.

Piaget, J. (1962). *Imitation in Childhood*. New York: Norton.

Plowman L, McPake, J. & Stephen C. (2010). The technologisation of childhood? Young children and technology in the home. *Children and Society,* 24 (1), pp. 63–74.

Salonius-Pasternak, D. E. & Gelfond, H. S. (2005). The next level of research on electronic play: Potential benefits and contextual influences for children and adolescents. *Human Technology: An interdisciplinary journal on humans in ICT environments,* 1(1), pp. 5–22.

Saltmarsh, S. (2009). Becoming economic subjects: Agency, consumption and popular culture in early childhood. *Discourse: Studies in the cultural politics of education,* 30 (1), pp. 47–59.

Schaefer, C. E. (1999). Curative factors in play therapy. *The Journal of Professional Counseling,* 14(1), pp. 7–16.

Siraj-Blatchford, I. (2009). Conceptualising progression in the pedagogy of play and sustained shared thinking in early childhood education: A Vygotskian perspective. *Educational and Child Psychology,* 26(2), pp. 77–89.

Sutton-Smith, B. (2009). *The Ambiguity of Play.* Cambridge, MA: Harvard University Press.

United Nations (1989). Convention on the rights of the child. Retrieved at: www.ohchr.org/Documents/ProfessionalInterest/crc.pdf.

Vasquez, V.M. (2014). *Negotiating Critical Literacies with Young Children* (10th Anniversary edn). New York: Routledge-LEA.

Vasquez, V.M. & Felderman, C. B. (2013). *Technology and Critical Literacy in Early Childhood.* New York: Routledge.

Verenikina, I. & Kervin, L. (2011). iPads, digital play and pre-schoolers. *He Kupu,* 2(5), pp. 4–19.

Vygotsky, L. S. (1978). *Mind in Society: The Development of Higher Mental Processes.* Cambridge, MA: Harvard University Press.

—— (2004). Imagination and creativity in childhood. (Trans. to English by M.E. Sharpe, Inc.). *Journal of Russian and East European Psychology,* 42 (1), pp. 7–97.

Waddell, M. & Oxenbury, H. (1991). *Farmer Duck.* London: Walker Books.

Wardle, F. (1996). *Of Labels, Skills, and Concepts.* Urbana, Ill: ERIC Clearinghouse.

CHAPTER 4

Talking to learn: Listening to young children's language

Through talking and listening we learn to interact with others and to learn about the world and how it works. In this chapter we will look at how we use language to explore the world and to share our thoughts and feelings with others. We will also look at the purposes for communicating and how these are related to the audience, and the mode of communication. Supporting young children to develop their oral language is dependent on a thorough knowledge of language development and how this provides the basis for literacy and learning. To support this understanding we will look at talk as both performance and process; the continuum from spoken to written language and three aspects of language: field, tenor and mode. We will also look at some practical strategies for supporting or scaffolding children to make the most appropriate choices for how to use language, depending on the subject (field), audience (tenor) and mode of communication.

Anticipated outcomes for the chapter

After working through this chapter, you should be able to:

- recognise how language develops
- identify the purposes for using language and the relationship to a child's first attempts to use language
- identify the differences between spoken and written language
- identify some ways to support oral language development.

SCENARIO: EPELI'S FAVOURITE TOY

My favourite toy is my car.
It is big and black and it goes really slow
But when you put the batteries in, it goes really fast.
I like it because it goes really fast.

When Epeli stepped forward in front of the group of four and five year olds who made up his kindergarten class, he was full of confidence and ready to share his opinion about his favourite toy. This was his first year at school but all the children in his class had been practising their speeches to present in front of their parents who were to attend the special event. They listened intently as Epeli described his favourite toy and then confidently returned to his place on the mat as the audience applauded.

For most very young learners, making a speech to a large group on a specific topic is very far removed from their usual experiences and use of language. For many adults this may be challenging but most young children will meet this challenge if they are given enough support. For instance, young children may listen to many weeks of speeches before they are confident enough to give one themselves. Like reading and writing, this is usually motivated by the desire to express themselves; in this case to share information about a favourite toy. To see what types of support can be offered in developing oral language it is useful to explore the concept of audience, and to think about the purpose and structure of spoken language interactions and how, for instance, a public speech differs from most of our day-to-day conversations.

Introduction

The vast majority of children enter school having mastered their mother tongue and sometimes another language or dialect but most young children have only used oral language in contexts and situations, like the home or an early childhood setting in which they were communicating with familiar adults or other children. In this chapter we will look at how we can help young learners to develop their oral language to communicate their ideas and feelings about a range of topics as well as learning to interact appropriately with others in a range of situations (Christie, 2005). For an educator, knowing what it means to master a first language is helpful in supporting young learners to further develop their oral language whether English is their first or an additional language or dialect. The special challenges for students learning English as an additional language or dialect (EAL/D) are explored in Chapters 5 and 6.

How language develops: Starting at home

Even in utero the unborn child can hear and respond to familiar voices, especially those of his parents (See Chapter 2 for more detail on early language development). From their first interactions babies are responding to and learning language (Halliday, 2004) and the Table 4.1 describes some of the ways that language is used even before a child can communicate fluently in their first language. This is called **protolanguage** and the table below describes the five functions proposed by Halliday to describe the very beginnings of language development. Each individual child develops these functions in their own way and only moves beyond the gestures and sounds they have chosen to express these functions when they are able to make new choices from the first language they are learning (Halliday, 2004). The functions are either mathetic, the reflective use of language, or pragmatic, using language to prompt an action. For instance, Halliday gives the examples of 'I want you to . . .' and 'I want . . .' as pragmatic demands for services and goods and 'What's that?' and 'That's what the world is like' as examples of the mathetic or reflective use of language when it reflects engagement, exploration or observation (Halliday, 2004, pp. 243–4).

> **Protolanguage** The means of communication developed by each child as they move towards the development of their first language, involving a set of sounds combined with a gesture that a child puts together.

Table 4.1 Asher's progress with developing protolanguage

Function	Meaning and example
Instrumental	**Give/Demand** Ten-month-old baby Asher is sitting in the high chair. He indicates he wants to feed himself the chicken with gesture and 'eh-eh' sounds.
Regulatory	**Do/Command** Asher is sitting on the floor but wants to be pulled into a standing position. He takes your hands, makes eye contact and utters 'up' as he pulls himself up.
Interactional	**Be with/Greeting** As his grandmother arrives, Asher smiles and waves in greeting.
	Be with/Engagement Asher lifts his arms up, smiles and moves up and down while saying 'uh-uh-uh', thus indicating he wants his mother to pick him up.
Personal	**See or like/Observation** As his Aunty shows him his favourite book *Where is the Green Sheep?* he smiles, waves his arms and bobs up and down to show his pleasure.
Imaginative	**Play** Asher initiates the peekaboo game with an item of clothing from the washing basket.

Source: Adapted from Halliday, (2004) Figures 11 & 12 (pp. 242–3)

Figure 4.1 Asher playing with one of his books

From your own experience with babies or very young children you will have heard the utterances or seen the gestures used to express these functions. If you do not know the child, you may not be able to understand the meaning being made. Carers and siblings will correctly interpret the consistent use of gestures or sounds because they will understand what food or toy is desired due to the repeated use of the sound or gesture in the same context. By the time young children have learnt their first language well enough to fulfil these functions in a way that satisfies their personal needs, they are ready to learn to use language in different contexts and for different purposes. This is true for both first- and second-language speakers. However, for those learning English as an additional language, there must also be opportunities to learn about the culture in which they are learning language as well as the vocabulary and grammar of English (Luke, 1993; Scollon & Scollon, 2001; Gibbons, 2006)

Building on the same functions represented by the development of protolanguage, in preschool and the early years of schooling we often focus on showing children how to appropriately demand or request goods and services using the polite and appropriate forms that our culture demands. Similarly we show children how to question, interact and play but, at the same time, we develop an educational discourse which is appropriate to the school or educational context and which will help children to move from commonsense to educational knowledge (Painter, 2006). That is, being able to develop knowledge that is not based on personal experience; it is to build knowledge systematically as it is presented in a topic rather than in a fragmented way over time (Painter, 2006, p. 71).

REFLECTION

Observe a young child that you know well and see if you can record some of their repeated sounds and gestures over time. Use Table 4.1 to try to understand the meanings being made and to differentiate the purposes of the child's interactive gestures and sounds.

Learning to represent knowledge through oral language

How did five-year-old Epeli learn to make a public speech about his favourite toy while only in his first year at school? The answer is that he was supported to explore language as a focus for his learning. He was learning about toys while being taught how to make appropriate language choices in describing, evaluating and presenting his ideas. The aspects of language being explored by the children in developing their public speeches were **field, tenor and mode**. They explored the topic and how to describe and evaluate, they considered the audience and what was necessary to clearly communicate with others and they considered the appropriate choices for the mode of communication.

Field The subject of spoken or written text.

Tenor The relationship between speaker and listener or author and reader.

Mode The means of communication, either spoken or written.

Field – What will you talk about?

Children in Epeli's kindergarten class of four and five year olds had been reading and writing about toys. Each week some children brought their favourite toy to school and were given the opportunity to practise their public speaking skills before several classes in the kindergarten hall. In this case the field or subject matter was toys and his topic was 'My favourite toy'. Public speaking can be encouraged with very young learners by providing

Figure 4.2 Building public speaking skills

picture prompts and clues that reflect the criteria used to judge public speaking and debating. These include the manner in which the speech is made, the quality of the content, matter (or content, especially in relation to young learners) and the method of organising the speech event (Cameron & Davey, 2012). One child is selected to be the 'adjudicator' and to point to the questions and then elicit a response from the children who listened to the speech. The adjudicator then ticks the aspects of the speech that receive a favourable response and the audience applauds the speaker.

When developing language and literacy, language itself should always be considered as part of the field. While the topic is toys the focus is not just toys but the way a text, whether it is oral or written, is constructed appropriately for the field. Educators can look at all activities in this way and ask themselves questions about the tenor and mode as well as the field. Whether language is the main focus or constitutive (main focus) of an activity, such as in a public speech, or ancillary to the activity, such as the asides made during a football game (Martin & White, 2005), it is important in understanding the tenor and the mode. In this case, making a public speech, language is central or constitutive to the activity but when children are playing a game like snakes and ladders language is used to interact with the central activity of a board game, and language is therefore ancillary to the task.

By making this differentiation it is clearer what type of support is needed and when it is needed. During interactions the use of home languages or dialects are not only acceptable but often very helpful in supporting learning but in this case the use of appropriate Standard Australian English (SAE) is the goal. By making this differentiation it is easier to evaluate the support children need and whether it should be to use any language resource to problem solve and complete a task or whether the support should be given to develop appropriate English language use. To this end the young learners engaged in speech making were given a pattern based on the prompts: *What is it? What does it look like? What does it do? Why do you like it?* These verbal prompts were used repeatedly to develop the children's speeches and to help them with the difficult aspects of composing a suitable oral text which they could remember and reproduce in front of a large group. The criteria for the adjudication were mainly focused on manner which strongly relates to the tenor, or relationship, developed between the speaker or writer and their audience.

Tenor – Who is your audience?

Tenor is the relationship developed between a speaker and listener or an author with a reader or viewer. In the initial scenario Epeli was able to speak in front of a large group on a set topic because he was aware of both the field, or subject matter, and those aspects of speech making that related to the audience, the tenor. Aspects of tenor include the social distance between the participants, their relevant status and the part they play in the discourse (Halliday & Hasan, 1985). In Epeli's case the social distance was close as his audience were his kindergarten peers; their status was also the same as there were no very important people in his audience. The children had also been guided in the appropriate participation in the discourse, the appropriate behaviour as a member of an engaged audience, so they listened intently and then applauded at the end of the speech.

Tenor is an aspect of language that many adults find difficult to explain but educator Genevieve Lempriere developed a diagram to work with her six-year-old, Year 1 students to help them to understand the importance of imagining an audience.

Lempriere's work with young learners on understanding tenor

I created a diagram with the same premise as Martin and Rose (2008) – to help students understand how we use language differently depending on whom we are speaking to. I showed the diagram to my students and spent time explaining each aspect with elaboration. After introducing the diagram to my students, I gave them some verbal examples to help them understand the concept of tenor more clearly. I explained that the message in this scenario was asking someone to shut the door.

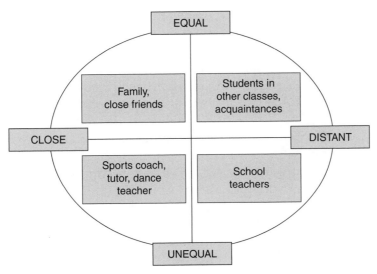

Figure 4.3 Tenor

The way you ask someone to shut the door varies according to *who* you are asking. The tone of voice is also important.

> 'Mrs Lempriere, can you please shut the door?' *addressing a teacher; formal*
>
> 'Mum, shut the door!' *addressing a parent*
>
> 'Hurry up and shut the door' *addressing a sibling*
>
> 'Hey, shut the door Duckie?' *using a nickname; addressing another from a close relationship*

The use of role plays benefit students by helping them understand the relationship. Give a common statement or question to a group of students and then give each group a different relationship status. Groups then share their expression with the whole class and have the rest of class guess/explain/elaborate on the relationship.

With my class, students were learning about weather as part of our Term 4 focus. I modelled a text on how rain is formed and facilitated a discussion about the language used in the text. I helped students consider how the author had used statements and technical language to create an authoritative status. With facilitation, the students were able to discuss their ideas about the author–audience relationships and were beginning to use the metalanguage (see Chapter 10). I found this task very worthwhile and, although it was challenging for my students, I believe it was a useful way to get students to start to think about how language is used for interaction and how the relationship between the author and audience influences the text.

Mode – How will you achieve your purpose?

Mode is the channel or way in which the message is made, which can be either spoken or written or a combination of both. This is a challenging concept in our

(a)

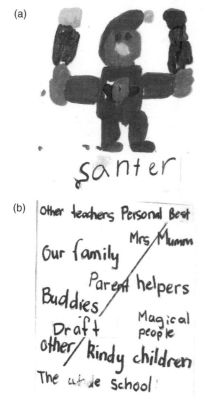

(b)

Figure 4.4 Lisa Mumm's young learners' class work on writing for an audience

modern era when there is no longer a clear distinction between speech and writing in the use of SMS messages, email, webpages and other media forms like film, radio and television. The written message can actually be verbal language written down. This is what happens in film and television scripts and in any novel that includes dialogue as well as in some emails and SMS messages on mobile phones, but not all. The genres, purposes and audiences for writing or talking about specific subjects require the use of particular modes; for instance, to persuade or explain (Halliday and Hasan, 1985). The mode can be seen 'as a cline from language in action to language as reflection' (Martin & White, 2005, p. 28) while at the same time ranging from monologue to dialogue.

In the following example Lisa Mumm asked her five-year-old kindergarten students to imagine the audience they might be addressing in their writing, thus addressing the tenor. She brainstormed with the children to create a list of all the people who might read their written work or to whom they might write a letter. She then asked them to rank the audience on a cline from 'draft' to 'personal best', developing the idea of tenor and its relationship to mode. At the draft stage at the bottom of the cline, children placed themselves and their peers. Perhaps unsurprisingly for the time of year 'magical people/ Santer' was placed at the top of the cline at the 'personal best' position. This very young group of learners demonstrated their understanding of an imagined audience and that appropriate choices in mode were vital in achieving the goal or purpose of the text; in this case their written requests for presents in a letter to Santa.

Moving from spoken to written texts

Mode continuum The continuum between spoken and written language which takes into account the many variables in field, tenor and mode.

The goal of education is to support the child to choose the most effective ways of communicating in the situation and the context in which they find themselves. This can mean that communicating in the child's home is quite different from how they choose to communicate in the early childhood centre, preschool or school. Exploring the concepts of field, tenor and mode is the first step in understanding the **mode continuum**, which refers to the range of ways that messages can be communicated, from talking to a friend to writing a book. Figure 4.5 shows situations in which a young child might communicate and they range from the most spoken-like to the most written-like (Jones, 1996).

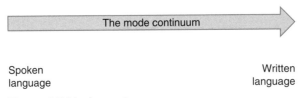

| Spoken language | | Written language |

Figure 4.5 Mode continuum

It is very important to recognise the different purposes, audiences and modes of communication so that they are able to provide the right type of support in the right contexts. As Gibbons states: 'If students are to learn to analyse and explain experience, solve problems and develop and challenge ideas, then sociocultural theory would suggest that what is needed is a critical examination of how far the discourse of the classroom and in particular the interactions between teacher and students, is likely to develop these modes of thinking' (Gibbons, 2006, p. 24).

Producing texts: A young learner's ability to choose

A child learning English as an additional language requires support and in many educational settings learning support is provided for these children and for those with learning disabilities. Educators also recognise that some homes provide children with the sort of support that aids their educational development such as reading stories and playing games like Scrabble or a range of board games that can prepare very young learners for learning at school. However, the diversity of language use in homes and how this impacts on learners is often not recognised. For children to be able to make appropriate choices when developing texts they need to be familiar with those texts at all levels (referred to in Table 4.2) and know which are the most appropriate choices to make in field, tenor and mode.

Social factors in language development

This diversity of language use in the home was addressed by Bernstein (1990). He identified four socialising contexts in the family: regulative, instructional, interpersonal and imaginative. These reflect the function that Halliday (2004) identified in the very earliest stages of language development, the development of protolanguage. Bernstein's theory of **elaborated** and **restricted** codes

Elaborated and restricted codes Orientation to a particular use of language (see Chapter 2 for further discussion).

provides an example of how disadvantage is realised in the personal language choices made by individual children (Bernstein, 1990). He suggests that children whose coding orientation is restricted are not as successful as children whose coding orientation becomes more elaborated as they proceed through the education system. A child's language is related to the social context in which it is learned (Halliday, 1985; Painter, 1996; Williams, 2000) and development of an orientation towards an elaborated or restricted code begins in the earliest years of a child's socialisation (Brice-Heath, 1982; Bernstein, 1990; Painter, 1996; Williams, 2000; Scollon & Scollon, 2001). In some families the socialisation and education of children does not reflect the pedagogic practices in schools and it is this dislocation in the use of language that Bernstein suggests becomes a barrier to educational success for some students.

This is best exemplified by Bernstein's (1990) study of seven year olds who were asked to sort pictures of food. The children were from what he describes as 'white middle-class' and 'lower working-class' groups. Using his classification it can be seen that one group, the 'lower working-class' was less socially and economically advantaged than the other group. When the children from the advantaged group chose ways of sorting, they demonstrated that they knew that choosing criteria for sorting in an educational context should be based on abstract principles related to the types or sources of food rather than personal experience. The principle of sorting that the socially and economically disadvantaged group chose was the one that most closely related to their own personal context, thus demonstrating what Bernstein describes as a restricted coding orientation. Both groups were able to sort the pictures in more than one way but it was knowledge about the most appropriate choice that separated the groups. The students who chose to sort the pictures according to their personal preference for the food, or because one food was served as part of a meal with another food, were focused on their own personal experiences. The other group used abstract principles and sorted the food into groups like fruits and vegetables. Bernstein was examining this orientation towards using abstract principles and using language to communicate them.

His study demonstrates that there are socially constructed barriers that prevent socially disadvantaged groups from participating equally in society and this is demonstrated even in the personal language development of individual learners. The type of language use experienced by children at home and in their community may not reflect that of the school while, in other families, the way language is used in the home makes a smooth transition to the discourse of the school (Williams, 2000). In Williams' study the families were all English speaking and yet he was able to identify huge differences in the use of language between families, reflecting the results of Bernstein's experiments with young children many years earlier. This theory of codes (Bernstein, 1990) provides a way of examining how social disadvantage is realised in the personal language development of particular children and, more importantly, how they can be helped to develop their oral language by recognising the important relationships between audience and purpose; between field, tenor and mode.

Identifying patterns from word to text

If we understand the challenges some children face it is easier to address their needs. Given that the child's most developed meaning-making system is oral language, as in the development of protolanguage, and this always precedes literacy, it is a child's oral language that is their greatest resource when learning to be literate. When this is understood we can select patterns to be repeated to support children to learn English, learn through English and learn about English (Halliday, 2004) whether they are speaking Standard Australian English (SAE) as a first or additional language or dialect.

In many instances oral language presentations are generated by young children bringing a treasured toy or object to show and talk about. However, this can result in a very one-sided dialogue as the adult poses many questions and the child may produce only one-word answers or a gesture like the nod of the head. For instance, T: *What is your favourite toy?* S: *Car.* For children who have well-developed oral language and a vocabulary enhanced through talking about texts as well as all the other aspects of daily life, talking about a familiar event or object might be easy but for many other children more help is needed.

As well as considering the field, mode and tenor of a text, if the levels of text are also kept in mind we can find an explicit way of supporting a young learner. For instance, the structure of Epeli's very short simple speech on his favourite toy was supported by developing patterns through the audience's prompts, *What is it? What does it look like? What does it do? Why do you like it?* which alert the speaker to the purpose and phases/stages of the text and its overall purpose. Repeating patterns such as *When I . . .* to start a sentence or clause complex develops cause and effect. Showing how to develop a noun group by offering synonyms and the development of the more concise noun group to replace 'The toy I like best is . . .' with 'My favourite toy', helps the child to move along the continuum from the use of language in a highly personal context to the more abstract use of language that is indicative of writing.

Table 4.2 Levels of text

Text level	Personal response	*My favourite toy*
Stage/phase level	Context/Description	*Big and black*
	Opinion	*Because it goes really fast*
Sentence (clause complex) level	The dependent clause located in the first position in a complex sentence	*When you <u>put</u> the batteries in / it <u>goes</u> really fast.*
Clause level		
Group/phrase level	Noun group	*My favourite toy*
Word level	Extending vocabulary	*favourite*

Source: Adapted from Derewianka & Jones (2012) p. 11

REFLECTION

Think about when you were at school and you shared something in front of the class, such as in news time or show-and-tell. Were you a confident speaker? Did the teacher support you with prompts or questions? Were you supported to develop an independent monologue like Epeli or were you taking part in a dialogue based on a question and answer format?

Learning through spoken interaction

Talk as process

To truly make text talk in the classroom, teachers and students must build semantic connections between the words of the text and other already familiar ways of speaking. More than this they must become familiar with speaking the more formal language of the subject and must integrate it into their own ways of speaking. (Lemke, 1989, p. 138)

Identifying the different roles of talk is also helpful in developing a pedagogy that supports language development. During activities in which talk is ancillary to the task, talk as process is enacted. In these situations the talk is usually interactive dialogue and the first language or home dialect is a very appropriate choice. Being orientated towards a restricted code is mediated by the close contact with other participants in a shared context. However, the purpose of education is to help children move beyond their current understandings to use language in new and different ways for a range of purposes.

Talk as process Talking to complete a task (talk is ancillary to the task).

Therefore in any shared activity language can be modelled. New and sometimes technical vocabulary related to the subject can be provided. For instance, when explaining cause and effect in science a *dependent clause* (for example, *when the sun heats the water*) could be modelled and some *relating* or *action verbs* (for example, *rain falls* and when *clouds form* could be modelled) that might be unfamiliar because the passive voice (for example, the glass *is filled* by . . .) is used but they may be needed to describe cause and effect.

Genevieve Lempriere's work with her Year 1 class was about 'How rain is formed' and this age group often looks at the water cycle. The language used to describe the water cycle is exemplified in Figure 4.6. This pattern differs from the more familiar language pattern that most young learners would choose of: actor, process, goal. For example, 'I <u>pressed</u> the button' as opposed to '*When the* button <u>is pressed</u> the iPad <u>is</u> ready to use.'

Figure 4.6 The water cycle

When the sun <u>heats</u> the water	water vapour <u>is formed</u>.
When clouds <u>form</u>	rain <u>falls</u> onto the surface of the earth.
Rain <u>is formed</u>	*when the droplets of water in the clouds <u>are pulled</u> to earth by gravity.*
Evaporation <u>is caused</u>	*when the sun <u>heats</u> the water.*

Young learners are not required to use this language but, in the context of shared activity and play, the language can be shared and reinforced through interaction with the educator and other children, and through shared reading of texts appropriate to the subject. These texts will also reflect the language choices that are appropriate to the subject. As Lemke (1989) suggests, there should be a constant movement between the familiar language of the home and the more formal written-like language found in the school and in written texts. If the adults are aware of the patterns of language appropriate to the task it is possible to explicitly model the patterns.

Talk as performance

Oral language games like 'Instructions' or 'Descriptions' can be played to develop children's abilities to describe or instruct (Rushton, 1996; Rossbridge & Rushton, 2010). Prompts are developed which support the child to create a monologue rather than the dialogue that often happens in news time. In 'Descriptions' the child is asked to describe an object or picture hidden in a box in response to whispered prompts from an adult. In other games like 'Instructions' the child instructs the group on an activity like making a sandwich or tying a shoelace, in response to prompts from the whole group of children (Rushton, 1996, p. 92).

Table 4.3 Oral language games

Games	Prompts: Display the game titles when playing them and display the initial statement with Descriptions to support young learners.
Descriptions Child shakes the box and says: *In my box is something which* . . . Children guess the answer.	Objects: What size? What shape? What colour? What do you use it for? example In my box is something which is big, round, yellow and you play with it at the beach – beach ball. Picture of an animal: What size? What colour? What special feature? Where does it live? What does it do? example In my box is something which is small and black, has sharp claws, and it lives at my house and gives me cuddles – cat. (An adult has to give these whispered prompts to support the child to develop a monologue.) Prompts – called out by all the children . . .
Instructions	First . . . Then . . . Next . . . Finally
Recount	When? Where? Who? What? What did you think of it (evaluation)?
Narrative	When? Where? Who? What? What went wrong? (complication) What happened in the end? (resolution)

Talk as performance Talking as a performance as in a speech, lecture or play (talk is constitutive).

In playing these games language does take a central place and the young learner is moving away from the use of language in a familiar context towards **talk as performance** as they present an instruction or description to a group. As it is developed orally and as a monologue it can easily be transcribed into a written text by an adult or, where possible, by a young learner. Playing games like this helps children make language choices that are appropriate to talk as performance and writing, at this stage of development.

The difference between spoken and written language

Lexical density The density or percentage of content words in a given text.

This move from spoken to written language is best described as a move away from grammatical intricacy and towards **lexical density**. It is a continuum and one that develops through the school years. Halliday (1985) states that lexical items are often called 'content words' (p. 63) but in the sort of texts that challenge literate adults, the content words are often presented in complex, content-filled noun groups such as this statement about the water cycle: *The water cycle* is *a process, which involves an exchange of energy that influences climate*, and can be described as *the movement of water from one reservoir to another* using *the physical processes of evaporation, transpiration, condensation, precipitation and accumulation*.

Even if you have a good understanding of the water cycle this one sentence carries a lot of information to process and this information is packaged in noun groups, made into things which can be discussed and written in a shorter, more concise way than if the same subject was being discussed verbally using the more familiar patterns of oral language. For instance, if the statement is unpacked (*Water* moves around in *a cycle* and uses energy when it does because *it* keeps changing from *one thing* to another and that makes *a difference* to *the weather*. It moves from *one place* to another because *the sun* makes *it* dry up and *it* keeps changing. It becomes *vapour which is a bit like steam* and then *it* turns into *clouds* and then *it* turns into *rain* and then *it* falls into *rivers and oceans*.) the first thing you will notice is the greater length of the unpacked version. The second is that it was easier to read and understand. This is because it is less lexically dense and the language pattern is more like how we speak: there are fewer noun groups with less information and content words.

In the early years the first texts we introduce to children often use spoken language to support emergent readers. Repeated refrains and rhyme are also supportive but it is the ability to predict the text as we are reading that is the most helpful. Even as a literate adult, reading more grammatically intricate text is relaxing and much easier (closer to spoken style) than lexically dense text (think of your holiday magazine compared with university study). In the previous example it is also important to note that it is not just the vocabulary that provides the challenge. Many very young children can identify technical words like 'dinosaur' or 'tyrannosaurus rex'; it is the packaging of the information, the lexical density, which is the most challenging. The more challenging sentence has more lexical items per clause than the more spoken-like sentence.

The pedagogical implication in the early years is the need to develop a clear view of the challenges that young learners will meet and to prepare them for success. Lexically dense texts are to be found in educational settings that begin in the early years of primary school and extend through to tertiary education. So where should we start? Firstly, with oral language. Support children by giving them many opportunities to use their home language and then build on the use of the home language in appropriate contexts. By this, we mean developing oral language with building on the noun group; for instance, helping children move from a nod of the head or a one-word answer (*car*) to *My favourite toy is my big black car*.

Scaffolding: Controlled, guided and independent practice

Central to a view of teaching as mediation, then, is the recognition that both language and content learning depend on the nature of the dialogue between teacher and students, the role that teachers play in the construction of discourse, and the specific assistance that the teacher gives to students in their role as apprentices in the subject learning. (Gibbons, 2006, p. 174)

Extending from the work of Vygotsky (1986) language scaffolding (Hammond, 2001; Hammond & Gibbons, 2001) uses the concept of the zone of proximal development (ZPD) to support the recognition of the zone in which learning is mostly likely to take place. The metaphor of scaffolding was originally developed by Wood, Bruner & Ross (1976) and is exemplified in the concepts of controlled, guided and independent practice. It is important to think of independent practice, especially when the focus is oral language, as not being an individual child but rather children working independently without direct support from an adult. The support for interaction needs to be carefully planned. If it is to have the desired impact on children's development, it has to be designed in scaffolding (Derewianka & Jones, 2012).

The purpose of this planning is, as Dufficy (2005) suggests, to help educators 'to loosen the reins on the minds of children in our classrooms and assist them to move into challenging new cognitive domains through dialogue.' (Dufficy, 2005, p. 39.) Scaffolding, by definition, is removed at a certain point and therefore the concepts of controlled, guided and independent practice point to that progression from strong support to independent production. While a single activity like making a speech about a favourite toy can be seen to cycle through these stages, it is the repetition of the same activity or aspects of the activity over time that will help every child move through those stages to independent production.

Drawing it all together

While getting children to talk is not an issue for most of us, helping them to develop talking and listening is much more challenging. That is why it is vital that educators understand the purposes, audiences and levels of text as well as the individual challenges that their young learners might face in developing their oral language. This is vital as learning language is not just learning to communicate but learning to think, to make choices and to make meaning. As Swain & Lapkin state:

A complementary perspective is that language serves not only a communicative function, but is, itself, a psychological tool. Like any tool, it facilitates task performance by mediating between us and the accomplishment of the task. The tool may facilitate our performance of the task and may make some things possible that were not otherwise. (1998, p. 320)

It is only when developing oral language is seen as developing the ability to think and choose that a pedagogy can be developed that provides opportunities for children to make language choices relevant to the many subjects and contexts that they will find in an educational context. Those choices need to be made for monologues, dialogues, performance and process and to enable children to express themselves in as many ways as they choose.

Questions for further discussion

- Can you identify examples of the use of protolanguage when observing a young child?
- Choose an activity you are preparing for children. Can you identify the field, tenor and mode?
- Think of your daily interactions with text. Can you place them on the mode continuum, (for example, speaking to your family, texting, checking Facebook, reading a magazine, making a presentation to colleagues)?
- When reading a story to children, can you identify some patterns from word to text level (refer to Table 4.2) that you can emphasise for the children's attention?
- Do all activities support language development? How could you adapt an activity to provide more opportunities for spoken interaction and language development?
- Can you identify which activities support talk as performance or talk as process?

Further reading

Anstey, M. & Bull, G. (2014). *Classroom Talk: Understanding Dialogue, Pedagogy and Practice.* Sydney: Primary English Teaching Association Australia (PETAA).

Edwards-Groves, C. (2014). PETAA Paper 195, Talk moves: A repertoire of practices for productive dialogue. Sydney: Primary English Teaching Association Australia (PETAA).

Rossbridge, J. (2014). PETAA Pen 161, 'Learning to Use' and 'Learning About' Language. Sydney: Primary English Teaching Association Australia (PETAA).

Rossbridge, J. & Rushton, K. (2014). PETAA Paper 196, The Critical Conversation about Text: Joint Construction. Sydney: Primary English Teaching Association Australia (PETAA).

Whorrall, J. & Cabell, S. (2015). Supporting children's oral language development in the preschool classroom. *Early Childhood Education Journal,* DOI:10.1007/s10643-015-0719-0.

References

Bernstein, B. (1990). Elaborated and restricted codes: overview and criticisms. *The Structuring of Pedagogic Discourse. Vol. 4: Class, Codes and Control.* London: Routledge, pp. 94–130.

Brice Heath, S. (1982). What no bedtime story means: Narrative skills at home and school. *Language in Society* 11(1) pp. 49–76.

Cameron, L. & Davey, T. (2012). *Taking the Initiative.* NSW Department of Education and Communities. Retrieved at: www.artsunit.nsw.edu.au/sites/default/files/Taking_the_Initiative.pdf.

Christie, F. (2005). *Language Education in the Primary Years.* Sydney: UNSW Press.

Derewianka, B. & Jones, P. (2012). *Teaching Language in Context.* Melbourne: Oxford University Press.

Dufficy, P. (2005). *Designing Learning for Diverse Classrooms.* Sydney: Primary English Teaching Association Australia (PETAA).

Gibbons, P. (2006). *Bridging Discourses in the ESL Classroom: Students, Teachers and Researchers.* London: Continuum.

Halliday, M. A. K. (1985). *Spoken and Written Language.* Victoria: Deakin University Press, pp. 61–7.

—— (2004). Three aspects of children's language development: Learning language, learning through language, learning about language. In J. J. Webster (ed.), *The Language of Early Childhood: M. A. K. Halliday.* New York: Continuum, ch. 14, pp. 308–26.

Halliday, M. A. K. & Hasan, R. (1985). *Language, Context, and Text: Aspects of Language in a Social-Semiotic Perspective.* Victoria: Deakin University Press.

Hammond, J. (2001). Scaffolding and language. In J. Hammond (ed.), *Scaffolding.* Sydney: Primary English Teaching Association Australia (PETAA), pp. 15–30.

Hammond, J. & Gibbons, P. (2001). What is scaffolding? In J. Hammond (ed.), *Scaffolding.* Sydney: Primary English Teaching Association Australia (PETAA), pp. 1–14.

Jones, P. (ed.) (1996). *Talking to Learn.* Sydney: Primary English Teaching Association Australia (PETAA).

Lemke, J. (1989). *Making Text Talk: Theory into Practice.* Columbus, OH: College of Education Ohio State University.

Luke, A. (1993). The social construction of literacy in the primary school. In L. Unsworth (ed.), *Literacy, Learning and Teaching: Language as Social Practice in the Primary School.* Melbourne: Macmillan, pp. 22–32.

Martin, J. & Rose, D. (2008). *Genre Relations: Mapping Culture.* London: Equinox.

Martin, J. & White, P. (2005). *The Language of Evaluation: Appraisal in English.* Hampshire: Palgrave Macmillan.

Painter, C. (1996). The development of language as a resource for thinking: A linguistic view of learning. In R. Hasan & G. Williams, *Literacy in Society.* Edinburgh: Addison Wesley Longman, pp. 50–7.

—— (2006). Preparing for school: Developing a semantic style for educational knowledge. In F. Christie (ed.), *Pedagogy and the Shaping of Consciousness*. London: Continuum.

Rossbridge, J. & Rushton, K. (2010). *Conversations about Text: Teaching Grammar Using Literary Texts*. Sydney: Primary English Teaching Association Australia (PETAA).

Rushton, K. (1996). Developing literacy skills through oral language activities. In P. Jones (ed.), *Talking to Learn*. Sydney: Primary English Teaching Association Australia (PETAA), pp. 89–95.

Scollon, R. & Scollon, S. (2001). *Intercultural Communication* (2nd edn). Malden, MA: Blackwell Publishing.

Swain, M. & Lapkin, S. (1998). Interaction and second language learning: Two adolescent French immersion students working together. *The Modern Language Journal*, 82 (iii).

Vygotsky, L. (1986). *Thought and Language*. Cambridge, MA: MIT Press, pp. xi–xliii.

Williams, G. (2000). The pedagogic device and the production of pedagogic discourse: A case example in early literacy education. In F. Christie (ed.), *Pedagogy and the Shaping of Consciousness*, London: Continuum, pp. 88–122.

Wood, D., Bruner, J. & Ross, G. (1976). The role of tutoring in problem solving. *Journal of Child Psychology and Psychiatry*, 17(2), pp. 89–100.

CHAPTER 5

Difference and diversity in language and literacy development

In this chapter we will explore the diversity in language and literacy development that reflects the multicultural and multilingual society comprising contemporary Australia. We will look at the relationship between language, culture and identity, and how language helps to shape identity. We will then explore some of the unique aspects of language learning for bilingual children. We will also look at the need for these young learners to learn English, learn through English and learn about English (Halliday, 2004; ACTA, 2015).

Anticipated outcomes for the chapter

After working through this chapter you should be able to:

- empathise with a child who is learning English as an additional language, learning through English and learning about English and support them to engage in learning using all their language resources
- draw on your understandings about language development to support bilingual learners
- explore strategies for communicating with the families and communities of bilingual learners.

SCENARIO: A FAMILIAR DAILY ROUTINE

Michel's mother, Catherine, is standing at the front door of the family home with Michel, her young preschool-aged son while they watch his father back the car out of the driveway and then head off to work for the day. She looks down at her little son and says: 'Michel, wave goodbye to Baba'. Her son waves to his father until the car disappears from view. He then looks up at his mother and says, 'Baba wented'.

This family speaks English at home but Michel's grandparents also speak to him in Arabic, Welsh and a dialect of Italian. Michel Idris has been named after his two grandfathers, one an Arabic speaker born in Lebanon whose second language is French and third language English, and the other who is a bilingual Welsh speaker from Wales in the UK. When Michel's father Jacob speaks with his parents and extended family he speaks Arabic and French as well as English. Michel's mother, Catherine, has mixed ancestry as her mother is Italian and the only language that her parents share is English. Catherine therefore speaks English with both her parents but also knows some Welsh and some Italian. Far from being confused by his multicultural, multilingual family, Michel Idris interacts happily with the speakers of all these languages, calling his father 'Baba' and his grandparents 'Daid', 'Nonna', 'Jiddo' and 'Tayta'. However Michel's mother tongue is English and, as we can see from this interaction with his mother, he has already learnt how to form the past tense by adding 'ed' to a verb. As he is only two years old, he needs some more time to learn about English and to learn that 'go' is an irregular verb that takes a special form in the past tense. Long before entering any formal educational context, Michel Idris is interacting in more than one language and learning about language while he learns it and learns through it (Halliday, 2004).

Introduction

The language and cultural diversity of Australia was examined in the 2011 Census by the Australian Bureau of Statistics (2011). The census showed that the majority of Australians have English-speaking ancestry so it is therefore not surprising that 76.8% of Australians reported that English was the only language spoken at home. However, all of these people are not necessarily speakers of only one language. Many Australian families may only speak English at home but have family members who speak one or more languages. These statistics indicate that most Australians view Australian society from the perspective of an English speaker with that cultural heritage. However, we are also a community in which a sizeable minority, almost 30% of people, speak a language other than English at home. Speaking a language opens a door to a culture; it maintains links to the traditions and ways of living and being that belong to the people who speak it.

This is a complex relationship because English speakers do not necessarily share a country, nationality or even a culture; English speakers span the world.

Other languages – such as Spanish, Chinese and Arabic – also have many dialects and are spoken by people from many countries and cultures across the world. So to understand the language and cultural heritage a child brings to an educational setting, it is very important to understand the language, or languages and cultures, in the family as well as the context in which the family is bringing up their child. Each family has funds of knowledge (Moll et al., 1992) that they share with their children and this great resource can provide a springboard for learning in an educational context if it is recognised and nurtured.

Supporting young students to develop their identities as bilingual and bicultural learners

The *Early Years Learning Framework* (EYLF) was developed by the Australian Government in 2009 to guide the practices of teachers and carers of children in the early years. It states that:

> There are many ways of living, *being* and of knowing. Children are born *belonging* to a culture, which is not only influenced by traditional practices, heritage and ancestral knowledge, but also by the experiences, values and beliefs of individual families and communities. Respecting diversity means within the curriculum valuing and reflecting the practices, values and beliefs of families. Educators honour the histories, cultures, languages, traditions, child rearing practices and lifestyle choices of families. They value children's different capacities and abilities and respect differences in families' home lives. (p. 13)

Chapter 6 explores some aspects of the rich cultural and linguistic heritage which Aboriginal children bring to an educational context, and the specific knowledge and understandings that teachers need to develop to be able to effectively support young Aboriginal learners. However all educators need to be aware of the other factors which may impact on many **bilingual** learners as they enter schools and preschools. In the *Elaborations of the Australian Professional Standards for Teachers* developed by the Australian Council of TESOL Associations (ACTA, 2015) these other factors are stated in *Standard 1 Know students and how they learn* and similarly in *Outcome 1 Children have a strong sense of identity* (EYLF, 2009).

Some of the factors outlined in these documents that may obviously impact on bilingual learners are the languages or dialects spoken at home, and the cultural heritage and beliefs of their families. In Australia, children from these families are currently identified as learners of English as an additional language/dialect (**EAL/D**) but at other times acronyms such as **NESB, LBOTE, ELL** and **ESL** have also been used to describe these

Bilingual Able to speak two languages.

EAL/D English as an additional language or dialect.

NESB Non-English speaking background.

LBOTE Language background other than English.

ELL English language learner.

ESL English as a second language.

learners. Sadly for many migrants, refugees and children from the families of the stolen generations, there can be an impact from the trauma associated with racism, dislocation and warfare. These factors potentially have a long-lasting impact on children and their families. Therefore one young child can take longer than another child to develop a sense of belonging and ease in an educational context, depending on these factors and their impact. Many young bilingual learners often respond to these challenges by remaining in a **silent period** of time. They choose not to respond until they have developed a sense of ease and belonging (Cummins, 1986; Krashen, 1992) For teachers, the challenge is the number of languages spoken by Australians and the variety of cultural backgrounds from which they come. However, young children are very happy to join in clapping songs and in reciting poems. Engaging in modern technology allows any teacher to easily learn a greeting in the languages encountered in the classroom. Just a few words of greeting or a song in the child's first language will almost certainly bring a smile to the child's face and make their family members feel welcome. Amenah Mourad, a bilingual educational leader shares her story and her knowledge that reflects her experiences both as a bilingual child and a very experienced teacher of bilingual children.

Silent period Period when a child chooses not to interact verbally.

SCENARIO: AMENAH

Figure 5.1 Amenah Mourad in her first year at school

I remember being in kindergarten, not being able to speak a word of English. I spoke Arabic only. I remember going into kindergarten and feeling so overwhelmed. You know when you see those Hollywood movies where you can feel the walls, the ceiling, the whole room coming down on you. I started school at four and a half and I remember feeling that way. Until Year 1, I wasn't really able to communicate in English. I remember my Year 1 teacher; she gave me a book and it had pictures in it with positional language. She'd say it orally and we had to tick the positional language picture, and I couldn't do it. It was just too much for me; it was information overload. There were too many words coming out of her mouth and I couldn't connect what she was saying with the picture. I got into trouble because I didn't do it; the anxiety was high.

If I had a child like that in my class I would turn over every stone to make sure I understood that child's background. I wouldn't just rely on media reports or what I read, I would go a bit further than that. With bilingualism in the classroom I think if you can connect those concepts in their first language it will make the connection easier in their second language. Just going straight into the second language, like with the positional language, if she'd asked me 'on top' in Arabic I would've answered it. But she asked me in English and I couldn't do it. Back then I thought I was a failure. I had a lot of anxiety growing up in regards to my academic ability but I developed resilience, knowing in my heart that I could do it but I couldn't show it. The same thing happened in high school. High school was tough for someone with a Muslim heritage . . . it upset me that teachers just assumed that my family didn't value education. I come from a family that values education. My parents did expect me to go to university and they did expect me to perform at school. My dad has a PhD and my mum has a Master's degree. In my family, there are six of us: one is a very successful businessman; five of us are university trained, with one doing his PhD. I grew up in a very strict Muslim family but for my parents educating both their boys and girls was a priority. When I attended university it was very different because the teachers were not judging me on ethnicity or religion. Because there was more independent research, I performed very well.

Interview with Amenah Mourad, a bilingual educational leader

How can a monolingual, English-speaking teacher best support bilingual learners?

Knowing what I know now as a teacher I would not use the same strategies that my Year 1 teacher used. I could understand a lot more than I could express. I think with bilingual students the oral practice is not enough, it has to be concrete. You can't just speak: you need to demonstrate, especially if they don't have a word of English, for instance with positional language. I'd actually physically demonstrate, I'd go through the whole process. Instead of the teacher just being out the front and teaching, I would bring that space a bit closer. I'd be more hands on and proactive. If you have an app or a wonderful website that can support the concept, you could teach it in the first language first, show it in the first language first and then you could translate it into English as the second language develops. Especially with the new syllabuses. There are so many different ways you can represent the cultures and languages in your school through your programming. That's not a hard thing to do any more with all the resources that are out there. Whether it's online, or support services or bilingual teachers in your school or being a network school or sister school or even connecting with schools overseas. You can go beyond your classroom.

How can we support young learners and honour their first language and culture?

Music, dance, celebration; anything that makes them feel included and welcome. Celebrating with food is always a bridge between the student's home and school. I just loved it when Mum used to send hummus dip to school and the teachers loved it. It made me feel special. Not stereotyping and not using what society thinks about this particular culture or about this particular religion. Looking at the child as an individual and knowing what you can do for this child. As an adult I think classroom teachers of bilingual students need to have empathy. They need to think, 'If I was in a classroom and couldn't speak a word of English, how would I feel?'

I remember I was in Year 5 and we had to complete a cloze passage on Mary Poppins, and I had no idea who Mary Poppins was. The book was never read to us in class. I remember the simple grammatical features like 'the' and 'a' I could fill in and then there was something like 'She needed her "something" to fly', and I put in 'plane'. You need a plane to fly, obviously, who would think that you need an umbrella to fly? I remember getting the test back and looking at it and feeling so devastated because there was no way in the world I would have known that answer. There was an assumption that my parents had taken us to see *Mary Poppins* or that we'd read the book.

For any teacher, don't assume that students all have that background knowledge and that they bring it to the classroom; they don't. Especially that cultural knowledge, the fairytales and the nursery rhymes. Don't leave the child alone, especially at recess and lunch. Develop little networks around the child. Use a lot of gestures, use body language, smiles. Are there any other speakers of the child's first language? Go online. There's a world of information out there that can help you with simple words, 'hello'. Just the greetings, if someone spoke to me in my first language, and I didn't have a word of English, it would absolutely make me feel welcome.

How can we best support refugee students?

[When considering] students are arriving as refugees and they've had any sort of traumatic experience . . . if you have a **refugee** child in your class, and you've never taught a refugee child or a child with a second language, I don't think that just reading books is going to be enough to get a real understanding. I would develop a relationship with the families. I would invite them in and

Refugee A person forced to leave their home due to a natural disaster, war or persecution.

celebrate who they are and open up those lines of communication with them. You make them feel comfortable, you make them feel welcome and you target their strengths. I would also target schools that have high refugee populations and I would try to develop a network so I could get into those classrooms and see how those schools function and see how they take care of those children. You can read about it, you can follow strategies but I don't think you'll be able to cater for that child if you don't actually see it or experience it. Experiment with the video conferencing, seeing it in action is the best thing.

REFLECTION

Reflect on your own feelings when you were in a situation where you couldn't communicate easily with those around you. Who made you feel comfortable? How were you helped to fit in? What strategies did you use to manage the situation in which you found yourself?

Learning to interact orally in English

Learning English refers to the challenge of learning a new language or dialect, namely Standard Australian English, as well as the cultures of Australian schools and the wider Australian society. (EAL/D Elaborations overview, ACTA, 2015)

The challenge for a teacher is to develop English with a focus on meaning and without trying to replace the first language with the second (Skutnabb-Kangas, 2013; Wong Fillmore, 1991). The first language should be supported and respected as the child's mother tongue, and students should be encouraged to use their first language to support learning in the second language. Learning English should be developed as a meaningful part of the child's development and engagement is key to this development. Amenah's story shows that she was seeking meaning in her learning and that she wanted to demonstrate what she could understand through language. Her story also shows how important it is to allow students to demonstrate what they can do or understand using either their first language (L1) or their second language (L2). It is therefore important to provide scaffolded opportunities (Hammond & Gibbons, 2001) with both high challenge and high support for children to successfully demonstrate their understanding, rather than just trying to test them in their second language (L2).

L1 First language.

L2 Second language.

While it is almost impossible to uncover all of the background history of each child, it is at least a positive step to be aware of what factors may impact on a child and to sensitively approach each child with this awareness. In educational settings the very best way to engage young students is to help them to enjoy a range of activities that support them to interact with confidence using both their first language and **Standard Australian English (SAE)**. Structured play activities, as discussed in Chapter 3, are

SAE Standard Australian English.

the most accessible to children especially if the group does not share a language background. If you have parents or colleagues who can help, learning greetings, poems and songs in your students' first language is a great start to developing their sense of belonging and encouraging them to interact orally with you and their peers. You do not have to be a fluent speaker to be able to say 'hello'.

Working with the children and their families or working with your colleagues and using the available resources, you could label the room with pictures and words from the children's first languages and English. For instance, label *door, window, table* and *computer*. Learning the word for 'thank you' in the child's first language and using it to thank a parent who brought home-cooked food to the school will both positively affirm the child's identity and open up the relationship between the home and school for all the children. Children do not have to be independent readers to recognise and say the words, especially if they are supported by pictures. For young children learning English, pointing and speaking both the familiar name from their own language and then in English will help their confidence as they build their English vocabulary (Gibbons, 2002; Dufficy, 2005; Hertzberg, 2012).

In play situations children will often happily interact using whatever language they have available to communicate their requests and comments. From these interactions young children often quickly develop **BICS** (Cummins, 1986) in English. Referring to the development of protolanguage (Halliday, 2004; Painter, 1996; Williams, 2000) as discussed in Chapter 4, it is helpful to remember that these oral interactions,

BICS Basic Interpersonal Communication Skills.

the requests and demands for goods and services usually take place in a shared context where eye contact and gesture can be used. A shared context makes it easier to communicate than, say, over the phone or in writing.

When students have little or no English language skills it is difficult to assess what they know and understand, so observation of how they interact in carefully selected activities will provide the best opportunities for the child to demonstrate understanding. These types of activities will be characterised by multiple access to materials as the teacher presents the same message in many ways (for example, orally, in writing, modelled with images or diagrams). This is what Amenah suggests when she says you need to be proactive and hands on instead of being out the front teaching. This is known as **message abundancy** (Gibbons, 2006) as the same message is presented in several ways. As a child, Amenah was asked to tick a box next to a picture that corresponded to positional language in English. To do this, her only reference point was the picture as she only knew the corresponding words in her first language. The English word was not given any context in the exercise and the only teacher-directed help was the instruction provided to undertake the task. There was no message abundancy and no scaffold; the activity just tested

Message abundancy Providing access to the same message using a range of modes.

the child's memory and listening skills but did not provide any opportunity for learning. It produced anxiety instead. To develop oral fluency and vocabulary teachers should encourage every student to use all their language resources from both their first and second languages when participating in activities dependent on interacting with others, and which are presented to the student using message abundance.

Developing literacy in English

Learning through English refers to the challenge of using English for social and academic purposes whilst still learning it. (EAL/D Elaborations overview, ACTA, 2015)

Developing Basic Interpersonal Communication Skills (BICS) often develops quickly as children interact with each other and adults use whatever language resources are available to them. This ability to interact in a familiar context can sometimes mask the lack of development in understanding language structures or appropriate vocabulary use as they are replaced by gesture and intonation because the speakers are interacting in a shared physical space. Developing language in educational contexts requires that the child moves from these types of interactions and begins to master more abstract thoughts in their communication, in contexts that are not physically shared in time and space. Think of a phone conversation you may have shared with a young child when they describe an event or object. The child will often assume your shared knowledge of their subject and you might need a parent or caregiver to explain what was being said because you have not shared the experience or seen the object. As an example of this task, a teacher of Year 1 students at school demonstrated the language demands of retelling a story and how oral language could be developed using tablets and an app that supported the children to move beyond interacting in a shared context (Jones, 2012).

For young children it is therefore vital to introduce the texts that English speakers will encounter in the early years to familiarise them with the patterns of language. Developing these oral language skills in the early years supports the later development of literacy (Griffin et al., 2004). Introducing the songs, poems, rhymes and traditional tales will help them gain a familiarity with the sounds and structures of the language. **Schema theory** relates especially to the knowledge we have developed in our minds through our interactions with texts and with the world. As Gibbons states, 'meaning does not reside solely in the words and structures of the text, but is constructed in the course of a transaction between the text and the reader' (2002, p. 80). For instance, as soon as an English speaker hears 'Once upon a time' they can accurately predict that a fairytale is about to begin. Amenah's first encounter with *Mary Poppins* exemplifies this very well as she had no prior knowledge to successfully complete the cloze passage she was given, while she understood all the words and concepts that related to flying.

Schema theory A theory that suggests that knowledge and understanding is built on patterns developed through previous experiences.

Developing Cognitive Academic Language Proficiency (CALP) is a much slower process and usually takes around seven years. Of equal importance is that, as Collier and Thomas (2001) state: 'Students who have lost their first language in early childhood or during the elementary school years, experience less success in school – this phenomenon, found in sociolinguistics research worldwide, is referred to as **subtractive bilingualism**' (Lambert, 1975, p. 69). For students who have already developed literacy in their first language the understandings and skills which they have developed are more easily transferred to the second language. This theory (Cummins, 1981) is known as **Common Underlying Proficiency (CUP)** and suggests that bilingual students may be advantaged academically if they have support in developing both languages. This is because the language skills and understandings needed to handle more abstract and decontextualised ideas are, as Cummins states, common in both languages. These are abilities like classifying, evaluating and inferring which can be developed and used in either language and are necessary for success in educational contexts.

The development of CALP refers to the development of both oral and written language as it relates particularly to register. **Register** is well explained by Gibbons when she states that, 'Since language reflects the use to which it is put, and because it varies systematically according to the situation in which it occurs, there will be certain recurring predictable features that occur each time a particular situation occurs.' (2006, p. 31). These are the three variables that make up any register and they are field, tenor and mode (Halliday, 2004). They refer to the subject of the interaction or text, what it is about (field); the relationship between the speaker and listener or reader and text (tenor); and finally how the text is delivered, whether it is oral or written (mode). To interact orally or to read effectively we need to be able to predict what the text will be about as the first step. This is by calling on our previous knowledge and making a connection between the text and our own experiences. This is especially important for bilingual learners whose cultural and linguistic experiences may be very different from those of English speakers. For instance, the kinds of knowledge we use to predict in a written text relate to the sounds, letters and words but also to the structure of language and to knowledge of the world.

> CALP Cognitive Academic Language Proficiency.

> Subtractive bilingualism Losing the first language in the school years and its negative impact on learning.

> CUP Common Underlying Proficiency.

> Register A specific instance of field, tenor and mode.

REFLECTION

Think about your own language development. Can you recognise any milestones? Do you know the first word your learnt? Do you remember when you first read something independently? What is the first song or poem you can remember learning? Can you remember learning another language or some words in another language? Observe a young child and see what language choices they are able to make in interacting in context and then in describing an object or retelling an event. Are they different? How?

Learning about the structures and features of English

> Learning about English involves understanding the systems of English and how they work together in different situations to produce appropriate spoken and written texts. (EAL/D Elaborations overview, ACTA, 2015)

There are many challenges when learning English and the best way to support young learners is to make sure that you have a good understanding of language development. The example at the very beginning of this chapter showed young Michel Idris overusing his knowledge of forming the past tense. For a well-informed teacher this can be seen quite correctly as a positive indicator of his language development, not as a 'mistake'. While the developmental aspects of young children's language are familiar in a commonsense way, for educators it is very important to recognise the difference between spoken and written language as this is key to recognising the development of children's literacy.

> The written language presents a SYNOPTIC view. It defines its universe as product rather than as process. Whether we are talking about a triangle, the layout of a house, or the organization of a society, the written language encodes it as a structure or, alternatively, as a chaos – but either way, as a thing that exists. (Halliday, 1985, p. 97)

The ability to identify the features of both spoken and written language will support young learners, especially bilingual learners who are learning a new language as well as learning through it. In oral language we usually present ideas and events in a continuous flow without punctuation, which is very familiar in young children's early attempts to write. They write what they say and young Michel would write 'Baba wented'.

For young learners it is very important that oral language is used as the starting point for writing as this is engaging and meaningful for the young writers who want to express themselves. Oral language is important as it is through the oral interaction with the writing process that students can learn how to write. Good language models can be provided through reading and listening. In the case of bilingual children, it is essential to build vocabulary prior to reading or writing a text. Providing explicit and detailed support to understand and create texts is the basis of scaffolding (Hammond, 2001). If students are given the tools they need, that is, familiarity with the grammatical features, the structures of texts and the key vocabulary, they can go beyond their own experiences to express themselves.

The spoken language brought by students to a school or preschool encompasses their culture and background experiences (Gibbons, 2002) and this language resource should be respected and fostered. For instance, if children or educators share a first language the discussion accompanying the writing process can be in both the first and second languages even if the text is being composed in English. If language is seen to be socially constructed it is easier to see that speaking and writing are developed through choices. Grammatical features can then be seen as an aspect of language open to choice like all others.

Having their lives reflected in the stories and activities which they encounter in English (see also Chapter 9) will support engagement and help to confirm the individual child's identity in the educational context. Children of any background will try to make connections with texts by drawing on their own experiences. In most children's lives this will include the daily family routines and interaction with animals or characters made familiar through television or film. It is also important that children interact with books and texts in which they see themselves. They may live in towns, cities or rural areas, and in flats or houses. At least some of the faces, homes, food and clothing encountered by them in texts in an educational setting should be familiar and reflect their own families and experiences.

This is especially important for communities that are socially marginalised as this may negatively impact on their educational outcomes. 'Educational responses to underachievement that fail to address the causal role of identity devaluation, and its roots in historical and current patterns of coercive power relations, are unlikely to be successful.' (Cummins et al., 2015, p. 556). In some educational settings there may be many children from a variety of language and cultural backgrounds; in other settings, a first language may be shared by most children in the class. Whether their families and traditions differ from the mainstream or just from the other children in the class, it is important to find a range of resources that positively reflect all the children's experiences and which develop a feeling of belonging (Baker & Freebody, 1987). These resources can be a starting point for their interaction and creativity. When responding to these texts children are given the opportunity to create their own meanings and to reflect on themselves as empowered learners.

Drawing it all together

Learning English, learning through English and learning about English should take place through engaging activities that support children to interact and play with language as well as learning language by interacting with texts. Supporting children to make language choices depends on the contexts provided by educators. Role play, drama, discussion about text, interaction around shared problems and tasks, are all ways that provide opportunities to learn, using both first and additional languages.

Questions for further discussion

- Evaluate some texts and resources for their suitability with young bilingual children. What criteria did you use?
- How can you best use your own language resources to support children to develop theirs?
- How can you support a child who does not share your language?
- Consider the many first languages Australian children might speak. Can you describe some ways you could support all of them to engage in learning?

Further reading

Some of these texts may reflect children's life experiences in your classroom or they can be shared with children to help them understand the many languages and cultures that are part of Australia. Books like *Cat and Fish* are also useful as they tell a story of two very different characters meeting and becoming friends. Their friendship develops despite, as one young learner pointed out (to one of our authors), the danger involved in a relationship such as theirs, when one partner is often the meal of the other. From his comment it was clear that he had connected with this story and understood that difference was not a barrier to friendship and harmony, a great observation for a young learner to make. It is in a critical response to texts that creativity can be fostered and it is when a sensitive teacher can support a young learner to build on their prior experiences to make new meanings (Gibbons, 2006).

Books

Title and publisher	Author	Special feature
Amelia Ellicott's Garden (Scholastic Press, 2004)	Liliana Stafford & Stephen Michael King	Set in an urban Australian multicultural suburb
Cat and Fish (Lothian Books, 2004)	John Grant	A story about two distinct animals creating a friendship
Cleversticks (Dragonfly Books, 1992)	Jena Chapman & Vilma Cencic	A hurricane story that will be relevant for any child from a Pacific island community
Handa's Surprise/Handa's Hen (Walker Books, 1997/ Walker Books, 2003)	Eileen Brown	An African story series
Isabella's Bed (Hachette Children, 2008)	Alison Lester	A migrant's story
Mother Goose's Action Rhymes (Macmillan Children, 2009)	Axel Scheffler	A book of traditional poems and rhymes accompanied with actions
My Two Blankets (Little Hare, 2014)	Irena Kobold	A refugee story
Rabbi Benjamin's Buttons (Charlesbridge, 2014)	Alice B McGinty	This story explores Jewish culture and religion
Refugees (Lothian Books, 2003)	David Miller	A refugee story that focuses on two birds who are searching for a home
So Much (Walker Books, 2008)	Trish Cooke	Set in a West Indian home in the UK
The Very Rich Kind Lady and Her One Hundred Dogs (Walker Books, 2003)	Chinlun Lee	A story about dogs and their kind lady benefactor. The dedication is written in Chinese language (Mandarin).
Ziba Came on a Boat (Penguin, 2007)	Liz Lofthouse	A refugee's story

Apps

The stories in these apps are told in clear voices in English. They are a great way to develop listening skills and encourage independent reading. These can be accessed by iTunes or Google Play. See Chapter 11 for a detailed discussion.

Lola's Alphabet Train – this provides interactive opportunities to learn sounds and letters in English and several other languages, using Lola the panda.

Playschool Artmaker – this facilitates the creation of pictures, animated films, story slide shows that include narration and photo uploads.

Popplet – this records and organises ideas and their interrelationships, where photos can be uploaded.

Interactive picture books

Animalia: The waterhole (Graeme Base)

Dear Zoo (Rod Campbell)

Duck in the Truck (Jez Alborough)

Hairy Maclary from Donaldson's Dairy (Lynley Dodd)

Kidzstory (Various) – this is a range of interactive fairy tales including The Ugly Duckling, Little Red Riding Hood and The Little Gingerbread Man

Olivia Acts Out (Ian Falconer)

PopOut! The Tale of Peter Rabbit (Beatrix Potter)

The Heart and the Bottle (Oliver Jeffers)

The Wonky Donkey (Craig Smith)

Organisations and resources for teachers

Australian Council of TESOL Associations (ACTA), www.tesol.org.au.

English as an Additional Language or Dialect: Teacher Resource (EAL/D), Australian Curriculum, Assessment and Reporting Authority (ACARA), www.acara .edu.au/curriculum/student_diversity/eald_teacher_resource.html.

EverythingESL.net, www.everythingesl.net/inservices/bics_calp.php.

Learning English through sharing rhymes, British Council, https:// learnenglishkids.britishcouncil.org/en/parents/articles/ learning-english-through-sharing-rhymes.

References

Australian Bureau of Statistics (2011). *2011 Census quick stats*. Retrieved at: www.censusdata.abs.gov.au/census_services/getproduct/census/2011/ quickstat/0.

Australian Council of TESOL Associations (ACTA) (2015). *The EAL/D Elaborations of the Australian Professional Standards for Teachers*. Retrieved at: www.tesol.org.au.

Australian Government Department of Education, Employment and Workplace Relations for the Council of Australian Governments (2009). *Belonging, Being and Becoming: The Early Years Learning Framework for Australia (EYLF)*, Canberra: Commonwealth of Australia. Retrieved at: www.mychild.gov.au/agenda/early-years-framework.

Baker, C. & Freebody, P. (1987). 'Constituting the child' in beginning school reading books. *British Journal of Sociology of Education*, 8(1), pp. 55–76, DOI:10.1080/0142569870080104.

Collier, V. & Thomas W. (2001). Literacy programs in prison: Ideas about purpose, culture, and content. *Journal of Correctional Education* 52 (2), pp. 68–73.

Cummins, J. (1981) Four misconceptions about language proficiency in bilingual education. *NABE Journal*, 5(3), pp. 31–45, DOI:10.1080/08855072.1981.10668409.

—— (1986). Empowering minority students: A framework for intervention. *Harvard Educational Review*, 56(1), pp. 18–36.

Cummins, J., Hu, S., Markus, P. & Montero, M. K. (2015). Identity texts and academic achievement: Connecting the dots in multilingual school contexts. *TESOL Quarterly* 49(3), Sept., pp. 555–81.

Dufficy, P. (2005). *Designing Learning for Diverse Classrooms*. Sydney: Primary English Teaching Association Australia (PETAA).

Gibbons, P. (2002). *Scaffolding Language, Scaffolding Learning: Teaching Second Language Learners in the Mainstream Classroom*. Portsmouth: Heinemann.

—— (2006). *Bridging Discourses in the ESL Classroom: Students, Teachers and Researchers*. London: Continuum.

Griffin, T., Hemphill, L., Camp, L. & Wolf, D. (2004). Oral discourse in the preschool years and later literacy skills. *First language*, 24, pp. 123–47, DOI:10.1177/0142723704042369.

Halliday, M.A.K. (1985). *Spoken and Written Language*. Victoria: Deakin University Press.

—— (2004). Three aspects of children's language development: Learning language, learning through language, learning about language. In J. J. Webster (ed.), *The Language of Early Childhood*. New York: Continuum, Ch.14, pp. 308–26.

Hammond, J. & Gibbons, P. (2001). What is scaffolding? In J. Hammond (ed.), *Scaffolding Teaching and Learning in Language and Literacy Education*. Sydney: Primary English Teaching Association Australia (PETAA), pp. 1–14.

Hertzberg, M. (2012). *Teaching English Language Learners in Mainstream Classes*. Sydney: Primary English Teaching Association Australia (PETAA).

Jones, M. (2012). iPads and kindergarten students' literacy development. *SCAN,* 31(4), pp. 31–40.

Krashen, S. (1992). *Fundamentals of Language Education.* Chicago: McGraw-Hill.

Lambert, W. E. (1975). Culture and language as factors in learning and education. In A. Wolfgang (ed.), *Education of Immigrant Students.* Toronto: Ontario Institute for Studies in Education.

Moll, L.C., Amanti, C., Neff, D. & Gonzalez, N. (1992). Funds of knowledge for teaching: Using a qualitative approach to connect homes and classrooms. *Theory Into Practice,* 31(2), pp. 132–41, DOI:10.1080/00405849209543534.

Painter, C. (1996). The development of language as a resource for thinking: A linguistic view of learning. In R. Hasan & G. Williams (eds), *Literacy in Society.* London: Longmans, pp. 50–85.

Skutnabb-Kangas, T. (2013). Today's Indigenous education is a crime against humanity: Mother-tongue-based multilingual education as an alternative? *TESOL in Context* 23(1&2), pp. 82–124.

Williams, G. (2000). The pedagogic device and the production of pedagogic discourse: A case example in early literacy education. In F. Christie (ed.) *Pedagogy and the Shaping of Consciousness,* London: Continuum, pp. 88–122.

Wong Fillmore, L. (1991). When learning a second language means losing the first. *Early childhood Research Quarterly,* 6(3), pp. 323–46. Retrieved at: www.sciencedirect.com.ezproxy2.library.usyd.edu.au/science/journal/08852006/6/3.

CHAPTER 6

Aboriginal perspectives in the early childhood literacy classroom

In this chapter we will consider the need for all early childhood educators to develop a rich understanding of and respect for Aboriginal* cultures and languages and how this respect can be shared with young children. We will also explore the importance for Aboriginal children of reflecting on Aboriginal culture and language in early childhood settings. This is challenging for many non-Aboriginal educators and we will look at the many respectful ways that both Aboriginal and non-Aboriginal people can bring these understandings into educational settings. The best ways are listening to authentic Aboriginal voices and using quality children's literature that genuinely reflects contemporary Aboriginal culture and language, thereby allowing Aboriginal authors to speak about their culture through their work.

Anticipated outcomes for the chapter

After working through this chapter, you should be able to:

- recognise that many Aboriginal languages and dialects are spoken and taught across the nation
- identify the languages or dialects spoken in your community using some of the resources supplied
- understand that many contemporary Aboriginal children may speak Aboriginal English, a dialect of English, and be aware of some strategies to support them

---

* I am writing in Sydney, New South Wales, and in this part of Australia, Aboriginal people have stated publicly that they wish to be referred to as 'Aboriginal' not 'Indigenous' people so I have chosen to respect their request throughout this chapter.

- evaluate the authenticity of contemporary texts to share with young children and identify stories with Aboriginal perspectives or written by Aboriginal authors
- share contemporary and Dreamtime stories by providing children with knowledge about the people who tell them, the languages in which they are told and the country to which the stories belong.

SCENARIO: KAY

Kay is reading to her young son, who is in the early years of primary school. She is reading a story written by an Aboriginal author and in the story the child lists the activities that he does with his mother and the illustrations show that the characters are Aboriginal. When Kay looks at her son, she notices from his expression how connected he is to the story because it reflects his life. They then read another story by an Aboriginal author about an emu egg in which the character makes a cake with her mother's help. This cake is special because it has been made with an emu egg. When she presents the cake to her family her Uncle says 'flamin' big cake, girl'. At this point in reading the story Kay's son says, 'Mum, read that again, read that again'.

> As his family lives in the city, this young boy's experience of emu eggs may be limited, but the characters, their interactions and the language, Aboriginal English, is very familiar because it reflects his contemporary Aboriginal culture and life.
>
> Adapted from Rushton (2015 pp. 232–3)

Not all children will have the same understandings and experiences of what most non-Aboriginal people would consider to be story (Disbray, 2008) as language choices and storytelling styles correlate to cultural practices and speech communities (Painter, 2000; Williams, 2000; Scollon & Scollon, 2001; Eades, 2013). The choice of both subject matter and language will therefore help a young reader to make connections to their own experiences. Helping students to make these connections can be supported by using a range of texts written by Aboriginal people such as those Kay was reading to her young son.

Introduction

Engaging young students is an important aspect of learning and Kay's scenario illustrates how important the choice of subject matter, familiar themes and connection to family is when engaging a young reader. Furthermore, the use of the home language, in this case Aboriginal English, is another key aspect of engagement. Books like *Why I love Australia* by Bronwyn Bancroft or *Shake a Leg* by Boori Monty Prior and Jan Ormerod are great stories and wonderful books for all readers. They will help young students to explore contemporary Aboriginal cultures and languages including Aboriginal English, as they provide engaging stories and illustrations. They are even more significant for an Aboriginal child as they make a clear connection to that child's linguistic and cultural heritage in their contemporary setting (Harrison & Greenfield, 2011). This connection with texts is the first step to encourage emergent readers and their communities in overcoming obstacles to literacy and address the problems posed in becoming literate (Exley, 2007; Goodson & Deakin Crick, 2009; Bamblett, 2013; Hill & Diamond, 2013).

Australia is (and always was) a multilingual, multicultural society

Identifying cultural and linguistic heritage is important because it supports an understanding of who Aboriginal people are, where they live and what languages they speak. Contrary to popular conceptions most Aboriginal people live in large cities or in regional areas rather than in the remote areas of Australia. There are approximately 66,000 Indigenous people in NSW major cities, which is more than the entire Indigenous population of the Northern Territory of 64,000 (Australian Bureau of Statistics 2006a). (Reeve, 2012, p. 20)

Aboriginal English A dialect of English spoken by many Aboriginal people.

Therefore most Aboriginal people speak English every day and many of them also speak **Aboriginal English**, which can include words from traditional languages as well as grammatical structures borrowed from a traditional language similar to many of the dialects of English spoken in the UK or the US. When Europeans first settled in Australia, Aboriginal people had already had contact with many other cultures from the Dutch to the Macassans. From the earliest days of the colony in New South Wales, Aboriginal people demonstrated their curiosity and willingness to explore foreign languages and cultures even though they were often forced away from their lands which posed a threat to their own languages and culture (Harris, 1993; Moses & Wigglesworth, 2008; Goodall & Cadzow, 2009). Aboriginal children, wherever they live, are the future custodians of the land and of the languages which Aboriginal people have used to describe and protect it for millennia (McLeod et al., 2014).

Languages spoken

At the time that Captain Phillip claimed the lands of Australia for the British crown by establishing a settlement at Sydney Cove, there were an estimated 250 distinct Aboriginal languages, each with their own dialects, being spoken in Australia (Schmidt, 1990). At this time of settlement, Aboriginal people showed their traditional flexibility and curiosity towards new learning experiences and their desire to maintain their own languages and cultures which many language groups still do (Bavin, 1993; Kral & Ellis, 2008). The land on which the Sydney Opera House is built, Bennelong Point, is named after Aboriginal leader Bennelong who travelled to England in the earliest days of the colony in the 18th century. Then in 1796, after this trip, he wrote a letter in English to those who had cared for him while he was there. Bennelong demonstrated both his understanding of a new culture and an attempt to participate in it without abandoning his own (Van Toorn, 2006). Bennelong's behaviour exemplifies the historical attempts of Aboriginal people to both maintain their own languages and cultures while simultaneously interacting with and learning from others.

Due to their cultural traditions, at the time of settlement most Aboriginal people would have been speaking more than one language or dialect. In the years after the invasion and settlement of Australia most Aboriginal people were forcibly removed from their lands and this led to changes in the languages that were spoken. Sadly, there are now very few traditional languages that remain strong, in the sense that the language is used as the main community language and that it is spoken across the generations of community members (Shnukal, 1985 & 2002; Schmidt, 1990). As Schmidt explains:

> In the post-contact period, relocation of Aboriginal people irreversibly altered the integral relationship between language, land and identity which had characterised distinct language speaking groups and their territories in the pre-contact era. (p. 13)

Language use is changing, for instance Kriol is a **creole** that is now the first language of many young children in remote areas of Australia. Creole languages often develop from **pidgin** which are 'the creation of skilled people faced with a sudden need to communicate with other people who do not speak the same language' (Harris, 1993, p. 145). Unlike pidgin languages that are not the primary language of any group, creole languages are created from pidgin in circumstances like this where the impetus is to communicate with people from many different language groups. These changes in language use are related to changes to the traditional organisation of communities. For instance, Aboriginal language and cultural groups may maintain links to their traditional lands but no longer live on country; rather, they live in communities which include many different language and cultural groups (Harris, 1993).

Creole A language developed from more than one language that becomes the first language of children.

Pidgin A hybrid language developed by at least two groups of people who do not share the same language and only use the hybrid language between each other in that situation.

Past government policies included forcibly removing Aboriginal children from their families and clan groups and this often resulted in their physical removal to places far away from their traditional lands and communities. They were often placed in institutions where they were not allowed to speak any language other than English. Aboriginal English developed in these conditions and should now be recognised as a legitimate dialect of English, because as Eades (2013) states, Aboriginal English is:

> the name given to dialects of English which are spoken by Aboriginal people and which differ from Standard English in systematic ways. The historical development of Aboriginal English is fascinating because it demonstrates how Aboriginal people have adapted their ways of communicating to English. (p. 79)

In contrast, Eades suggests that Standard English is 'simply the dialect of English which is spoken by the more powerful, dominant groups in society' (p. 78) and these dominant dialects will therefore differ across English-speaking countries such as the UK, the US, Canada, New Zealand and Australia where Standard Australian English (SAE) is the dominant dialect. Many linguistic and cultural groups who now live in cities can however still identify their traditional lands and maintain links to their traditions and languages. There are also movements to teach and revive traditional languages (Zuckermann & Walsh, 2011).

The importance of teaching children about their local Aboriginal communities

Naming is powerful and as Linda Tuhiwai Smith (1999) states:

> It is about retaining as much control over meanings as possible. By 'naming the world' people name their realities. For communities there are realities which can only be found in the Aboriginal language; the concepts which are self-evident in the Aboriginal language can never be captured by another language. (pp. 157–8)

It is therefore important to make as many links as possible between the cultural heritage of the child and their community, especially if their language heritage is at risk. The fact that Bennelong Point is named after Bennelong provides a starting point for examining the story of his people and their culture. The history of modern Australia has included the dispossession of Aboriginal people across all states and territories, but in many cases Aboriginal people have been able to maintain their links to their land and their cultural heritage. A surprising example is that of the home of the 18th-century warrior Pemulwuy, the Bediagal lands which are now known as the Georges River area in the middle of Sydney (Goodall & Cadzow, 2009). It was not until the 1960s with the spread of industrialisation and urbanisation that the Aboriginal people living in this area were suddenly noticed although they had lived there, on their traditional lands, from before the colony was formed.

> Living in the centre of the growing city, Aboriginal people survived the expectations that they would disappear. They have explored different strategies to rebuild communities from the fragments of early groups and the incoming travelers from across the eastern states. This has been the transformative process of resilience in conditions of stress, trauma and change: drawing on the past to create new futures. (Goodall & Cadzow, 2009, pp. 278–9)

Like the people from this area, other Aboriginal people are also able to trace their ancestry back to lands on which they have maintained their presence up to today, despite those lands having now been enveloped by cities. Looking at our own local areas through this lens provides an understanding of our own local history and landscape, to see how our community has changed over time. It also provides opportunities to explore the language and culture of the traditional owners of the land.

The importance of the home language as a starting point for reading and writing

Learning to read and write does not start on the first day of school. Many students come to school already well developed in literacy practices. However, in some remote communities the first day of school may be the first time students have encountered Standard Australian English. Moses and Yallop (2008) state:

> Like most Aboriginal children in remote area schools in Australia, the children . . . have found themselves in the charge of a newly graduated monolingual teacher who has never had sole responsibility for a class, has never had contact with remote Aboriginal children, and has no training in teaching English to speakers of other languages.(p. 52–3)

While this may not be the experience of most Aboriginal children, learning to read and write for a student who speaks the dominant dialect and is a member of the dominant culture will differ in some very important ways from members of disadvantaged minority families (Hill & Launder, 2010; Compton-Lilly, 2011). For instance, Aboriginal students have been over-represented in the lowest category in international tests for reading (Lokan, 2001) and therefore represent a disadvantaged minority group in this sense (Burney, 2006). Many Aboriginal students may come to school speaking Aboriginal English and may therefore need the support of educators to develop **bidialectally** just as other students, such as those in remote schools, may need support to develop bilingually.

Bidialectal The ability to speak two dialects of English.

Wherever they live in Australia and whether a young learner is speaking a creole language, an Aboriginal language, Aboriginal English or Standard Australian English, it is still important to respect, reflect and where possible use the language of the home and community to engage students and to provide a bridge between the language and culture of the home and the school (see Chapter 5 for a discussion of supporting bilingual children). Finding the place where cultures and languages meet and finding a way to balance these is a challenge.

Story has been identified as one of the eight ways of learning in an Aboriginal language classroom that helps to meet this challenge (Yunkaporta, 2009). Aboriginal ways of learning and making meaning have also been expressed in the concept of **two-way schooling**. This concept was developed by Aboriginal Elders who wanted their language and culture to be respected and taught in schools like those at Yirrkala and Yipirinya. The term was developed to describe what was special about these schools in which Aboriginal language and culture were taught. As Harris (1990) notes:

Two-way learning/schooling A term, attributed to an Aboriginal Elder, which reflects a method of engaging children to learn about both cultures; not just western culture, as in one-way learning.

> The history of the term two-way school goes back at least to the early 1970s . . . The term was used in contrast to the government school which was a one-way school. (p. 13)

It is important to recognise this principle of two-way schooling and to try and teach all students about Aboriginal culture.

REFLECTION

Think about your local area. Are there any Aboriginal street names or suburb names? Can you identify the language they were taken from? Do you know the name of the Aboriginal custodians of the land in your local community? Are you familiar with any of their stories?

Learning about culture through story

Story provides a window into any culture and Aboriginal stories provide knowledge about land, culture and language. For children in the early years of school, story can be one of the most engaging aspects of learning. As long ago as 1839 the Reverend Watson wrote about the Wiradjuri children in his Mission school in Wellington, New South Wales:

> [T]he children taught to read at the Mission House are much attached to books, consider it a severe punishment to be deprived of them, and prefer the present of a new one to almost anything else. While they are learning the Alphabet, and to spell, they feel no interest, and the work of instruction is tedious to both the teacher and the pupil; but when they have overcome these preliminary difficulties, and are able to read so as to understand, their attention becomes excited; they begin to feel a pleasure in the employment, and never appear to be wearied with it. The Aboriginal natives are indeed capable of attaining to the knowledge of any thing in which they may be instructed. (Van Toorn, 2006, p. 35)

This is the level of engagement that we should aim for today so that the descendents of the Wiradjuri are as engaged in learning as their ancestors were. However, Aboriginal children, unlike children from the dominant culture, often find that their lives, social values and language patterns are not reflected in the texts, cultural practices and stories that they encounter at school. Many children will have interacted with texts from their earliest years and will find them again in the educational settings but some children may be excluded from the texts read and produced, particularly in the school (Bishop, 2003).

Helen Empacher is an Aboriginal woman and school principal and in the following interview she shares some suggestions on how to develop an Aboriginal perspective. Helen is a descendant of the Yuin people from the south coast of New South Wales and later in this chapter she shares some practical strategies as she teaches a lesson using a book written for and by preschool children from the Little Yuin preschool.

Interview with Helen Empacher, school principal and Aboriginal woman, descendant of the Yuin people of NSW

How would you include an Aboriginal perspective in the classroom?

- Make contact with the local Aboriginal people and if there's not someone in the school, make contact with any Aboriginal families and with the Aboriginal Land Council and start talking to somebody; it's all about communication and relationships.
- Network with other schools because there could be somebody who can provide a lesson model or discuss what a lesson should include.
- Research appropriate ways to teach Aboriginal history, culture and language.
- Find resources such as using the Aboriginal language map. Finding appropriate resources can suffice for the lack of culturally connected people in the school setting. Examples of these resources are using the Aboriginal language map or contacting the Aboriginal Land Council.

What preparations are needed for reading a Dreamtime story?

It is really important to know who wrote it, what purpose was behind it, where that story is actually from and whether or not it is actually accepted by that community. *My Little Yuin* is an example of the community getting that book written and supporting it quite obviously and so there's no question about using that as a resource.

How can you check that a text or resource is acceptable?

Check with the Aboriginal Education Unit with the department or with your local Aboriginal Education Consultative Group (AECG) and again your Aboriginal Land Council.

There are many wonderful books available for non-Aboriginal and Aboriginal educators to choose from in developing a culturally inclusive pedagogy that honours both language and culture. It is through story that Aboriginal people have kept their culture alive over many millennia despite invasion and colonisation and it is through story that we can make our pedagogy inclusive. 'You tell your personal stories about any topic right at the start and make sure you give the students a chance to share their stories as well. That way you are drawing on everybody's home culture and knowledge for the lesson.' (Yunkaporta, 2009, p. 4) For non-Aboriginal educators, bringing books of authentic Aboriginal stories into the classroom is one of the best ways to start this sharing. This is because for Aboriginal people stories were always very important because they provided information about the land and how to protect it and in this way knowledge was passed down the generations. As Martin and Rose (2008) state:

> Every landform in the entire Australian continent was once associated with . . . a sacred story, interconnected in complex networks of 'Dreaming tracks' or 'songlines', where the ancestor beings travelled over the country in creation times. (p. 74)

There was therefore always a central place for story in Aboriginal culture as it was through learning the stories that related to the land, that men and women became the Elders and leaders of their communities. Telling and listening to stories was the way information about sources of food and water were learnt as families walked across their lands. The Dreaming stories explained both the creation of the land and also provided guidelines for living on and protecting the land that sustained life itself. Dreaming stories are not simple stories created to entertain children; a version of a story may have been told to children but all Dreaming stories are complex, layered and relate important information to those who have been authorised and inducted into the culture and can correctly interpret the story's deeper meaning (Martin & Rose, 2008). It is therefore very important when introducing Dreaming stories to acknowledge their religious and scientific importance of Aboriginal people, and the country from which they came.

Story has also provided a way for individual Aboriginal people to share their family histories and it is through these stories that their fellow Australians have come to better understand their own history. Well-known Aboriginal people like Sally Morgan and Archie Roach have shared their personal stories in pictures, words and songs and in doing so have shared the wisdom of their people. Traditionally, Elders carefully selected stories according to the audience and Aboriginal storytelling was most often accompanied or expressed through song and dance. Contemporary Aboriginal people still practise storytelling or 'yarning', stories often told with a lot of humour in families and communities (Mills, Sunderland & Davis-Warra, 2013). While there are many more texts available than those listed in this chapter (see Further reading) we have tried to provide a list that includes a variety of special features. All of the books are written or illustrated by Aboriginal people or produced by Aboriginal communities and the subject matter suits all young children but each text explores at least one very important aspect of Aboriginal language and culture. The stories include both contemporary and traditional stories and some are told in Aboriginal English or use words from traditional languages, but all provide an opportunity to share an Aboriginal story and could therefore be used to develop a culturally inclusive Aboriginal perspective.

Developing an Aboriginal perspective

Choosing authentic texts that reflect the language and culture of Aboriginal people provides opportunities for all children to explore Australia's rich linguistic and cultural heritage and also provides a focal point for Aboriginal children to make connections to their own cultural heritage. The text *Our Little Yuin* was produced by the Little Yuin Aboriginal Preschool and it uses the Yuin language to describe the animals in their country. The preschoolers provided the illustrations and the text is a walk through Yuin country, describing what the children see and do. The following lesson provides opportunities for children to develop English as well as naming their surrounds using one of Australia's traditional languages.

Figure 6.1 Book cover of *Our Little Yuin*

This is the lesson plan that Helen used and it provides a starting point for lesson planning with an Aboriginal perspective, perhaps using some of the texts suggested in the Further reading section. This lesson plan transcribes the lesson to demonstrate the language used throughout and some of Helen's strategies including the use of puppets and dramatic play (See Chapters 3 and 9).

Helen Empacher's lesson plan example

Discussing *Our little Yuin*

Learning intentions:

- Learn about Aboriginal culture and some words from one Aboriginal language spoken in New South Wales. (*Australian Curriculum* Cross-curriculum priority: Aboriginal and Torres Strait Islander histories and cultures).
- Compose simple texts to convey an idea or message by using pictures and graphics to support your word choice.

- Demonstrate developing skills and strategies to read and comprehend a short, predictable text on a familiar topic, identifying unfamiliar words and attempting to use experience and context to work out word meanings.
- Demonstrate developing skills and knowledge in grammar, punctuation and vocabulary when responding to a text and composing a description.
- Identify how circumstances of place add information to a description and experiment with adverbial phrases in structured and guided activities to indicate when, where and how actions occurred, for example last week, at home.

Before reading: Talk about Yuin country, who and what you would find there and what it looks like. Introduce the puppet, *koogoonyaroo*, who will feature in the story.

Ask the children if they know his name, and if they know that he has more than one Aboriginal name (*kookaburra*, the Wiradjuri name and *koogoonyaroo*, the Yuin name). Tell the children that Aboriginal people have many languages and that they are going to learn some words in one of them.

Modelled reading: Read the book and focus on the Yuin words – *umbarra* (black duck); *gurrie* (snake); *koogarty* (tree frog); *djunga* (octopus); *koogoonyaroo* (kookaburra); *janan-gabitch* (echidna).

After reading: Model 'walking in role' as *koogoonyaroo* (for example flapping his wings, pecking at the ground).

Ask some children to 'walk in role' as each of the characters such as *koogoonyaroo*, *gurrie*, and *djunga*. Arrange the whole class in a circle and walk around the circle in the role as *umbarra*, making his familiar sound.

Joint construction: Use action verbs to describe the behaviour of these animals. *display* with pictures from the book: *umbarra* waddles, *gurrie* slithers, *koogarty* jumps, *djunga* swims, *koogoonyaroo* flies; and *janan-gabitch* walks.

Independent writing: Pairs of students pick their favourite animal and write (or cut and paste) a sentence that finishes with an adverbial phrase of place (circumstance) to be displayed in the room and accompanied by a picture:

to the water

across the grass

in the trees

under the sea

up in the sky

through the bush

Helen Empacher teaches the lesson on *Our Little Yuin* to a kindergarten class

This beautiful lady over here, who I look a lot like, that's my mum, and that's my pop. Do you have a pop as well? [children's response] 'No'. You might call him something else. What do you call your granddad? Some people call him granddad, grandpa. Here are some other people who are from my family. Some of them still live in Yuin country but some of them live in other places like me, because I live in Sydney now.

Other than telling you about Yuin country and my family I would like to read you a story *Our Little Yuin*. Some children from a preschool down in Yuin country actually made this book. Aunty GG gave me this as a present. Aren't I lucky? So this is all about Yuin country and the animals that we find in Yuin country and sometimes you might hear me say words that don't really look like that. What does

Figure 6.2 Helen Empacher shows pictures of Yuin country and her relatives and gives the children some background information

that look like to you? [children's response]'Duck'. Yes that's what you say, but Yuin people, we say *umburra*.

Helen reads *Our little Yuin* to the class

Aren't they great colours? They work very nicely together. Can you see the beach? That's the end. So who would like to have a turn at being our Kookaburra? Try and make the noises as well. What did Yuin people call the kookaburra? Kooganyarroo.

(*Child puts on the kookaburra puppet.*) What sound are you going to make early in the morning?

(Helen plays the sound of kookaburras on the IWB and children copy.)

Who thinks they can be Aboriginal dancers like we were in our warm up? I'm going to put that music on again. Use all of the space that's in here, so spread out. I'm going to call out the name of the animal. You're going to have to think about what animal I'm talking about because I'm going to use the Yuin words and then you've got to be that animal. Let's see how you go. (Didgeridoo music starts) *Djunga!* Floating around, floating in the water and then shoot off, and floating again. *Gurrie!* Snake! Floating like a *djunga* again, *umbarra* black duck, waddle, waddle. *Koogoonyaroo, koogoonyaroo.* Fly, fly…

What have we learnt about? What about the *kooganyaroo*? Can I tell everyone about *kooganyaroo*? You say *kookaburra*, but *kookaburra* is actually already an Aboriginal word. It's not from Yuin country, it's from another country in Australia called Wiradjuri. So there's another group of Aboriginal people called Wiradjuri people. I'm a Yuin person but there are Wiradjuri people and their word is actually *kookaburra*. We think it's English, well it is English but it's taken from the Wiradjuri

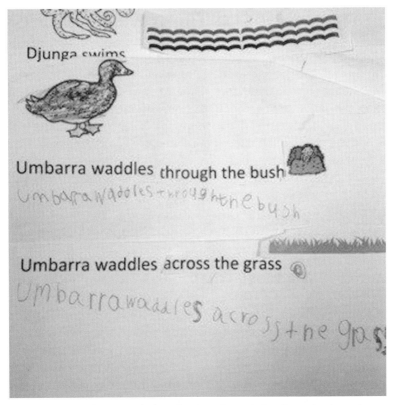

Djunga swims

Umbarra waddles through the bush

Umbarra waddles across the grass

Figure 6.3 Children match the Aboriginal words for the animals to the landscape

people. There are lots of words that we have taken from Aboriginal people, even places like *Maroubra*. We take words all the time. *Pizza* comes from Italy, *bonjour* comes from France, so I'm speaking lots of languages at once. So *kooganyaroo* is Yuin but *kookaburra* is Wiradjuri, still an Aboriginal word.

These samples of the children's work demonstrate how they were able to make meaning from the text choosing their own adverbial phrases of place to cut and paste a comprehensible sentence, so *Umbarra* can both waddle across the grass and through the bush (Rossbridge & Rushton, 2010). Some students cut and pasted their sentences using picture clues to complete them and others were also able to write their sentences.

REFLECTION

Consider Helen's advice and the principles of inclusion in the lesson she taught. Choose a text written by a contemporary Aboriginal author. Can you prepare some activities for children that engage them in learning about Aboriginal culture using some of Helen's strategies?

Cultural inclusion: Learning who 'we' are

Who 'we' are as a pedagogical construction (Alton-Lee, 2003, p. 26) needs to actively include all children and include all the cultures and languages of their families and communities. Choosing materials in which the 'we' includes an Aboriginal perspective will develop this sense of inclusion. In this one question 'Who thinks they can be Aboriginal dancers like we were in our warm up?' Helen involves all the children in the class. At the same time she aligns them with herself as an Aboriginal woman and includes them in the cultural practice of naming by using the Yuin language. She engages the students using drama and challenges them to use their memories and imaginations to move like the animals she names. 'I'm going to call out the name of the animal. You're going to have to think about what animal I'm talking about because I'm going to use the Yuin words and then you've got to be that animal.'

Drawing it all together

Respecting Aboriginal culture includes respect for Aboriginal knowledge and ways of learning. Therefore developing an Aboriginal perspective means respecting the way children use language to communicate, especially if the language used is Aboriginal English. Non-Aboriginal people can use the organisations and resources listed below to support their personal journeys in finding out about their local Aboriginal communities. There are also the wonderful resources produced by Aboriginal people to support non-Aboriginal educators in developing an inclusive pedagogy and to present the authentic voices of Aboriginal people.

Questions for further discussion

- How would you describe who 'we' are as Australians?
- How can you best start to learn about and communicate with your local Aboriginal community?
- What criteria can you use to decide which stories are inclusive and respectful to Aboriginal people?
- How can you include drama, song, dance and play in an inclusive pedagogy?
- How can you best support the child's home language in your setting?

Further reading

For an understanding about Aboriginal life in New South Wales, refer to Nigel Parbury's book, *Survival*. For stories to use in the class, here is a table of recommended titles.

Parbury, N. (2005). *Survival: A History of Aboriginal Life in New South Wales*. Surry Hills: NSW Department of Aboriginal Affairs.

Title and publisher	Author	Special feature
A is for Aunty (ABC Books, 2000)	Elaine Russell	Artwork by an Aboriginal artist and illustrator from Tingha, New South Wales
An Australian ABC of animals (Little Hare Books, 2004)	Bronwyn Bancroft	Artwork by a Bundjalung artist and illustrator (New South Wales)
As I Grew Older (Working Title Press, 2014)	Ian Abdulla	Created by an Aboriginal artist using Aboriginal English
Butcher Paper Texta Black board and Chalk (One Day Hill, 2012)	Ruby Hunter & Archie Roach	A songbook prepared by two Aboriginal musicians and illustrated by Ruby Hunter
Me and My Mum (Indij Readers, 2003)	Anita Heiss & Jay Davis	Created by a Wiradjuri author and Biripi illustrator (New South Wales)
Our Little Yuin (Little Yuin Aboriginal Preschool, 2015)	Children of Little Yuin Aboriginal Preschool	Explores Yuin language (New South Wales) and is a story written by children
Possum and Wattle: My Big Book of Australian words (Little Hare Books, 2010)	Bronwyn Bancroft	Artwork by a Bundjalung artist and illustrator (New South Wales)
Shake a Leg (Allen & Unwin, 2010)	Boori Monty Prior & Jan Ormerod	Boori Monty Prior, an Aboriginal man from North Queensland tells a contemporary story that includes traditional ones using some words from the local area's Aboriginal language
The Emu Egg (Indij Readers, 2003)	Sharon Thorpe and David Leffler	Written in Aboriginal English by a Ngiyampaa author (New South Wales) and Bigambul illustrator (Queensland)
The Naked Boy and the Crocodile (Indigenous Literary Foundation, 2011)	Edited by Andy Griffiths	Stories by children from remote Aboriginal communities told in Aboriginal English
Tucker (Omnibus Books, 1994)	Ian Abdulla	Created by an Aboriginal artist using Aboriginal English
When I Was Little, Like You (Allen & Unwin, 2003)	Mary Malbunka	Stories told by an Aboriginal artist using Luritja language from the Papunya region (Central Australian Western Desert)
When the World was New: in Rainbow Snake Land (Bookshelf, 1988)	Catherine Berndt & Raymond Meeks	Shares stories that were originally told to the author in the Gunwinggu language (Northern Territory)
Why I Love Australia (Little Hare Books, 2012)	Bronwyn Bancroft	Created by a Bundjalung artist and illustrator (New South Wales)

Useful websites

Many of the New South Wales websites provide links to national websites and they are typical of online resources available in most states of Australia.

Australian Institute of Aboriginal and Torres Strait Islander Studies, http://aiatsis.gov.au

Koori Mail, www.koorimail.com

Language maps (see Our languages below)

Magabala Books, www.magabala.com

NSW Aboriginal Education Consultative Group, www.aecg.nsw.edu.au

NSW Aboriginal Land Council, www.alc.org.au

NSW Reconciliation Council, www.nswreconciliation.org.au/resources

Our languages, www.ourlanguages.net.au/languages/language-maps.html (includes resources for Language maps)

References

Alton-Lee, A. (2003). *Quality Teaching for Diverse Students in Schooling: Best Evidence Synthesis*. Wellington: Ministry of Education. Retrieved at: www.educationcounts.govt.nz/publications/series/2515/5959.

Bamblett, L. (2013). Read with me everyday: Community engagement and English literacy outcomes at Erambie Mission. *Australian Aboriginal Studies Journal of the Australian Institute of Aboriginal and Torres Strait Islander Studies.* 1, pp. 101–9.

Bavin, E. (1993). Language and culture: Socialisation in a Warlpiri community. In M. Walsh & C. Yallop (eds), *Language and Culture in Aboriginal Australia*. Canberra: Aboriginal Studies Press, pp. 85–96.

Bishop, R. (2003). Changing power relations in education: Kaupapa Māori messages for 'mainstream' education in Aotearoa/New Zealand. *Comparative Education*, 39(2) (27), pp. 221–38. Retrieved at: www.jstor.org/stable/3099882.

Burney, L. (2006). Education as the cornerstone of social justice. *Developing Practice: The Child, Youth and Family Work Journal.* 17, pp. 5–7. Retrieved at: http://search.informit.com.au.ezproxy1.library.usyd.edu.au/documentSummary;dn=838073187998823;res=IELHSS> ISSN: 1445–6818.

Compton-Lilly, C. (2011). Literacy and schooling in one family across time. *Research in the Teaching of English,* 45(3), pp. 224–51, DOI:849266511.

Disbray, S. (2008). Storytelling styles: A study of adult–child interactions in narrations of a picture book in Tennant Creek. In J. Simpson & G. Wigglesworth (eds), *Children's Language and Multilingualism: Indigenous Language Use at Home and School*. London: Continuum, pp. 56–78.

Eades, D. (2013). *Aboriginal Ways of Using English*. Canberra: Aboriginal Studies Press.

Exley, B (2007). Meanings emerging in practice for linguistically and culturally diverse students: An early years multiliteracies project. *International Journal of Pedagogies and Learning*, 3(3), pp. 101–13. Retrieved at: http://search.informit.com.au.ezproxy1.library.usyd.edu.au/documentSummary;dn=307035082006640;res=IELHSS> ISSN: 1833–4105.

Goodall, H. & Cadzow, A. (2009). *Rivers and Resilience: Aboriginal People on Sydney's Georges River*. Sydney: UNSW Press.

Goodson, I. & Deakin Crick, R. (2009). Curriculum as narration: Tales from the children of the colonized. *The Curriculum Journal*, 20(3), pp. 225–36, DOI:10.1080/09585170903195852.

Harris, J. (1993) Losing and gaining a language: the story of Kriol in the Northern Territory. In M. Walsh & C. Yallop (eds), *Language and Culture in Aboriginal Australia*. Canberra: Aboriginal Studies Press, pp. 145–54.

Harris, S. (1990). *Two-Way Aboriginal Schooling*. Canberra: Aboriginal Studies Press.

Harrison, N. & Greenfield, M. (2011). Relationship to place: Positioning Aboriginal knowledge and perspectives in classroom pedagogies. *Critical Studies in Education*, 52 (1), DOI:10.1080/17508487.2011.53651, pp. 65–76.

Hill, S. & Diamond, A. (2013). Family literacy in response to local contexts. *Australian Journal of Language and Literacy*, 36 (1), pp. 48–55. Retrieved at: http://search.informit.com.au.ezproxy2.library.usyd.edu.au/fullText;dn=196644;res=AEIPT> ISSN: 1038–1562, viewed 22 January 2014.

Hill, S. & Launder, N. (2010). Oral language and beginning to read. *Australian Journal of Language and Literacy*, 33(3), pp. 240–54.

Kral, I. & Ellis, E. (2008). Children, language and literacy in the Ngaanyatjarra lands. In J. Simpson & G. Wigglesworth (eds), *Children's Language and Multilingualism: Indigenous Language Use at Home and School*. London: Continuum, pp. 154–72.

Lokan, J. (2001). *15-up and Counting, Reading, Writing, Reasoning: How Literate are Australian Students?: The PISA 2000 Survey of Students' Reading, Mathematical and Scientific Literacy Skills*. Melbourne: ACER.

Martin, J.R. & Rose, D. (2008). *Genre Relations: Mapping Culture*. London: Equinox.

McLeod, S., Verdon, S. & Bennetts Kneebone, L. (2014). Celebrating young Indigenous children's speech and language competence. *Early Childhood Research Quarterly*, 29, pp. 118–31. Retrieved at: www.sciencedirect.com.ezproxy2.library.usyd.edu.au/science/article/pii/S0885200613000975.

Mills, K., Sunderland, N. & Davis-Warra, J. (2013). Yarning circles in the literacy classroom. *National Report on Schooling in Australia. The Reading Teacher*. 67(4), pp. 285–9, DOI:10.1002/trtr.1195.

Moses, K. & Wigglesworth, G. (2008) The silence of the frogs: Dysfunctional discourse in the 'English-only' Aboriginal classroom. In J. Simpson &

G. Wigglesworth (eds), *Children's Language and Multilingualism: Indigenous Language Use at Home and School*. London: Continuum, pp. 129–53.

Moses, K. & Yallop, C. (2008). Questions about questions. In J. Simpson & G. Wigglesworth (eds), *Children's Language and Multilingualism: Indigenous Language Use at Home and School*. London: Continuum, pp. 30–55.

Painter, C. (2000). Preparing for school: Developing a semantic style for educational knowledge. In F. Christie (ed.), *Pedagogy and the Shaping of Consciousness*. London: Continuum, pp. 66–87.

Reeve, R. (2012). Indigenous poverty in New South Wales major cities: A multidimensional analysis. *Australian Aboriginal Studies Journal of the Australian Institute of Aboriginal and Torres Strait Islander Studies*. 1, pp. 19–34.

Rossbridge, J. & Rushton, K. (2010). *Conversations about Text: Teaching Grammar Using Literary Texts*. Sydney: Primary English Teaching Association Australia (PETAA).

Rushton, K. (2015). Learning to be literate in Aboriginal communities: The significance of text. PhD thesis, University of Sydney. Retrieved at: http://hdl.handle.net/2123/12779.

Schmidt, A. (1990). *The Loss of Australia's Aboriginal Language Heritage*. Canberra: Aboriginal Studies Press.

Scollon, R. & Scollon, S. (2001). *Intercultural Communication* (2nd edn). Malden, MA: Blackwell Publishing.

Shnukal, A. (1985). Why Torres Strait 'broken English' is not English. In M. J. Christie (ed.), *Aboriginal Perspectives on Experience and Learning: The Role of Language in Aboriginal Education*. Victoria: Deakin University Press.

—— (2002). Some language-related observations for teachers in Torres Strait and Cape York Peninsula schools. *The Australian Journal of Indigenous Education*, 30 (1).

Smith, L. Tuhiwai (1999). *Decolonizing Methodologies: Research and Indigenous Peoples*. Dunedin: University of Otago Press.

Van Toorn, P. (2006). *Writing Never Arrives Naked: Early Aboriginal Cultures of Writing in Australia*. Canberra: Aboriginal Studies Press.

Williams, G. (2000). The pedagogic device and the production of pedagogic discourse: A case example in early literacy education. In F. Christie (ed.), *Pedagogy and the Shaping of Consciousness*. London: Continuum, pp. 88–122.

Yunkaporta, T. (2009). *Aboriginal Pedagogies at the Cultural Interface*. PhD thesis, James Cook University, Australia. Retrieved at: http://eprints.jcu.edu.au/10974.

Zuckermann, G. & Walsh, M. (2011). Stop, revive, survive: Lessons from the Hebrew revival applicable to the reclamation, maintenance and empowerment of Aboriginal languages and cultures. *Australian Journal of Linguistics* 31(1), pp. 111–27, DOI: 10.1080/07268602.2011.532859.

CHAPTER 7

Reading with children: Quality literature and language development

Reading with children is one of the most important ways that children can develop their language and be supported in becoming literate. This chapter uses excerpts from a range of contemporary picture books alongside reading expert Margaret Meek's concept of the 'reading lessons' that emerge from reading quality literary texts with children (1988). It provides a set of criteria as a basis for choosing quality literature. The role of talk in the reading process using Carol Fox's 'talking like a book' and Aidan Chambers' 'tell me' framework is also explored. Responding to literature through related creative arts activities concludes the chapter.

Anticipated outcomes for the chapter

After working through this chapter you should be able to:

- develop your understanding of the importance of reading quality literature with young children
- choose appropriate literary texts to share with young children
- plan and implement rich language experiences that provide spaces and places to play with the language in imaginative literary texts.

SCENARIO: READING WITH 15-MONTH-OLD JORDAN

Fifteen-month-old Jordan toddles excitedly across the room with one of his favourite stories, *Where is the Green Sheep?* (Fox & Horacek, 2004). He gives it to his father who asks, 'Would you like this book AGAIN?' Jordan nods. 'Shall Daddy read to you?' Jordan nods, smiles and waits expectantly for his father to lift him up beside him onto the lounge. Together they share the book with Jordan turning the pages, sometimes with a little help from his father. With each familiar rendition of 'Here is the___sheep' Jordan points to it and repeats the adjective that is associated with this sheep as they are encountered. His father stops frequently and asks Jordan what each sheep is doing. He affirms Jordan's response and extends his single word answer, 'Yes. You're right, this is the red sheep.' At each question about the whereabouts of the green sheep Jordan puts both hands in the air, with palms facing upward, and shrugs. He giggles in delight when they turn to the final page and find the green sheep sleeping.

Postscript: It soon becomes clear to Jordan's father that one book is not enough for this reading session and Jordan then chooses Rod Campbell's *Dear Zoo*. Jordan takes great pleasure in lifting each flap on the page, when appropriate, to discover the animal below. He and his father make the noise of each animal together before moving on. Finally there will be another reading of *Where is the Green Sheep?* before his father finishes.

Figure 7.1 An example of reading to babies: Asher's father and big brother share the reading experience

Introduction: Shared reading of literature

> Children depend upon us for their future. We have to read aloud to them. There is no choice. We have to allow their ears to be their teachers. As we read to them they will learn about language, and all the ways of using it, and about life, and all the ways of living it. How can we not read aloud to the children in our lives? (Excerpt from Mem Fox's website (memfox.com))

Chapter 2 focus on the importance of reading with babies from the moment they are born – even in utero Initially babies will be soothed by the regular patterns and voice inflections of the parent, caregiver or older sibling but soon they will display pleasure when a book is held up to them, especially if it is a favourite story. Educational theorists including Vygotsky (1978) and Bruner (1990) have theorised about the interdependent relationship between thought, language and cognitive development. Quality literary texts are wonderful models for a child's developing language skills and the shared reading of literature is a cornerstone of both *The Early Years Learning Framework* (2009) and *The Australian Curriculum: English* (2015).

Reading aloud to children and the type of talk that accompanies such **shared reading** is a critical factor on the road to independent reading for young learners. While most children will have been immersed in all types of reading, from watching their parents send text messages to looking at cereal boxes, junk mail and other print materials, there is a particular importance in experiencing books and stories. Literature is an artform often not mentioned with the other creative arts (Ewing, 2010) yet it is the art form that most Australian parents will have some experience with (Australia Council, 2010). It is not only beneficial for language and academic learning but also provides a window onto how others think and feel, how the world can be understood and wondered at, as well as helping children (and adults) learn empathy, compassion and integrity from the stories they encounter.

Shared reading An interactive reading experience where one or more children join with an adult to listen and discuss a shared book. Shared reading can be a parent reading with a child, a childcare worker reading with a small group or a teacher reading with a whole class.

We should always remember that sharing literature is about enjoyment. It should never be regarded as a chore. The intimacy of sitting together to share a story at any time of day or snuggling down at bedtime to read together is special. Computer games, DVDs and TV, while also important at appropriate times, should never be offered as a replacement. Reading with children is at once a fun activity and one of the most important ways children can be supported as they continue to learn through and about language. In the scenario above, Jordan is learning lots of vocabulary (such as several colours, weather terms, position, shapes) as well as the repetitive question-and-answer sequence. He is learning how to turn the pages as well as how to play with language (for example 'the star sheep'). There is a distinct pattern coupled with lots of repetition in both of the books his father is reading with him. Interestingly, humour is also an important part of both books – the green sheep is depicted as a rebel character – while all the other sheep are actively engaged in some activity, the green sheep is fast asleep. The person in *Dear Zoo* (Campbell, 1982) is obviously having fun sending lots of animals who would make inappropriate pets.

An early writer about the importance of reading with young children, Dorothy Butler (1979, 1980), wrote about how reading with Cushla, her profoundly disabled granddaughter, not only provided comfort during many painful times, but also helped Cushla defy many odds about her intellectual development. Butler attributed Cushla's almost miraculous progress to the reading of stories.

Even when accomplished as readers, many older children and adults find it is pleasurable to be read to and it is no different for the young child. Listening to an accomplished reader also provides a less experienced listener with a model of how words can fit together seemingly effortlessly to make meaning. At first, the attraction will be the uninterrupted attention as well as the lilting sound of the human voice and the patterns of language that a baby will enjoy. They will soon begin to respond with vocal interaction and gesture well before they can speak. And a range of research over decades (for example Butler, 1980; Meek, 1982, 1988; Saxby, 1997; Krashen, 2010) demonstrates unequivocally that children are empowered by literature: it encourages them to see their own thoughts, anxieties and imaginings articulated through the lives of others, and stretches their understanding of their own and others' worlds. For example, through a story like *How to catch a star* (Jeffers, 2005) a child will learn about not giving up even when things seem impossible, while learning more about what a star is. *Banjo and Ruby Red* (Gleeson & Blackwood, 2014) might help children learn about friendship and loyalty – and also realise that it is okay to be a little different. Anthony Browne's *Silly Billy* (2006) might help anxious children feel a little less so when they understand that everyone has worries. A discussion about compassion and tolerance might emerge from a shared reading of *The Very Best of Friends* (Wild & Vivas, 2004).

Reading aloud thus provides opportunities to enjoy text at a variety of levels. Books with rich and interesting words, rhymes and vocabulary are not only fun to listen to but also assist in developing phonemic awareness which are explored in more detail in Chapter 8.

REFLECTION

In *Reading Aloud to Children* Bill Spence suggests a number of excellent reading aloud principles for reading aloud including:

- becoming familiar with the book before it is read aloud (for example leafing through the book or examining a few images)
- creating interest in the book by first exploring the front and back covers
- encouraging prediction as the story unfolds
- asking questions and allowing opportunities for the child, or children, to do so
- reading expressively

- involving the listener
- talking about the story after the reading
- responding through related arts activities (story drama, painting and drawing characters, movement, related poetry or songs (2004, p. 2).

Experiment with reading aloud a favourite story to a young child, a family member or even into the mirror using Spence's principles above. Would you add other principles to the list? Take the time to play with voice inflection, pace and pitch. Does this kind of play encourage you to explore the language and, at the same time, to focus on your vocal skills? Why might young children enjoy the repetition of favourite words and phrases? What does the use of facial expression and gesture, rhyme and rhythm add to the reading? Why?

Literature 'lessons'

No philosophy, no analysis, no aphorism, be it ever so profound, can compare in intensity and richness of meaning with a narrated story. (McGowan, 2003, p. 138)

In her book *How Texts Teach What Readers Learn*, Margaret Meek (1988) examines the process of reading a story from the child's perspective. She demonstrates clearly how listening to and sharing stories not only helps children make meaning about who they are and how they relate in their worlds; it also implicitly teaches many other things about language. Children learn that narratives are set in time and space; stories are usually about things that happen to people or animals in a particular place or across several settings. While they may be imagined stories, children learn that there may still be a lot of truths in these stories. Learning a much loved and often read story by heart then enables children to 'bring the words to the page' and discover how language can be played with. They come to understand that the author's voice and viewpoint might be different from theirs as they begin to interpret a story for themselves.

Narrative A narrative is the story of events or experiences, whether real or imagined, often presented with a number of problems that are resolved at the conclusion of the story.

Author's voice An author's choice of language allows readers to hear and feel the particular personality of the author, which is often similar across their various stories.

Building on Meek's work, Carol Fox's research (1993) documents how young children who were read to frequently absorbed the ability to talk more formally, in her words, to 'talk like a book'. She asserts that this oral kind of literacy provided confidence in telling stories and helped extend their imaginations but also provided a transition to learning to read. Timothy's drawing of *Ugly Sluggly* and character profile (Figure 7.2) followed by his oral story about *Cuddly Ugly Sluggly*, as scribed by his grandmother (Figure 7.3) supports Fox's assertion that the interactions with words and images helps the child create his or her own stories.

A child's ability to think imaginatively is thus extended through stories and they learn how they can evoke feelings through sharing their own stories with others.

Figure 7.2 Drawing of *Ugly Sluggly*

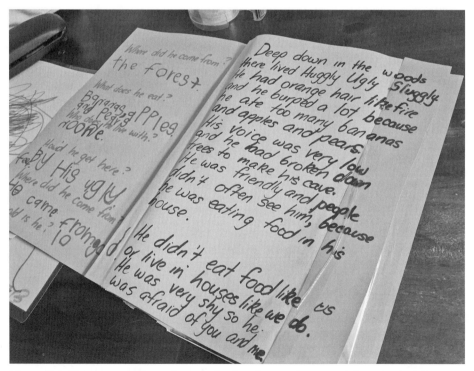

Figure 7.3 Character profile and transcribed oral story about *Cuddly Ugly Sluggly*

Seeing self in stories

All children must be able to find themselves, their families and their lives reflected in stories. Too often, and often inadvertently, stories from the dominant cultures in a community are privileged and this leaves some children confused about the relevance of literature for them. Stories must be selected from a range of different cultures, traditions and perspectives to enable children from all backgrounds to feel a sense of belonging. Aboriginal Dreamtime stories, creation myths and legends from other cultures, rhymes and poems and traditional tales from around the world will enable children to develop a rich **intertextuality** that will be valuable throughout their education and beyond. Early childhood educators need to ensure shared story reading and talking about texts are part of the daily routine and that those children who are not familiar with books at home are introduced to shared reading experiences. Scheduling parent information sessions will also be important (EYLF, 2009). Multilingual children also need opportunities to hear stories told and read in their mother tongues. Where possible, accessing books in their language will help build their sense of self and belonging, and ensure they become literate in their mother tongue.

> **Intertextuality** The relationships between one text and another impacts on the reader's understanding and interpretation of the text.

REFLECTION

Make a list of myths, legends, traditional tales, rhymes and picture books that come to mind easily. Analyse the list. Is there a diversity of cultural understanding reflected in your repertoire? What are the implications?

Book talk: Aidan Chambers' *Tell Me* framework

This chapter emphasises that quality literature should be shared with children every day in different forms including picture books, nursery rhymes and poems, song lyrics, graphic novels and visual texts. Children and adults should both select the books they would like to read, share and have read to them. In early learning, childcare and preschool contexts well-resourced bookshelves should be accessible for very young children. There should be attractive and comfortable spaces to relax in and read, perhaps with large cushions or pillows. Opportunities for young children to visit libraries, book fairs, fetes and bookshops are also important.

Reading aloud at least two or three stories or poems a day provides opportunities for children to see and experience what it means to be an engaged and effective reader. However, merely reading aloud without thoughtful discussion and meaningful activities has little value, as shown by a recent Swedish study, where some preschools used reading aloud to simply quieten children before or after play (Damber, 2015). Meyer et al (1994) make the point about reading *with* children not just *to* them, involving them in meaningful dialogue, including implying ideas, looking for patterns and clues in a story as well as connecting stories and characters to their own lives (Unsworth & Williams, 1990). Play activities can also flow once a story has been shared, where acting out a story, dressing up, painting and drawing of characters further deepens children's story and literacy development.

Celebrated author Aidan Chambers developed a framework, *Tell Me*, to encourage deeper 'book talk' or thinking about stories. He originally developed this concept in the 1980s and in the revised 2011 version, Chambers suggests:

> In any group of children . . . we find that if they begin by sharing their most obvious observations, they soon accumulate a body of understanding that reveals the heart of a text and its meaning(s) for them all. (www.aidanchambers.co.uk)

The first part of the framework involves the children sharing any enthusiasms for a book. The second part is where they share any dislikes, puzzles or questions. Finally any connections that they make with personal experience, another book or story to a broader understanding of the world are discussed. Chambers stresses the centrality of listening to each other's responses. He also provides a detailed list of questions that can be adapted and shaped to ask about the plot and the characters in one-to-one or group situations.

REFLECTION

Develop some questions for a new picture book using Chambers' framework. If possible trial them with a group of young children. Provide opportunities for them to ask questions of their own. Reflect on the kinds of questions the children asked. What did they tell you about the children's understanding of and response to the book? Were there some questions that surprised you?

Quality literature

> It is not enough to simply teach children to read; we have to give them something worth reading. Something that will stretch their imaginations – something that will help them make sense of their own lives and encourage them to reach out toward people whose lives are quite different from their own (Paterson, 2005).

There are many definitions of quality children's literature but award-winning author Katherine Paterson's comment about the importance of giving children books that are worthy of them – books that will stretch their imaginations – is an excellent start. Contemporary children's literature is rich with titles that will enable children and young people to develop empathy for others who live in quite different circumstances.

Many criteria have been developed about choosing literature for children and our book stresses the centrality of authentic or quality literary texts.

Consider the following suggestions as a starting point. A quality literary text:

- engages the child and adult alike; it relates, but is not limited to, the children's interests and experiences
- is rich in its use of language and image (rather than overly contrived with very limited vocabulary or ancillary images)
- merits multiple readings and triggers lots of 'why' questions or 'I wonder' discussion questions
- is multi-layered (there are a range of interpretations possible rather than only one dimension)
- evokes a range of different communities, worlds, cultures and ways of being
- is aesthetically designed.

Source: Adapted from Ewing, 2013

REFLECTION

Use the most recent Australian Children's Book Council awards and list of notable books to investigate the above principles. Are there other titles that you need to add? Develop your own list of criteria. *The Australian Curriculum: English* (2015) emphasises the use of Asian and Aboriginal literature. Are these texts well represented in the above award lists? Are they listed in the Copyright Agency's *Reading Australia* texts? (See Useful websites.)

Rich learning experiences with literature

The value and importance of play and exploration in early childhood learning provides a seamless connection to reading stories and exploring literature. While the move into school settings will introduce more formalised reading and writing activities and strategies, there are key principles that create the foundations for young learners engaging with books and stories. This chapter focuses on imaginative literature and picture books, but other types of reading including popular culture, screen-based texts, advertising materials and non-fiction are also an important part of a literacy diet. We argue that understanding the benefits and use of children's literature also informs the use of other texts. One of the key tenets of this book is that reading to children should begin from birth, a point made well by Dorothy Butler (1979, 1980). The core principle of reading and being read to should be the notion of pleasure and enjoyment; this seems self-evident, but this key belief is often lost when one considers the training, rules, testing and other educational detritus that can accompany and overshadow the teaching of reading (Meek, 1982; Krashen, 2010).

Engaging learning experiences with literature, including books, poetry, rhymes and songs as well as other media forms, should be underpinned by some key principles which include:

- the need for a rich variety of quality children's literature in the early childhood centre or classroom
- the critical role of talk when reading and negotiating meanings from narratives and literature
- the importance of time and opportunities to read regularly and widely
- the provision of 'space to play', both metaphorically, linguistically, dramatically and physically with the ideas, stories and characters that are drawn from stories
- the creative blending of arts-based learning with the reading experience.

Responding to books and stories is meant to extend the enjoyment, story, ideas and questions that books provide for readers. Many children have enthusiastically participated in a wild rumpus after reading Sendak's (1963) book *Where the Wild Things Are*, where they get the chance to feel what the characters Max and his friends are experiencing. Taking children on a bear hunt around the classroom after reading Rosen's *We're Going on a Bear Hunt* (1989) can be followed up by spontaneous play, using a soft toy to show the bear going through a tunnel, under a blanket and over the chairs. Get outside for water play in tubs (what does the cold water feel like), combine sand and water for 'mud' and listen to the squelching it makes. There are many ways to link books to outdoor play activities.

Other ways to respond to literature can include drama, song, dance, visual arts and craft. Classic stories like *The Jolly Postman* (Ahlberg & Ahlberg, 1986) invite postcard and letter-writing activities. *A Bus Called Heaven* (Graham, 2011), shows a wonderfully multicultural community. An accompanying activity for the story could be to set up chairs to create a classroom bus, which children can 'catch', greet friends and sing *The Wheels on the Bus* together. Alternatively the children might paint a bus mural on the wall, and draw and label themselves inside it.

Related arts activities to deepen the experience of and response to the story include:

- making finger puppets and using them to retell or innovate a variation of the story
- using paper plates to make simple character masks and then walking in role as that character
- incorporating percussion and sound effects in a re-reading or retelling of a story. The children can decide which instruments can be used at different places in the story. Books like *Peace at Last* (Jill Murphy), *Monkey and Me* (Emily

Gravett) and *Bumpus Jumpus Dinosaurumpus* (Tony Mitton) are a few examples of books that lend themselves to sound play.

- being in pairs and taking turns to sculpt each other as characters in the story
- depicting an important scene in the story as a frozen moment or tableau. Afterwards the children can discuss how the characters act and feel at this particular moment.
- miming or acting out a short sequence from the story either in small groups or as a whole group simultaneously. Dress-ups and props can be added.
- creating a stage play version. Some big books have traditional tales in playform, while other books such as *Farmer Duck* (Martin Waddell and Helen Oxenbury) have been adapted as plays for young children (see www .picturebookplays.co.uk)
- adapting the story as an early readers' theatre script (this can easily be done for many books)
- making your own version of the book either as a class or individually, such as a tiny concertina book, a pop-up book with a main character, a large jointly made story map or a big book.

There are many useful books and resources that show early childhood reading and writing contexts and classrooms with literature as a core focus including Gibson and Ewing, 2011; Leland, Lewison & Harste, 2012; Ewing, 2013; and Cremin, 2015. See the table in the Further reading list for suggested classroom texts.

REFLECTION

Make your own book after responding to one of the arts-related activities listed. Ask a child or group to work with you on the project. Record the conversation and listen to it afterwards. What do you notice about the children's developing language? Is their talk enhanced by the reading and related activity? If so, how?

Drawing it all together

In one sense, children start to become readers of their culture from the moment they are born. Developing in a rich environment of talk and other modes of communication, such as gesture, facial expressions and tone of voice, a baby quickly learns about meaning in all types of ways. Various 'texts' quickly become part of a young child's life, from 'performance' texts that are part of being in a family with various parents, siblings, uncles, aunts and friends, to early experiences of listening to a book being read aloud, where the matching of words, meaning and story begins. Early play like peek a boo, enjoying the rhythm and rhyme of a lullaby, singing along with a television show or interacting with a popular culture character on a screen app are all examples of a developing knowledge around how texts work. Later, substantial conversations and creative arts responses to the ideas or characters will continue this orientation to literature, language and literacy.

Questions for further discussion

- Did your family value stories in the way this chapter suggests? Do you have a rich repertoire of literary books and related resources? How will you continue to develop this?
- Watch ABC's *Life Series* (www.abc.net.au/tv/life/) which tracks eleven young children and their families from birth. Which families embody a sound orientation to literature and literacy? What factors are highlighted?

Further reading

Cairney, T. (2016). 230 Great Books for Children in 2016. Available at: http://trevorcairney.blogspot.com.au/search/label/children%27s%20literature.

Chambers, A. (2011). *Tell Me (Children, Reading and Talk) with The Reading Environment*. Stroud, Glos: Thimble Press. Available at: www.thimblepress.co.uk.

Here is a short selection of texts, with many in big book format, that show the diversity of choice teachers have when selecting quality literature in early childhood contexts.

Title	Author	Special features	Big book available
Each Peach Pear Plum (Viking, 1999)	Janet and Allen Ahlberg	Includes well loved nursery rhyme characters, repetition of words, phrases, questions and sequences	
Who Sank the Boat? (Penguin, 2007)	Pamela Allen	Includes repetition of words, phrases, questions and sequences	BB
E is for Echidna: My Australian WordBbook (Little Hare, 2011)	Bronwyn Bancroft	Alphabet book	
Why I Love Australia (Little Hare, 2010)	Bronwyn Bancroft	Has Aboriginal themes	

Title	Author	Special features	Big book available
A Dark Dark Tale (Anderson Press, 2012)	Ruth Brown	Includes repetition of phrases	
Silly Billy (Walker Books, 2006)	Anthony Browne	Builds a story and includes some repetition	
Mr Gumpy's Outing (Red Fox, 2001)	John Burningham	Builds a cumulative story	
Dear Zoo (Macmillan, 1982)	Rod Campbell	Includes repetition of phrases	BB
Do You Want to be My Friend? (Penguin, 1979)	Eric Carle	Includes repetition of phrases	
The Very Busy Spider (Puffin, 2011)	Eric Carle,	Includes repetition of phrases, questions and sequences	
The Very Hungry Caterpillar (Puffin, 2011)	Eric Carle	Includes repetition of words, phrases, questions and sequences	
One Leaf Rides the Wind (Viking, 2006)	Celeste Davidson Mannis	A Japanese counting book	
Hairy Maclary from Donaldson's Dairy (Puffin, 2005)	Lynley Dodd	Includes rich, playful language	
The Gruffalo (Macmillan, 2000)	Julia Donaldson	Includes repetition of phrases	
Boo to a Goose (Hachette, 1997)	Mem Fox	Includes repetition of words, phrases, questions and sequences	
Shoes from Grandpa (Scholastic, 1989)	Mem Fox	Builds a cumulative story	
Millions of Cats (Putnam, 2004)	Wanda Gag	A pattern story that includes repetition of phrases	
Mum Goes to Work (Walker Books, 2015)	Libby Gleeson and Leila Rudge	Shows parent roles	
Banjo and Ruby Red (Walker, 2015)	Libby Gleeson and Freya Blackwood	Builds a cumulative story; some repetition	
A Bus called Heaven (Walker, 2011)	Bob Graham	Themes of community and diversity	
Monkey and Me (Pan Macmillan, 2008)	Emily Gravett	Imitation of different animals, repetitive phrases	

(continued)

Title	Author	Special features	Big book available
This is the Bear (Walker Books, 2003)	Sarah Hayes	Builds a cumulative story	BB
The Doorbell Rang (Greenwillow, 1994)	Pat Hutchins	Builds a cumulative story	BB
How to catch a star (Collins, 2004)	Oliver Jeffers	Themes of perseverance and imagination	
Over in the Meadow (Swindon, 2002)	Ezra Jack Keats	Includes repetition of phrases	
There Was an Old Woman (Simon & Shuster, 1984)	Steven Kellogg	Cumulative Story	
Brown Bear Brown Bear (Henry Holt, 1996)	Bill Martin	Includes repetition of phrases	BB
Polar Bear, Polar Bear, What Do You Hear? (Puffin, 2007)	Bill Martin Jr	Includes repetition of words, phrases, questions and sequences	
Bumpus Jumpus Dinosaurumpus (Hachette, 2003)	Tony Mitton and Guy Parker-Rees	Rhyme, onomatopaeia	
Peace at Last (Puffin, 1999)	Jill Murphy	Repetition, onomatopaeia	
It's My Birthday (Walker Books, 2010)	Helen Oxenbury	Builds a cumulative story	
We're Going on a Bear Hunt (Walker, 1989)	Michael Rosen	Includes repetition of phrases	BB
The Great Big Enormous Turnip (Mammoth, 1998)	Alexei Tolstoy and Helen Oxenbury	Builds a cumulative story	
Henny Penny The Gingerbread Boy The Three Bears The Three Bears Three Billy Goats Gruff	Traditional children's stories; various versions are available	Involves a pattern story with repetition of phrases	BB
Farmer Duck (Walker Books, 2001)	Martin Waddell and Helen Oxenbury	Repetition of phrases, builds a story that lends itself to prediction	BB
The Very Best of Friends (1994)	Margaret Wild and Julie Vivas	Themes of friendship and loss	
I Went Walking (Omnibus, 2010)	Sue Williams	Includes repetition of words, phrases, questions and sequences	

Title	Author	Special features	Big book available
Goodnight Moon (Macmillan, 2012)	Margaret Wise Brown	Includes repetition of words, phrases, questions and sequences	
Let's Eat	Ana Zamorano and Julie Vivas	Includes repetition of words, phrases, questions and sequences	

Useful websites

Aidan Chambers' website: www.aidanchambers.co.uk

The Children's Book Council of Australia: http://cbca.org.au

Picture Book Plays interactive website: www.picturebookplays.co.uk

Reading Australia: http://readingaustralia.com.au (created by the Copyright Agency, this showcases the work of leading Australian writers and illustrators online to enrich our own diverse cultural identity).

References

Ahlberg, J. & Ahlberg, A. (1986). *The Jolly Postman or Other People's Letters*. London: Heinemann.

Australia Council for the Arts (2010). *More than Bums on Seats: Australian Participation in the Arts*. Sydney: Australia Council for the Arts.

Australian Curriculum, Assessment and Reporting Authority, ACARA, (2015). *The Australian Curriculum: English*. (Version 8.0) Retrieved at: www .australiancurriculum.edu.au.

Australian Government Department of Education, Employment and Workplace Relations for the Council of Australian Governments (2009). *Belonging, Being and Becoming. The Early Years Learning Framework for Australia (EYLF)*. Canberra: Commonwealth of Australia. Retrieved at: www.mychild.gov.au/agenda/early-years-framework.

Bruner, J. (1990). *Acts of Meaning*. Cambridge, MA: Harvard University Press.

Butler D. (1979). *Cushla and Her Books*. Auckland: Hodder & Stoughton.

—— (1980). *Babies Need Books*. London: The Bodley Head.

Campbell, R. (1982). *Dear Zoo*. London: Macmillan.

Cremin, T. (2015). *Teaching English Creatively*. London: Taylor & Francis.

Damber, U. (2015). Read-Alouds in Preschool: A matter of discipline? *Journal of Early Childhood Literacy*. 15(2), pp. 256–80.

Ewing, R. (2010). *The Arts and Australian Education: Realising Potential.* Melbourne: ACER.

—— ed. (2013). *The Creative Arts in the Lives of Young Children: Play, Imagination and Learning.* Melbourne: ACER.

EYLF (2009)—see Australian Government Department of Education, Employment and Workplace Relations for the Council of Australian Governments, (2009).

Fox, C. (1993). *At the Very Edge of the Forest: The Influence of literature on Story-telling by Children.* London: Cassell.

Fox, M. & Horacek, J. (2004). *Where is the Green Sheep?* Melbourne: Penguin/Viking.

Gibson, R. & Ewing, R. (2011). *Transforming the Curriculum Through the Arts.* Melbourne: Palgrave Macmillan.

Jeffers, O. (2005). *How to Catch a Star.* London: HarperCollins.

Krashen, S. (2010). The Goodman-Smith hypothesis, the input hypothesis, the comprehension hypothesis, and the (even stronger) case for free voluntary reading. Paper presented to the Defying convention, inventing the future in literacy research and practice: *Essays in tribute to Ken and Yetta Goodman.* New York: Routledge.

Leland, C., Lewison, M. & Harste, J. (2012). *Teaching Children's Literature: It's Critical!:* London: Taylor & Francis.

McGowan, J. (2003). *Hannah Arendt.* Minnesota: University of Minnesota Press.

Meek, M. (1982). *Learning to Read.* London: The Bodley Head.

—— (1988). *How Texts Teach What Readers Learn.* Stroud, Glos: Thimble Press.

Meyer, L. A., Wardrop, J. L., Stahl, S. A. & Linn, R. L. (1994). Effects of Reading Storybooks Aloud to Children. *The Journal of Educational Research,* 88(2), pp. 69–85, DOI: 10.1080/00220671.1994.9944821.

Paterson, K. (2005). *A Sense of Wonder. On Reading and Writing Books for Children.* Accessed from Katherine Paterson (n.d.), AZQuotes.com. Retrieved at: http://www.azquotes.com/quote/810363, viewed 6 January 2016.

Saxby, M. (1997). *Books in the Life of the Child.* Melbourne: Macmillan.

Sendak, M. (1963). *Where the Wild Things Are.* New York: Harper Row.

Spence, B. (2004). PEN 146, Reading aloud to children. Sydney: Primary English Teaching Association Australia (PETAA).

Unsworth, L. & Williams, G. (1990). Big books or big basals? The significance of text form in constructing contexts for early literacy development through shared reading. *Australian Journal of Reading,* 13(2), pp. 100–11.

Vygotsky, L. (1978). *Mind in Society: The Development of Higher Psychological Processes.* (Trans. M. Cole). Cambridge, MA: Harvard University Press.

CHAPTER 8

Supporting the emergent reader

Supporting emergent readers requires teachers to have a clear understanding of how readers develop in the early years. Building on the importance of children's literature discussed in previous chapters, this chapter explains the reading process and the role of language development, with a focus on the meaningful integration of letter–sound knowledge. Using a rich selection of texts with explicit guidance and support, children can develop the various skills and reader roles that lead to successful literacy learning.

Anticipated outcomes for the chapter

After working through this chapter, you should be able to:

- define the main elements of the reading process
- understand some of the key issues in reading development
- appreciate the history of reading instruction and the various approaches
- understand the role that phonics and phonemic awareness has in learning to read
- explore a variety of strategies for teaching reading in the early years of schooling.

SCENARIO: AMY AND LOUIS

A two year old, four year old and five year old gather excitedly around a new book. They discuss the cover and then a quick picture walk reveals the two main characters, Amy and Louis, are quite similar in many ways to these young readers – they like to play and visit each other, but are also quite sad when one has to leave.

Pictures of clouds inspire imaginings – a sea-horse! A dragon!

Settling down to read together, small eyes watch and listen intently. Upon hearing the refrain 'Coo-ee Amy!' they happily join in as the story unfolds.

Sadly, one character has to move across the oceans, away from her friend. 'Oh, they don't live together' comments the four year old, while the two year old points to the picture and says, 'He looks a bit sad'.

When Louis shouts out with all his might to his friend Amy across the world, the children spontaneously join in, willing Amy to hear her friend. They all agree that Amy does hear her friend from across the oceans.

Discussion ensues about the pictures, where favourite pages are noted. 'I love her calling 'Coo-ee' to her friend but I don't like it that they are lonely' explains the four year old.

'Louis is very small in this picture' observes the five year old, when seeing a picture of a truck driving away with Louis's friend inside. The five year old continues, 'Sometimes they draw people small to make them look sadder'. Discussion about the page ensues while the two year old happily chants, 'Coo-ee Amy Louis'.

After the reading, the group spontaneously composes new refrains, 'Coo-ee Daddy!', 'Coo-ee Mummy!' and coo-ees ring through the house until bedtime.

The children reading *Amy and Louis* (Gleeson & Blackwood, 2006) were intent on understanding the story, connecting it to their own emotions and experiences, predicting the outcome of events, hearing the rhyme and rhythm of the words and joining in with repeated phrases and sentences. While the two year old happily chanted the words, the five year old was noticing the specifics of print and words, becoming aware of how the code of letters and sounds worked together. In one sense, these features reflect an understanding of reading, where meaning and enjoyment are at the core. A combination of letter–sound knowledge allows words to be decoded while at the same time sentences build layered stories, which are embedded in a family's social and cultural activities. Reading, much more than simply decoding words, is a skill and a social process with a number of layers and aspects that teachers need to understand.

Introduction

A consistent theme throughout this book is the importance of understanding how language and literacy develop and are used within social and cultural contexts. The teaching of reading itself has developed and has been influenced by changing theory and practice over time. While Chapter 7 presents the importance of reading quality literary texts and the role of talk in learning to read, this chapter will explicitly outline the reading process, and its associated theories and practices for early childhood and classroom settings. By providing a historical overview of some of the key approaches to reading over the past century, including the controversies and discussions that have formed this history, we argue for a balanced approach that understands reading and literacy as a social practice, with meaning making at its core.

What happens as we read together

Whether it is reading at bedtime, after lunch, sitting in a favourite sunny place or spread out across the floor of a bookshop, being deeply engaged in a shared book reading is both a wonderfully pleasurable yet deceptively simple experience. Babies and young children who have had books read to them from before they can remember seem to naturally understand how to predict from the cover what the story may be about, express their opinions regarding a character, foresee a looming problem, then look forward to the conclusion where all is made right in the story world they have entered. Many parents easily take on the role of the storyteller, sharing amusing anecdotes, cultural practices or reading aloud to the family. Various family members may model the joy of reading, consistently reading and sharing books while encouraging children to talk, question and enjoy the experience. Given the diverse cultural population of Australia, with many children speaking multiple languages, home literacy practices will vary widely. Valuing students' home languages and practices, their 'funds of knowledge' (Moll et al., 1992) means knowing each child well, welcoming their family to the learning environment and helping them to see themselves as successful literacy learners who bring valuable skills and knowledge (Arthur, Ashton & Beecher, 2014).

Teachers of young children not only emulate a variety of family storytelling and reading practices, but carefully craft experiences which see the beginning of more sophisticated and complex aspects of reading taught to young learners. Some families' home literacy practices reflect the language and practices of school so the transition to learning can be relatively smooth. However, some children experience the move to school as challenging and unfamiliar because the culture of school is very new and different from home (Cairney, 2003). Aware of the importance of supporting schooling success as well as valuing home cultures, mindful teachers use a variety of engaging books, popular culture texts and other literacy resources that reflect the interests and values of their students. At the core of their work is both a philosophical commitment and a theoretical foundation which places meaning making as central when teaching reading.

Reading is of course one aspect of what it means to be literate. The term literacy is often a shorthand way of describing reading, writing, talking, listening and viewing, as well as a number of other communication modes such as gesture and design. Most current definitions of literacy acknowledge that it is a dynamic concept, shaped by culture and practice, and informed by political, social and economic factors to name a few (UNESCO, 2005). Peter Freebody argues that literate individuals are able to use a variety of communication modes fluently and effectively, 'communicating productively, responsively and responsibly' (Freebody, 2007, p. 9).

A visual model is a helpful way of seeing how the various facets of reading work together (see Figure 8.1). Historically this model draws on reading print, but given the widening sets of meaning making resources that are now considered part of 'reading', the model also reflects broader tenets of literacy learning in general.

In order to make meaning from a text, readers draw on the combination of different sources of information or *cues*, in order to begin the process of reading. Very young children listening to adults read to them, or reading a well-loved story by memory, will often use the visual cues from pictures as well as attend to some aspects of print that they have seen demonstrated. Depending on the development of the child before they enter formal schooling, they may begin to draw on a number of other cues as they begin to deepen their knowledge of what reading entails.

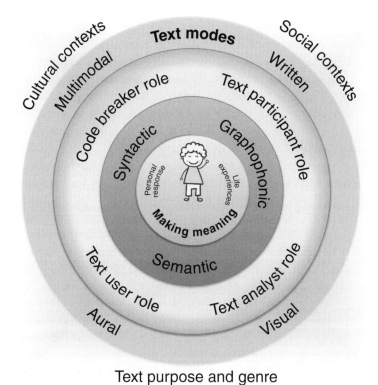

Text purpose and genre

Figure 8.1 A sociocultural model of reading and literacy practices

In order to make meaning from any written text, a reader will draw upon a combination of cues. **Semantic cues** involve knowledge about a field or topic in which the words are set. Consider the opening line of this story:

> Once upon a time a kind woman found a minute girl looking through the leaves of a tulip.

A reader will need to draw not only on their knowledge of fairy tales, prompted by the first phrase, but also their own reading experiences, cultural knowledge and vocabulary. At the same time, **syntactic or grammatical cues** draw on a reader's knowledge of how sentences are structured. If you misread the word 'minute' to be a measure of time, rather than a description of the girl's size, you drew on your grammatical knowledge to expect an adjective and may have re-read the word accordingly. **Graphophonic cues** (sometimes separated into graphological and phonological) are the knowledge of the letters (grapho) and associated sounds (phonemes).

Some words in the opening line are easily decoded such as *upon* and *tulip* where single letters and sounds easily match. However, other words reveal the complexity of English orthography with a soft *c* sound in words such as *once,* the combination of *ou* making what is known as a diphthong in *found,* and then a silent *gh* in the preposition *through.*

Reading any type of text – be it a bedtime story, academic journal, text message or a sticky note with the grocery list – is all about making sense of what we read. But as our opening vignette reminds us, making meaning always happens in some type of context and setting, which will play a part in how we interpret what we read. Working with a sociocultural approach to reading and literacy, Freebody and Luke's work explains that meaning making is not only based on the written text, but on the genre or text type, the purpose of the text, the background of both the reader and the writer and the wider cultural context where the text and reader are situated (Freebody & Luke, 1990; Freebody, 2007). Therefore, to be able to read a range of texts meaningfully and critically, a reader needs to participate in four reader roles: **code breaker**, **text participant**, **text user** and **text analyst or critic**.

Reading is a process where these roles are interrelated and work together. In one sense they are enacted recursively, where readers develop more sophisticated ways of undertaking each role, given their age and context. Even young readers who are beginning to develop initial code-breaker knowledge may already be excellent at meaning-making roles as they read

Semantic cues – The meaning of particular words.

Syntactic or grammatical cues Knowledge of how sentences and word order are used in English.

Graphophonic cues Letter–sound knowledge.

Code breaker role This involves breaking the code of written text (graphophonic knowledge) as well as the codes of other modalities such as the visual, gestural, aural and spatial.

Text participant role This focuses on making meaning and comprehending what is read, interpreting literal and inferential meanings across vocabulary, grammatical features and other modalities.

Text user role The understanding of how texts achieve their social and practical purposes, through the choice of genre (factual, persuasive, imaginative), text type structures and design, as well as the intended audience.

Text analyst or text critic role The discovery and questioning of the cultural assumptions and world views present in texts, which may influence, empower or marginalise readers and their communities.

Reader roles These are practices that allow readers to engage meaningfully and critically with a range of texts.

Modalities Different communication resources often categorised as linguistic, visual, aural, spatial and gestural.

books with enabling adults. Similarly, the simple idea that authors make choices as to what ideas they put into books is the beginning of the text analyst role for young children.

Understanding literacy and reading as a sociocultural process, as conceptualised in Figure 8.1, forms the foundation on which sound pedagogical practices and strategies are based. Not only do we understand that books have cultural histories but also that each learner, classroom and community has a unique context and history. *Sam's Bush Journey* (Morgan, Kwaymullina & Bancroft, 2010) explores the importance of connecting with Aboriginal culture and the land, so young learners with experience here will already have important prior knowledge to bring to this story. Similarly, a teacher whose students live on the coast may choose a book about seaside adventures, such as *Grandpa and Thomas* (Allen, 2003) and develop the discussion and semantic meanings in a different way to children with little beach knowledge (Callow & Hertzberg, 2006).

In terms of the teaching of reading, it is instructive to have something of an understanding of the history of reading theory and practice. Controversies about approaches to teaching reading in current contexts are better understood when placed in a historical perspective.

REFLECTION

Think about the variety of reading you do each day including texts, email, magazines and online shopping. What does it feel like to read an unfamiliar text, such as a dense academic article or some legal documents? It can often feel very overwhelming and challenging. As carers and teachers, it is very helpful to keep in mind the challenges that young children have when they encounter unfamiliar texts and new literacy experiences. We need to set our learners up for success, particularly when social or cultural aspects of school or preschool may be part of the issue.

A short history of reading

The preface and introductory chapters of this book emphasise the importance of understanding the social, cultural and contextual features of language and literacy development. As such, we are acknowledging that our foundational ideas draw on sociocultural and sociolinguistic theories, where reading and literacy are understood as social practices (Freebody & Luke, 1990; Luke, 2012; Comber, 2015). The specific area of teaching reading has a varied and rich history, where different researchers and disciplines have tried to work out the 'puzzle' (as Freebody puts it) as to what reading entails and how to best teach it (Freebody, 2007 p. 16). Some very different approaches have been put forward, with various controversies ensuing.

We would argue that reflective practitioners understand that education draws on a history of theory, policies and beliefs as well as received professional wisdom. Having a sense of this history provides teachers with a richer understanding of their profession as well as shaping the principles and practices they will employ in the classrooms of today.

The broader story of education and learning is entwined with the evolution of how reading (and writing) have been taught since the early twentieth century. As such, the work of early theorists like Dewey (1916), who championed the importance of curiosity and collaboration in classrooms using an inquiry approach, still informs learning and teaching in classrooms today. His commentary on the social nature of learning and language, and how meaning is made when children and parents communicate with each other, reflects key principles about the purpose and teaching of reading still utilised today. If you had a teacher who encouraged you to make connections with what you read and other experiences or knowledge in your life, you have an example of how Dewey's ideas are still influential today (Groundwater-Smith, Ewing & Le Cornu, 2014).

Classrooms in the first half of the twentieth century often had large numbers of children, usually seated in rows, and many of the learning activities were formal and somewhat factory-like in process. While reading aloud from popular books and respected literature would be part of the day, the process of learning to read was often understood as developing a set of cognitive skills to decode print. Learning to read would involve a selection of discrete activities, often described as a 'transmission model' (Skinner, 1957). Teachers would teach sound–symbol relationships about letters or groups of letters, as well as encourage students to memorise vocabulary, such as key sight words (Chall, 1967). Often described as a behaviourist approach, this theory of reading is based on the work of researchers such as Skinner (1957) as well as Bandura (1969). Children learn to read in small, logical steps, developing reading behaviours that a teacher carefully orchestrates. You may have memories of learning about letters and sounds using various activities and games where rules and patterns were taught in a prescribed sequence. The various **phonics** programs and approaches that are commonly promoted today as teaching the basics of reading draw on these behaviourist models. However, given the reading model from this chapter's introduction, it becomes clear that focusing exclusively on letter–sound knowledge at the expense of the other reader roles and cues offers a limited view of reading instruction.

Phonics An understanding of the relationship between the sounds of spoken language and the letters that represent these sounds.

Approaches to teaching reading have also been influenced by constructivist theories, where children are actively involved in exploring and developing their knowledge and skills. Building on Dewey's concepts of education, teachers take an active role in engaging students in learning, providing age-appropriate opportunities to question what they are learning. Piaget's work has been significant here, where his observations about children's development led him to propose stages of cognitive development (Piaget, 1959). While debated and refined by others in the field, his concept of learners developing and building knowledge in the form of *schemas*, which are continually added to when new information is learnt, has complemented approaches to the teaching of reading. Research in the field of reading instruction from the 1960s to the 1980s by Frank Smith (1978) acknowledged the active role that readers must undertake, while Kenneth Goodman (1968) argued for the active role of the reader in using various cues as well as context to make meaning. Researchers like Brian Cambourne further developed these ideas by proposing the conditions for language learning (Cambourne, Handy & Scown, 1988), which argued the importance of active involvement on the part of the learner and the teacher in both reading and writing. The interactive nature of language and reading was also emphasised by the work of Sylvia Ashton-Warner (1986) in her Language Experience Approach as well as Don Holdaway's (1979) research on the impact of shared reading on children's reading development prior to formal schooling. The term 'whole language' was often applied to the practices that flowed from the reading approaches above. Since the 1980s there have been recurring and rather unproductive arguments which attempt to pit more behaviourist phonics approaches against whole language approaches. However, as we will see, the emergence of other perspectives about the nature of reading since the 1990s has more helpfully characterised the complex question of how reading works as a balanced combination of cues and roles which are part of learning to read.

The belief that reading and writing are at their core meaning-making processes not only informed constructivist approaches, but also cognitive and information-processing theories. Acknowledging the complex interactions that occur in the reading process, theorists here posit that readers focus on comprehension using information from print as well as their background knowledge (Sousa, 2014; Stanovich, 2000). The importance of the individual's interpretation of texts is described by Louise Rosenblatt (1978) as transactional theory. She contends that readers make very personal interpretations of what they read, depending on the purpose of the task and whether they are reading for pleasure or to locate information. The impact of cognitive and information-processing theories is evident in classroom activities where readers are encouraged to make meaning from what they read and write, as well as value and describe the interpretations they make of stories and texts. The influence of this aspect of reading theory development is also evident in the central place of meaning making in our reading model (see Figure 8.1).

Since the late 1980s, sociocultural understandings of literacy have emphasised the importance of understanding language, both written and spoken, as situated in the social experiences and cultural settings in our lives. As discussed in Chapters 2 and 4, the role of oral language is a key aspect of literacy development. Linguists such as Michael Halliday (1978) argued that the function of language and language development is always part of a social system. The work of Shirley Brice-Heath (1983) not only examined the role of oral language as part of literacy development but also considered how language is used and valued differently across various cultural and socioeconomic communities. Sociolinguist Lev Vygotsky's (1978) concept of scaffolding and the zone of proximal development holds the central concept that learning and language cannot be separated from social experiences and contexts. This has particular significance in reading pedagogy, where teachers move between highly supported explicit teaching towards more independent learning as part of reading pedagogy, as well as valuing the importance of social interactions and discussion with and between students about what is being read.

During the 1990s, sociocultural approaches to literacy began to add another layer to the literacy discussion. These approaches highlighted the importance of readers learning to read both for enjoyment but also at a **critical literacy** level, where we recognise that because all texts are socially constructed, they will reflect particular values and world views. Unquestioned, powerful texts and discourses can empower some readers and communities while disenfranchising and even discriminating against others (Lankshear, 1994; Luke & Elkins, 2002). This work's impact on how reading is taught is reflected in teachers helping students comprehend deeper meanings from stories and encouraging them at certain points to question whose views and voices are heard, and whose may be silent. Such discussion applies to books and stories as well as factual, persuasive, media and electronic texts. The inclusion of the text user and text analyst role in our reading model (see Figure 8.1) demonstrates the more recent changes in teaching approaches to reading.

> **Critical literacy** Linked to the text analyst role, critical literacy assists learners to question and discuss the ideas that a story, video or game might present, particularly in terms of attitudes to cultural representation, gender and belief.

The influence of this aspect of the history of reading is seen in the model of reading presented at the beginning of this chapter, which include **cue systems** and a focus on meaning as well as context. Teaching practices such as shared and modelled reading, where a teacher builds context and background knowledge about a story before reading to a class, are informed by both constructivist as well as sociocultural understandings about reading.

> **Cue systems** Sources of information which readers use to make meaning with print (graphophonic cues, syntactic or grammatical cues, semantic cues).

Phases of reading and literacy development

Reading development is part of children's social, emotional and physical growth (EYLF, 2009) as well as their literacy development. While we can consider general stages of reading and literacy development, we need to be mindful that children will develop at different rates and stages. Some of this will be biological. For some students it will be the nature of their learning experiences, or the ones they are yet to have, that will influence the ways they come to reading. An emergent approach to literacy development from early childhood settings to formal schooling affirms the meaningful use of spoken and written language as the context for reading and writing (Teale & Sulzby, 1986), utilising 'play-based, child-centred activities such as singing, rhymes, dramatic play and shared reading' (Campbell, 2015 p. 13).

Experienced teachers draw on various theoretical and practical approaches when teaching literacy and reading. Although a continuum of development such as Table 8.1 gives a general sense of children's reading and literacy development, reflective practitioners understand that each child will have varying needs and developmental trajectories, which are influenced by individual qualities, family, communities, health needs as well as political and social circumstances.

Table 8.1 General phases of reading and literacy development

	Reading	Other literacy behaviours
Exploratory	• Listens to books read aloud • Holds books, turns pages • Looks at pictures and begins to name objects and characters.	• Scribbles and draws • Pretends to write by using symbols and pictures • Responds to visual and screen-based texts.
Emergent	• Selects favourite books, requests repeated readings • Joins in and memorises the story and rhymes • Understands that print contains meanings • Reads familiar signs and symbols • Knows print reads from left to right, top to bottom.	• Experiments with writing and letters, including numbers • Begins to write letters and simple words • Asks for writings to be read • Draws and explains visual texts • Uses simple screen-based technology.
Developing	• Retells simple stories • Reads simple texts with support as well as independently • Asks questions and discusses story ideas and themes • Uses appropriate intonation when reading or pretending to read • Joins in rhyming games • Begin to develop awareness of syllables and sounds of language • Identifies some letters and letter–sound matches • Learns sight words.	• Begins to write sentences and longer texts • Develops early spelling and punctuation skills • Uses models of text to support writing • Creates visual and multimodal texts using drawing, painting and technology • Engages with screen-based games, texts and stories.
Extending	• Begins to read with fluency and expression • Understands different genres of texts, such as informative, story, persuasive, digital media • Reads independently • Uses a variety of comprehension strategies to make meaning and self-correct.	• Develops ideas in writing across multiple sentences • Understands simple grammatical features such as noun groups and verbs • Begins to check writing and edit spelling • Creates visual and multimodal texts with drawing, painting and technology.

Making meaning using letter–sound knowledge

From our reading model (Figure 8.1), we have seen how the various cue systems and reader roles work together in a balanced fashion. Comprehension is often linked to the text participant role and involves readers using the cue systems as well as a number of other strategies as they read. Even with very young children, teachers and caregivers can nurture literal and inferential comprehension as they read, discussing not only how many little pigs were in the story (literal information), but what it must feel like to have your house blown down (which must be inferred). More explicit comprehension strategies are often introduced when children enter formal schooling, but a number of key strategies for teaching comprehension have been identified. These include the importance of predicting a story before and during reading, using the visuals and pictures, continuing to check whether what is being read makes sense, asking questions about what we read as well as inferring meanings from our own experience and other aspects of the story (Block & Duffy, 2008). There are a number of very helpful publications in the references to further support the teaching of comprehension such as those by Holliday (2008), Hoyt (2009) and Hertzberg and Freeman (2012).

While the model and principles presented here make it very clear that children all need to understand the graphological and phonological aspects of decoding print, they work as part of the reading process, not the most important nor the least. The particular area of phonics instruction, as it is often referred to, has been the site of much controversy in the past 30 years.

The seminal work of Marie Clay (1979) and Uta Frith (1985) provides a helpful framework for understanding how the brain begins to process words and letters. Frith's reading acquisition model, while refined and developed since her initial work (Sousa, 2014), draws on an information-processing concept, proposing a three-phase model to explain the stages of reading and word acquisition. In the *logographic* phase, three year olds and four year olds are likely to see a word like a photograph in terms of its overall shape and visual features, seeing and 'reading' various common signs, names and advertising logos. Reading with young children should involve much discussion of pictures as well as building a strong oral base around storybook language and vocabulary.

At around five or six years of age, the brain begins to decode letters (graphemes) into sounds (phonemes), and children begin to enter the *alphabetic* phase. Beginning readers have to work slowly and steadily as they attend to both individual letter sounds as well as identifying larger sound components such as syllables, and **onset and rime** (Goswami & Bryant, 1990). It should be noted here that as children move into this phase, the importance of shared reading, discussing story meanings, pictures and exploring the ideas in stories continues. We must remember that the ideas of reading for meaning, asking questions and reading for enjoyment are still the goal, even as they move through this alphabetic phase. The other key aspect to keep in mind here is the importance of writing development. Children focus on letters and sounds in what they read, and their writing activities are also critical for demonstrating their developing knowledge as they begin to write their name, make short lists, create labels, retell events and perform other purposeful writing tasks (Annandale et al., 2005; Cunningham, 2009).

Onset-rime – In one-syllable words, the onset is the part of the word before the vowel example the letters 'br' in the word 'brake', or the letter 's' in 'sat'. The remaining section, including the vowel and any other consonants, is termed the rime.

Hornsby and Wilson (2011) use a variety of children's work samples to show the development of letter–sound knowledge as well as the purpose, structure, grammar and enjoyment that writing entails.

As children become more proficient at cracking the alphabetic code, the process becomes more automatic. There will be times, as with adult readers, when slowing down to work out a word will be necessary (consider the word sesquipedalian, which means having many syllables). This final phase is what Frith named the *orthographic* phase. Not all children will progress at the same rate through these stages. Teachers need to plan thoughtfully to meet the needs of learners, providing support for learners who may vary in their reading and writing development.

While Frith's three stages belie more complex neurological processes, they provide a helpful frame to understand the stages that reading development is likely to take for most children. Teachers then need to have a solid understanding of how to teach children as they develop through the alphabetic phase to become proficient readers. While some call for a simple or basic approach to teaching reading and phonics, the richness and complexity of English needs to be considered.

English orthography

The English language has complex orthography; that is, the spelling of words, compared to, say, Finnish or Spanish. So while 'cat' and 'dog' can be sounded out one letter at a time quite successfully, words such as 'said', 'could', 'does' and 'two' reveal the challenges of simply teaching letters and sounds. Dombey argues that English is a 'vowel-rich language', where there are 12 single phoneme vowels, supplemented by eight vowel combinations (diphthongs), such as /oi/ as in 'noise' and /ow/ as in 'cow'. Even the letter 'a' can have four different sounds in words such as 'cat', 'call', 'car' and 'cake' (Dombey, 1999a p. 13). While children will need to develop specific letter–sound correspondences, it appears that recognising syllables happens and then the concept of onset-rime develops before individual phoneme identification occurs (Port, 2007). Using analogy, children can use a relatively small number of rimes (sometimes referred to as word families) to assist them in reading other similar words, so knowing 'ap' in 'tap' will assist in reading other words with the same rime, such as 'lap', 'nap', 'flap' and so on (Goswami & Bryant, 1990; Wyse & Goswami, 2013).

Why is understanding something about the complexity of orthography and learning to read important? A recent study about teaching phonics in early childhood settings revealed some early childhood educators were influenced to adopt commercial phonics programs based on media or marketing approaches, without these educators understanding the research that informs the most appropriate ways to introduce this aspect of reading (Campbell, 2015). Becoming a fluent and accurate reader means utilising all the cue systems, as well as having an understanding of the various roles readers utilise, so teachers need to understand the important role of phonics as part of a balanced approach. Given that reading and literacy are learnt in sociocultural contexts, where meaning, purpose and enjoyment are the focus, then a teacher's approach to teaching phonics should complement these important philosophical foundations. Choosing such a balanced approach 'requires teachers to have their own clear agendas, their own understanding of the system and how it is structured. It also requires them to make adjustments between this agenda and the children's interests, observations and inferences. It demands an inventiveness in finding texts worthwhile in their own right, that also provide the context for appropriate phonic lessons' (Dombey, 1999b p. 57).

Phonemic awareness

In early childhood settings, not only does the inclusion of singing, rhymes, chants and all sorts of oral language play make for enjoyable and creative learning experiences, it also begins the foundations for phonological awareness as well as developing phonemic awareness (Goswami & Bryant, 1990; Moustafa & Maldonado-Colon, 1999; Yopp & Yopp, 2000). **Phonemic awareness** is hearing, identifying and manipulating the sounds or **phonemes** in spoken words.

> **Phonemic awareness** The ability to hear, identify and manipulate individual sounds or phonemes in spoken words.

Activities that foster this should be playful and enjoyable, yet deliberate in focusing on the sounds of language. Hornsby and Wilson (2011) suggest teaching phonemic awareness in the following developmentally appropriate order, but also note that the activities will overlap and that development may be recursive, in that children will return to rhyme play even as they begin to read. They suggest the following, with some examples given but there are many other good activities from the resource list in their publication:

> **Phoneme** The smallest speech sound in a language. The phoneme is distinct from the letter name. The English language has 44 phonemes, where some letters may represent a variety of phonemes or sounds. For example, the letter 'c' can represent the hard /c/ in 'cat', or the soft /c/ in 'nice'.

- Tuning in to the sounds and listening – activities that involve listening for playground sounds, making sounds with our mouth, hands and feet, and introducing concepts such as *first*, *middle*, *last*, *sound*, *letters*, etc. as necessary vocabulary in order to develop phonological knowledge.
- Playing with rhyme – days or sessions can begin with songs, chants, action or counting rhymes ('Down by the Bay', 'Incy Wincy Spider', 'Row Row Row Your Boat'). Nursery rhymes are perennial favourites which model rhyme, including 'Hickory Dickory Dock', 'Humpty Dumpty', 'Jack and Jill', 'Baa Baa Black Sheep'. There are also many nursery rhymes from across the world such as 'Mosquito One, Mosquito Two' (Jamaica), 'Ride the Horsey' (Pakistan), 'The Cuckoo Calls, Coo, Coo, Coo' (India) and 'Peas, Potatoes, Beans' (Ukraine) (Toronto Public Library, 2015). Popular rhyming children's songs include 'Miss Mary Mack', 'Teddy Bear Teddy Bear', 'Bananas in Pyjamas', 'Old MacDonald' and 'This Old Man'. Read aloud stories with strong rhyming patterns and draw attention to the words that rhyme.

- Developing an awareness of words in spoken language – highlight an interesting word as part of news time, repeating it with the class ('You saw a *kookaburra* in the tree! It's such a great word to say – let's say it together'). Oral cloze helps children attend to specific words. When reciting a familiar rhyme or chant, the teacher recites the first part of the line and asks the children to complete the final rhyming word.
- Developing an awareness of syllables – clapping the syllables in children's names is a good beginning. Model how to do this, ask the children to join in, and add various other familiar words, when reading a story together or observing activities in the playground or garden. Have a 'feely bag', with objects such as a marble, 'pencil,' toy dinosaur, which children feel, guess the object then clap or say the syllables (include two-syllable or three-syllable words to vary the activity).
- Developing an awareness that words contain phonemes – model saying the initial sound of children's names and have them repeat back to you. Teach *I spy* where the teacher chooses an object to find. 'I spy with my little eye, something beginning with /p/' then repeat the phoneme *pppppppp* (model saying the *sound* of the initial letter, not the letter name).

(Hornsby & Wilson, 2011 pp. 48–63)

Some children may enter school with limited experience of books, story reading and word play and will need many opportunities to hear, enjoy and begin to play with language before they may be ready to move into learning about phonics and the alphabetical principle. Others may have had a very rich experience of story reading and engaging with print but still need support in making the link between spoken language and written text.

Developing phonological knowledge as part of learning to read

While phonemic awareness activities can be applied appropriately across both early childhood and formal schooling, the more explicit teaching of letter–sound correspondence is usually appropriate once children have entered school and are moving towards the alphabetic phase (Frith, 1985). Broadly speaking, there are several different methods for teaching phonics. Synthetic phonics uses a part-to-whole approach that teaches students letter–sound relationships in an incremental sequence. Small groups of letter sounds are taught during short sessions, allowing children to begin blending and segmenting letters when reading and writing (NSW Department of Education and Training, 2009). Many commercial programs use this approach. Analytic phonics tends to begin with known language and shared books, then focuses on words from these sources, explicitly teaching letter–sound correspondences which they can begin to apply to unknown words (Moustafa & Maldonado-Colon, 1999). Analogy phonics teaches children to use parts of known words to decode new words, such as the use of onset and rime, where once *boat* is known, then the rime '–oat' can be used to read 'coat', 'moat', 'float' etc. (Goswami, 1992). Teachers who understand the need to integrate letter–sound knowledge across reading and writing activities as well as meeting individual children's needs will use all three methods in a systematic yet flexible approach (Pressley, 2006). A recent study in New Zealand that focuses on the reading needs of children from low socioeconomic backgrounds compares three broad approaches. The experimental study compares the use of big-book reading combined with embedded phonics instruction, in contrast to a phonics-only program with no use of books, and a big-book shared reading program with limited focus on letter–sound teaching. They found that the combined embedded instruction, compared with big-book reading and phonics-alone programs, appeared to have no comparative disadvantages but it had considerable advantages in supporting low socioeconomic students' literacy. They concluded that 'the combined instruction was as effective as explicit phonics for basic decoding skills and was superior to phonics for all other measures of literacy' (Tse & Nicholson, 2014, p. 17).

The following example of a literacy plan (Table 8.2) across the beginning months of formal schooling embeds both practical suggestions as well as key concepts about where letter–sound learning might occur across the days and weeks. Some children will move quickly while others will need meaningful revision of key concepts when learning to read. In the first few weeks of school, teachers help children to socialise and feel settled in a new environment. Routines are important for young children – sitting together on the classroom rug, reading the day and a description of the weather, learning new songs and rhymes and checking the roll are all part of setting up daily practices.

Daily activities

As part of the daily literacy and English session, focused phonics activities should generally be no more than 10 to 20 minutes long for early years students. There are other opportunities throughout the session and the day to focus on aspects of letter–sound knowledge. Phonics teaching must be explicit and logical for children, which then assists them to learn the skills as well as make connections back to the purpose of reading and writing. Many curriculum documents provide a suggested scope and sequence to aid teachers plan systematic instruction. Assessment of student needs is an important part of the teaching process to ascertain what may already be known, what to revise and where to move to next (Hill, 2012).

Recognising single letter–sound (grapheme–phoneme) correspondences may run parallel to phonemic awareness development. Learning the names of letters often comes before children understand the various sounds associated with the letter. Making a list of children's names and saying the name of the first letter of each, reading alphabet books, making an alphabet frieze and singing the alphabet song (slowing to clearly enunciate l, m, n, o and p) are all ways to introduce and revisit letter names as well as reinforce alphabetical order. Often curriculum documents will outline a sequence of single letter–sound sequences, which allow students

Table 8.2 Literacy plan for kindergarten, prepatory or reception students in their first few months of school

	Beginning of the school year	During the year	Informal and formal ways of building letter–sound knowledge
Morning welcome: Shared songs, chants and rhymes, class names, news time	Welcome children and caregivers, teach new songs and chants, read and listen to class names as the roll is marked, introduce news time routines.	Activities like 'secret sentence' involve children building up information about the sentence (the letters, words and punctuation) as you write together.	Once roll-taking routines are familiar, highlight initial sounds of names. Then letter names of children's names builds phonemic awareness then phonological knowledge.
Reading aloud	Read at least two or three stories a day to enjoy and discuss.	Continue to read stories each day to extend children's repertoires of authors, story knowledge and comprehension.	While enjoyment is the focus, discuss and point out the natural patterns in stories with strong alliteration and rhyme. Children listening to quality literature develops story language awareness and new vocabulary.
Shared and modelled reading	Use big books, poems or rhymes on charts to allow concepts of print, directionality (reading print from left to right), fluency, expression and comprehension to be modelled to children. Repeat readings of a story across a week-long period. Common sight words and new vocabulary are taught as children join in with the shared reading.	Select a variety of more challenging books to read across each term and the whole year. This continues children's skills in attending to print, images, characters, themes and layers of meaning. Comprehension strategies are also integrated into shared reading with explicit instruction.	Focus explicitly on letter–sound correspondences after reading. This allows for phonics work to flow from a meaningful story context. Teachers can teach initial sounds, blends and digraphs using suggested orders from scope and sequence plans. Word families, rhymes, alliteration, onset and rime, teaching by analogy and more complex phonic patterns can all be taught in shared and modelled reading.

	Beginning of the school year	During the year	Informal and formal ways of building letter–sound knowledge
Exploring the story	Engage in post-reading activities including oral retelling to partners, character hot seating, creating story maps, innovating on the story, making a class big book or small concertina books, dressing up to act out the story and other arts-based literature responses.	Introduce more complex drama- and literature-response activities over the year, including readers' theatre, frozen tableaus, video and multimedia creation, story innovation and multimodal responses.	Introduce activities including writing which allow children to demonstrate growing understanding.
Literacy-centre activities: 10- to15-minute activities to rotate through the day and week	Arrange four groups of five to six children, which is a manageable number. While a teacher reads with one group, other groups engage in purposeful activities such as: reading alphabet books; a listening centre with books and headphones; a drawing/writing centre; word/letter activities; free-choice reading; story or letter activities on iPads/tablets.	As children develop, provide activities that include sorting cut-up sentences from known stories; readers' theatre; making little books; partner reading and buddy reading with older children.	Introduce word-level activities such as 'fishing' games (use magnets to pick up and read sight words); Snap using word/picture cards; bingo games. Introduce letter-level: activites such as sorting and matching magnetic letters; tracing cut-out letters; letter naming (throw a bean bag onto floor chart and name the letter it falls on).
Word work time: 10–15 minutes per day	Encourage phonemic awareness: say rhymes and change the rhyme; change a word in a favourite rhyme that does not match and then identify it; read stories with alliteration, repeat sounds together; read alphabet books.	Use children's names to explore sound–letter matching; read the alphabet together; create alphabet frieze or walk; name sounds and letters in alliteration texts; focus on hearing syllables; teach single letter and sound using suggested order, using book and classroom print as examples; segment and blend activities using known letters. When appropriate, move into more specific phonic activities, drawing on shared books for context, as well as suggested letter-and-sound sequences and associated activities.	

(continued)

Table 8.2 (*cont.*)

	Beginning of the school year	During the year	Informal and formal ways of building letter–sound knowledge
Writing	Using shared experience of starting school or shared book, model writing a simple sentence, and demonstrate basic features. Provide opportunities to draw and write each day as well as practice more formal handwriting instruction to develop proper grip and fine motor control.	As well as providing simple recounts of stories, allow for modelled and guided writing opportunities including list making, labels, simple procedural and factual texts. Teach spelling through word walls, links to phonic knowledge and sight words.	Offer time to compose texts as this allows teachers to see how children are using phonic knowledge, as well as giving opportunities to link reading and writing, and letter–sound skills. Writing from shared experiences and shared books provides further links between reading, writing and how letter–sound knowledge is used.
Free reading time	Provide free reading as part of the centre time as well as a regular whole-class activity. A well-stocked class library is central for this activity.	Allow children the chance to re-read well-loved stories and big books as well as new stories, peruse factual texts and explore new authors and books, while they enjoy classroom spaces with pillows and reading nooks.	

to begin blending and segmenting simple words quite quickly. One sequence is *a m t s i f d r o g l h u c b n k v e w j p y x q* (Carnine, Silbert & Kameenui, 1997), which also avoids introducing letters that look and sound alike at the same time such as *b* and *d*, *a* and *u*. Introducing small groups of letters in quick succession (not a letter a week) allows children to begin to manipulate them with hands-on activities as well as orally and in their writing.

Teaching phonics with formal lesson instruction in preschool is problematic, both developmentally as well as pedagogically. This is particularly when some preschool teachers adopt commercial programs which can be at odds with early-childhood emergent literacy approaches (Campbell, Torr & Cologon, 2012). Schools, districts and countries vary in what approaches they may advise (or insist) teachers use to teach phonics. While in the UK, there has been a strong emphasis on implementing synthetic phonics programs in schools, other countries provide extensive support for teachers to integrate explicit phonic instruction in a number of ways. The principles, activities and sequence suggested here are one example of how a teacher might envisage a reading program that reflects the key aspects of the reading model presented at the beginning of the chapter, set in the context of a balanced, literature and text-rich classroom environment.

Drawing it all together

In our opening scenario, we observed children across a range of ages who were not only learning lessons about reading from the text itself (as outlined in Chapter 7) but were also developing aspects of comprehension, letter–sound knowledge and playful interactions with an engaging story. This chapter emphasises the importance of understanding how the reading process works, where a number of roles and facets work together to support beginning readers. Young children make meaning from stories from very early shared reading to the development of independent reading. Teachers, informed by professional knowledge and theory, plan reading and literacy learning where children develop a range of roles and skills. Using a range of engaging and culturally relevant texts, learning to read in the early years should set a strong foundation for enjoying, questioning and exploring all types of literature in a child's life.

Questions for further discussion

- If someone now asked you what the concept 'reading' entails, how would you answer them, incorporating the main ideas from this chapter?
- Frith's reading acquisition model sets out general phases about children's readiness to decode letters into sounds. What implications does this have for teaching reading in early childhood and preschool settings?
- Choose a favourite picture book and re-read it, thinking about the various cue systems you use, as well as story themes and ideas that it holds. How could you begin to draw children's attention to specific letter–sound patterns? What activities would enhance their enjoyment and understanding of the story?

Further reading

Hornsby, D. & Wilson, L. (2011). *Teaching Phonics in Context*. Melbourne: Pearson Australia.

McLachlan, C., Nicholson, T., Fielding-Barnsley, R., Mercer, L. & Ohi, S. (2012). *Literacy in Early Childhood and Primary Education: Issues, Challenges, Solutions*. Cambridge: Cambridge University Press.

Tompkins, G. E., Campbell, R. & Green, D. (2012). *Literacy for the 21st century: A Balanced Approach* (1st Australian edn). Sydney: Pearson Australia.

Useful websites

Booktrust: www.booktrust.org.uk – an extensive site from the UK with book reviews, lists and resources.

Primary English Teaching Association Australia (PETAA): www.petaa.edu.au – research-informed books and practical teaching resources and ideas.

References

Allen, P. (2003). *Grandpa and Thomas*. Melbourne: Penguin/Viking.

Annandale, K., Western Australia Department of Education Training, Bindon, R. & Broz, J. (2005). *Writing Resource Book: Addressing Current Literacy Challenges*, Ascot, WA: STEPS Professional Development.

Arthur, L., Ashton, J. & Beecher, B. (2014). *Diverse Literacies in Early Childhood: A Social Justice Approach*. Melbourne: ACER.

Ashton-Warner, S. (1986). *Teacher*. New York: Touchstone.

Australian Department of Education, Employment and Workplace Relations for the Council of Australian Governments (2009). *Belonging, Being & Becoming: The Early Years Learning Framework for Australia*. Canberra: Commonwealth of Australia. Retrieved at: www.mychild.gov.au/agenda/early-years-framework.

Bandura, A. (1969). *Principles of Behavior Modification*. New York; London: Holt, Rinehart and Winston.

Block, C. C. & Duffy, G. (2008). Research on teaching comprehension: Where we've been and where we're going. In C. C. Block & S. R. Parris (eds), *Comprehension Instruction Research-Based Best Practices* (2nd edn). New York; London: Guilford Press, pp. 19–37.

Cairney, T. (2003). Literacy within family life. In N. Hall, J. Larson & J. Marsh (eds), *Handbook of Early Childhood Literacy*. SAGE, pp. 85–98.

Callow, J. & Hertzberg, M. (2006). Helping children learn to read. In R. Ewing (ed.), *Beyond the Reading Wars*. Sydney: Primary English Teaching Association Australia (PETAA).

Cambourne, B., Handy, L. & Scown, P. (1988). *The Whole Story: Natural Learning and the Acquisition of Literacy in the Classroom*. Auckland: Ashton Scholastic.

Campbell, S. (2015). Feeling the pressure: Early childhood educators' reported views about learning and teaching phonics in Australian prior-to-school settings. *Australian Journal of Language and Literacy*, 38(1), 12–26.

Campbell, S., Torr, J. & Cologon, K. (2012). Ants, apples and the ABCs: The use of commercial phonics programmes in prior-to-school children's services. *Journal of Early Childhood Literacy*, 12(4), pp. 367–88, DOI:10.1177/1468798411417377.

Carnine, D., Silbert, J. & Kameenui, E. J. (1997). *Direct Instruction Reading* (3rd edn). Upper Saddle River, NJ: Merrill.

Chall, J. S. (1967). *Learning to Read: The Great Debate: An Inquiry into the Science, Art, and Ideology of Old and New Methods of Teaching Children to Read, 1910–1965.* New York: McGraw-Hill.

Clay, M. M. (1979). *Reading: The Patterning of Complex Behaviour* (2nd edn). Auckland: Heinemann.

Comber, B. (2015). Critical literacy and social justice. *Journal of Adolescent & Adult Literacy*, 58(5), pp. 362–7, DOI:10.1002/jaal.370.

Cunningham, P. M. (2009). *Phonics They Use: Words for Reading and Writing.* Boston, MA: Pearson.

Dewey, J. (1916). *Democracy and Education: An Introduction to the Philosophy of Education.* New York: Macmillan.

Dombey, H. (1999a). Picking a path through the phonics minefield. *Education 3–13*, 27(1), pp. 12–21, DOI:10.1080/03004279985200031.

—— (1999b). Towards a Balanced Approach to Phonics Teaching. *Reading*, 33(2), pp. 52–8, DOI:10.1111/1467–9345.00111.

EYLF (2009)—see Australian Government Department of Education, Employment and Workplace Relations for the Council of Australian Governments (2009).

Freebody, P. (2007). *Literacy Education in School: Research Perspectives from the Past, for the Future.* Melbourne: ACER.

Freebody, P. & Luke, A. (1990). Literacies' programs: Debates and demands in cultural context. *Prospect*, 5, pp. 7–16.

Frith, U. (1985). Beneath the surface of developmental dyslexia. *Surface Dyslexia*, 32.

Gleeson, L. & Blackwood, F. (2006). *Amy & Louis.* Sydney: Scholastic.

Goodman, K. S. (1968). *The Psycholinguistic Nature of the Reading Process.* Detroit, MI: Wayne State University Press.

Goswami, U. (1992). *Analogical Reasoning in Children.* Hove, UK: Lawrence Erlbaum Associates.

Goswami, U. & Bryant, P. (1990). *Phonological Skills and Learning to Read.* Hove, UK: Erlbaum Associates.

Groundwater-Smith, S., Ewing, R. & Le Cornu, R. (2014). *Teaching: Challenges and Dilemmas* (5th edn). Melbourne: Cengage.

Halliday, M. A. K. (1978). *Language as Social Semiotic: The Social Interpretation of Language and Meaning*. Baltimore, MD: University Park Press.

Heath, S. B. (1983). *Ways with Words: Language, Life, and Work in Communities and Classrooms*. New York: Cambridge University Press.

Hertzberg, M. & Freeman, J. (2012). *Teaching English Language Learners in Mainstream Classes*. Sydney: Primary English Teaching Association Australia (PETAA).

Hill, S. (2012). *Developing Early Literacy: Assessment and Teaching* (2nd edn). Melbourne: Eleanor Curtain Publishing.

Holdaway, D. (1979). *The Foundations of Literacy*. Sydney: Ashton Scholastic.

Holliday, M. (2008). *Strategies for Reading Success*. Sydney: e:lit.

Hornsby, D. & Wilson, L. (2011). *Teaching Phonics in Context*. Melbourne: Pearson Australia.

Hoyt, L. (2009). *Revisit, Reflect, Retell: Time-tested Strategies for Teaching Reading Comprehension*. Portsmouth, NH: Heinemann.

Lankshear, C. (1994). *Critical Literacy*. Belconnen, ACT: Australian Curriculum Studies Association.

Luke, A. (2012). Critical literacy: Foundational notes. *Theory Into Practice,* 51(1), pp. 4–11, DOI:10.1080/00405841.2012.636324.

Luke, A. & Elkins, J. (2002). Towards a critical, worldly literacy. *Journal of Adolescent & Adult Literacy,* 45(8), pp. 668–73.

Moll, L. C., Amanti, C., Neff, D. & Gonzalez, N. (1992). Funds of knowledge for teaching: Using a qualitative approach to connect homes and classrooms. *Theory Into Practice,* 31(2), 132–41, DOI:10.1080/00405849209543534.

Morgan, S., Kwaymullina, E. & Bancroft, B. (2010). *Sam's Bush Journey*. Sydney: Little Hare.

Moustafa, M. & Maldonado-Colon, E. (1999). Whole-to-parts phonics instruction: Building on what children know to help them know more. *The Reading Teacher,* 52(5), pp. 448–58, DOI:10.2307/20202102.

NSW Department of Education and Training (2009). *Literacy Teaching Guide: Phonics*. Sydney: NSW Department of Education and Training.

Piaget, J. (1959). *The Language and Thought of the Child* (3rd edn). London: Routledge and Kegan Paul.

Port, R. F. (2007). The graphical basis of phones and phonemes. In J. E. Flege, O. S. Bohn & M. J. Munro (eds), *Language Experience in Second Language Speech Learning: In honor of James Emil Flege*. Amsterdam: John Benjamins Publishing Company, pp. 349–65.

Pressley, M. (2006). *Reading Instruction That Works: The Case for Balanced Teaching* (3rd edn). New York: Guilford Press.

Rosenblatt, L. M. (1978). *The Reader, the Text, the Poem: The Transactional Theory of the Literary Work*. Carbondale: Southern Illinois University Press.

Skinner, B. F. (1957). *Verbal Behavior*. Acton, MA: Copley Publishing Group.

Smith, F. (1978). *Reading*. Cambridge: Cambridge University Press.

Sousa, D. A. (2014). *How the Brain Learns to Read* (2nd edn). Thousand Oaks, California: Corwin Press.

Stanovich, K. E. (2000). *Progress in Understanding Reading: Scientific Foundations and New Frontiers*. New York: Guilford Press.

Teale, W. H. & Sulzby, E. (1986). *Emergent Literacy: Writing and Reading*: Ablex Pub. Corp.

Toronto Public Library. (2015). Kids Space. Retrieved at: http://kidsspace. torontopubliclibrary.ca/earlyreading.html, viewed 24 November 2014.

Tse, L. & Nicholson, T. (2014). The effect of phonics-enhanced Big Book reading on the language and literacy skills of 6-year-old pupils of different reading ability attending lower SES schools. *Frontiers in Psychology*, 5, 1222, DOI:10.3389/fpsyg.2014.01222.

UNESCO. (2005). *Education for All – Literacy for Life*. Paris: United Nations Educational, Scientific and Cultural Organization.

Vygotsky, L. (1978). *Mind in Society: The Development of Higher Psychological Processes*. (Trans. M. Cole). Cambridge, MA: Harvard University Press.

Wyse, D. & Goswami, U. (2012). Early reading development. In J. Larson & J. Marsh (eds), *The SAGE Handbook of Early Childhood Literacy*. London: SAGE, pp. 379–95.

Yopp, H. K. & Yopp, R. H. (2000). Supporting phonemic awareness development in the classroom. *The Reading Teacher*, 54(2), pp. 130–43, DOI:10.2307/20204888.

CHAPTER 9

Storying and the emergent storyteller and writer

It has been argued that many western cultures have almost lost the art of storytelling but we all live our lives by storying. This chapter, co-authored by Victoria Campbell, University of Sydney, looks at how oral storying is critical for developing a child's sense of self and identity, and how oral storying can facilitate the writing process.

Anticipated outcomes for the chapter

After working through this chapter, you should be able to:

- articulate why storying and storytelling are important in the lives of young children
- acknowledge the importance of being able to tell stories in your role as a teacher
- understand the relationship between telling stories, drawing and emerging as a writer.

If you don't know the trees
you may get lost in the forest
If you don't know the stories
you may get lost in life.   (Agard, 2014, p. 11)

SCENARIO: JORDY

In earlier chapters we have seen how from birth the young child is on a lifelong journey to make sense of who they are in the world. By around three years old, many children are becoming confident storytellers, especially when sharing stories with their loved ones. Consider two-and-a-half-year-old Jordy's story below:

> Once upon a time a shark with very large teeth comes out of the leaves and ROARED! The shark was SCARY and he scared Manon and he bit Manon. Poor Manon!! He climbed up a cliff to get away from the shark.

> 'ROAR!' Manon and his baby went to a different country and they were safe.

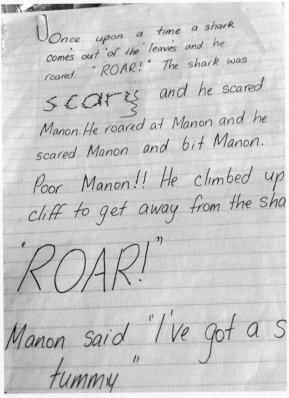

Figure 9.1 Two-and-a-half-year-old Jordy shares one of his first stories, as transcribed by his grandmother

Jordy had been watching a film for the first time, but he used his own understandings to make sense of some of the characters and the context as he retold it to his grandmother. Can you guess what story inspired Jordy's? What conventions has he incorporated in this story? After listening to his story, Jordy's grandmother responded by writing it down as Jordy retold it. She used capitals to represent the emotion that Jordy had used in the retelling. Because she had not seen the film that Jordy had been watching, she had no context and was a little unsure of how a shark could emerge from a clump of trees and roar; nor what kind of creature 'Manon' was. Nevertheless she was impressed that he was already demonstrating an understanding of narrative form.

Introduction

We live our lives through story without always being conscious that we are doing that. Story is one of the few universal cultural traits. All people in all cultures weave their life experiences into stories; they use language to shape and share their understandings (Rosen, 1972; Minns, 1997), and establish both personal and cultural identities. In our oldest cultures, stories were often told by a highly respected leader and were related to illustrate an important life lesson. Stories were also usually the way that history, laws and customary ways of living were communicated. Yet some would argue that many western communities are losing the art of sharing important life stories with one another and that the media, internet, film and television have taken over this storytelling role. Others, however, suggest that children are just telling stories in different ways by creating them using storytelling apps or digital puppets, as examples, to tell their stories. Similarly Facebook, Twitter and blogs are enabling adults to share their stories.

Storying A term used by Australian educator Kaye Lowe to refer to meaning-making activities that make sense of our life events where a story works as a metanarrative, 'something that threads between the many separate fragments of information and experience that we encounter' (2002, p. 7).

This chapter closely examines the role of story in developing who we are. It demonstrates how **storying** is strongly linked to the *EYLF* (2009) outcomes because it is critical for establishing a child's sense of self, identity and sense of wellbeing as well as being an important way of communicating. The chapter also provides suggestions for educators who need to become more confident at storytelling, and highlights the importance of actively listening to children's stories. Finally, it explores how oral storying and drawing are significant precursors to learning to write stories.

REFLECTION

Think about a way you have used a story, or stories, to make sense of something that happened today? Who did you share this story with? Did you share it differently with several people? Are you a natural storyteller? Did your family tell lots of stories? Do you enjoy listening to others tell stories? What medium or mode do you use to tell these stories? Is there a reason for your choice?

The narratives of young children: Establishing a sense of self and identity through story

When we story our lives for others, we reveal who we are: our hopes and dreams, our likes and dislikes, what makes us laugh and what makes us cry. Like adults, children's stories can range across the continuum, from the deadly serious to the wonderfully humorous. Young children create meaning and make sense of their world through narrative. Bruner (1990) suggests that our storying (Lowe, 2002) is much more akin to the way we think than reasoning or what he calls logico-scientific ways of talking/reporting. Research conducted by Engel (1997) into emergent **storytelling** in the first three years of a child's life supports this view. For Engel when children share personal stories, 'one of the things they do is to narrate an inner life, and an identity, and share that inner life and identity with others' (para. 46).

> **Storytelling** Telling or writing a story (events located in time and space). This term is often used more narrowly to convey the sharing of a narrative orally using words, sounds and gesture.

Listening to children tell stories, Engel also observes:

> Creating a story does many things for a child, just as it does for the storytelling adult. One function storytelling serves for the young child is to create a bridge between the self and important others (friends, teachers, and parents). (2000, p. 196)

As Carol Fox (1983, 1993) has argued, children's stories provide us with a window into their imaginations. When children story, they are engaged in socially constructed activity that depends on the relational aspects of talking and listening. In this way their *identity* is being socially constructed and assisted through storying. For Bruner (1990) this 'narrative sense' (p. 68) or ability to construct coherent narratives is crucial for the formation of self and thus important for a healthy mind. Many psychologists (see for example McAdams, 2006) argue that being able to tell stories about our own experience is important for our emotional and social wellbeing. Certainly it is true that from the time they can talk, children make sense of themselves and others through varying forms of storying.

Becoming a confident storyteller: The teacher as storyteller

'Tell us another one!' I had already spent the better part of an hour telling several folktales with a group of young children. Together we had crossed over a threshold into lands where giants roamed, kings cried, and elephants grew new trunks. But now it was time for me to leave. As I was packing up one child came to me and whispered urgently, as though he did not want the teacher to hear 'Will you come again tomorrow?' When the teacher walked with me from the room she marveled at how engaged her children had been, particularly for that length of time. She went on to confess that she had difficulty getting them to sit still for 15 minutes even when reading a book. I paused and said 'I would be happy to help you discover how to tell tales of your own.' Over several weeks she learned to tell stories without a book. The last time I spoke with her she said 'I am amazed, the children now say to me – tell us another one!' (Victoria Campbell)

When a teacher decides to share a story without referring to a book, something unique happens – the teacher and children make eye contact and actively listen to each other. There is no third person in the guise of the author or illustrator to mediate. Together, the class crosses the *once upon a time* threshold, toppling into fantastic worlds, where wolves blow down houses, and terrorise grandmothers, where genies emerge from lamps, princesses grow hair as long as bell ropes, tortoises win races, and princes have the uncanny knack of showing up at the right time. Teacher and children go on a story journey together, forging new terrains as storying co-creators. The teacher, as guide, weaves words and gesture together to form a coherent narrative, but the storytelling space becomes charged with children's imaginations as they imbue the story with meaning drawn from their own experiences and personal references. The teacher responds to the children's reactions and adapts accordingly, thus making it more personalised and alive. Livo and Rietz (1986) eloquently describe the nature of this experience:

> The oral story is soft and malleable. It yields to the pleasures and needs of its audience. Its language is not the precise and unchanging form of the written story, created by a single author, but the evolving, flowing language of the community. (p. 15)

Oral storying is a personal and immediate form of communication that depends on a flowing exchange between the teller and listener. When she tells a story, the teacher acknowledges that children are co-creators in the storytelling experience and as a consequence children feel valued in that space. Egan (1986, 1997) suggests that once we recognise the important role story structure plays in human understanding 'then we are led to reconceive the curriculum as a set of great stories we have to tell children and recognise . . . school teachers as the storytellers of our culture' (1997, p. 64). Daniel (2007) also argues:

> unless teachers feel that they themselves are equipped to be classroom storytellers, then the activity of classroom storytelling delivered by an adult will remain the preserve of the professional teller of tales instead of its being regarded as a general teaching method, rich in potential for assisting children to become effective learners. (p. 735)

So teachers need to see themselves as storytellers. When teachers *do* become storytellers and use it as regular part of their pedagogy, it becomes a natural and pleasurable way to enhance students' learning. By developing their skills in this area, teachers are able to model explicit forms of narrative structure including character motivation, setting and place, sequence of events, plus examples of purposeful language, vocal expression and body language. Storytelling also develops children's social and cultural understanding, and builds a sense of community, particularly if stories are chosen that are inclusive and representative of the range of children's and teachers' cultural backgrounds.

When we story, whether it be a personal story or fictional tale, we reveal who we are (Lowe, 2002). It allows for the natural language, grammar, syntax and physicality of the storyteller. A teacher needs to become comfortable to stand, or sit, in front of a group of children and tell stories. It is an art form, but as Kuyvenhoven (2009) reassures 'it is the lightest of arts' (p. 195). And it is not acting. Birch (2000) describes the difference between acting and storytelling as follows:

> Storytelling is most interesting when the storyteller is not acting out a part, but rather doing two things simultaneously. Through verbal *and* nonverbal clues, effective storytellers bring out nuances, both large and small, which delineate characters within the story and direct the point of view of an audience toward the characters. Actors may use sense memory to bring the character to life, but they submerge their own *selves* in service of character. Storytellers are not hidden. (pp. 20–21)

When storying a fictional tale such as a fairy tale or folktale, the teller expresses their point of view and personality as they move between narrating events and demonstrating character. They do this by using their own voice, own rhythms, own gestures and personal references to bring the story to life for the listeners. In Walter Benjamin's essay *The Storyteller* (in Hale, 2006) he says 'traces of the storyteller cling to the story the way the handprints of the potter cling to the clay vessel' (p. 367). The identity of the storyteller is at the heart of any successful storytelling encounter.

When adults share stories with children, they share a part of themselves. This was true for early career teacher Bianca who was keen to reconnect with her cultural identity and to explore ways to introduce it into her teaching. She chose to tell a true family story set in rural China, about her great grandmother's children who where kidnapped by bandits and returned through a noble deed. Bianca observed that storytelling was effective because it 'brings *you* fully into the classroom' (Campbell, 2008, p. 43). Her comment is supported by Palmer's (1998) claim that 'good teaching comes from the identity and integrity of the teacher . . . personal identity infuses their work' (p. 10).

Beginning

The first step is to find a story to tell. Like Bianca you may like to modify a personal tale or prefer to start with a traditional tale. For young children, a simple nursery story such as *Three Billy Goats Gruff, Goldilocks, The Giant Turnip* or *The Three Little Pigs*, could be chosen. These kinds of tales have a repetitive rhythm and pattern, and often appeal to younger children. Older children who are in the early years of school may enjoy the more complicated narrative aspects of the fairytale, myth or folktale; for example, *King Midas, Arachne, Rumpelstiltskin*, and the Celtic myth of the

Selkie. These are not prescriptive as older children may enjoy returning to simple stories while younger ones can travel happily into a classical myth or legend.

After choosing a story, the teller will need to develop confidence to orally tell the story. Often an appropriate place to start is to reflect on the key moments of the story. Many storytellers like to think of these critical moments as the *bare bones* or *skeleton* of the story, which they will *flesh* out with their unique way of telling. Here is an example of the *bare bones* of a version of the Greek myth *Arachne*:

- Arachne is a great, yet boastful weaver
- People warn that her pride may offend the gods
- An old lady appears who challenges Arachne
- The old lady transforms into the goddess Athena
- A competition is held between Athena and Arachne
- Arachne wins
- Her tapestry makes fun of the gods
- For her pride, Arachne is turned into a spider.

Now the storyteller needs to *flesh* out the bones of the story with their unique way of telling. Another important thing to remember is that there is no need to memorise the story, the teller needs only to become familiar with it. In this way the storyteller is free to use their own words, grammar, syntax and rhythms to bring the story to life for the listeners.

When learning the story, it is helpful to think of linking images together, by asking what happens next? Experienced storyteller Solis (2006) poetically recommends that we 'connect these images like pearls on a necklace. Or even like stepping stones across a river. Each image leads to another, moving the story along.' (p. 9).

Finally, it is important to remember that the listeners in the storytelling experience are co-creators, they are actively engaged in helping create story images, effectively doing 50 per cent of the work. While the storyteller *fleshes out* the story using their own individual style, the imaginations of each listener will also create unique images and sensations prompted by the words of the teller.

After telling an oral story, the teacher can build on the experience by using the strategies listed below to assist children's ability to retell and develop their own versions of the stories. Of course stories can be read too, but with an oral tale the listener is actively engaged in co-creating the story.

'Advance/detail' game: Retelling a story with a partner

Students have an opportunity to retell the story using their own words. There is no right or wrong way to tell the story, however they need to include a sequence of events that involves important characters. The narrative form provides the structure within which children can improvise/play. Before starting this activity decide upon the key moments, or plot points. As a whole class, or in small groups depict these on A4 pieces of paper (or whiteboard) with a sentence accompanied by an image (children can draw these images). Arrange the story in a narrative order. These will serve as visual prompts for young storytellers.

Arrange partners so they sit opposite each other. One child tells the story while the other child listens. The child who is listening also directs the story by saying either '*Advance*' or '*Detail*'. When *advancing* the teller moves forward in the story, following the plot line. When *detailing* the teller stops, or 'drills down' into the story by adding detail, such as colour, shape, size, smell, etc. Halfway through the story the children swap roles; the child who was telling the story becomes the listener/director and the child listening/directing becomes the teller. For younger children 'forward' or 'description' may be more appropriate words. This could be modified as a whole-group experience with the teacher providing guidance. (Adapted from Johnstone, 1989)

When teachers develop their artistry in this way, their classroom becomes a learning community that harnesses children's already powerful imaginations.

Supporting children's storying development in the early years: Listening to each other

Supportive environments, where talking and listening are valued, allow children to share their stories. Listening to children as they share their narratives of experiences supports the young storymaker and assists them as they make sense of their world. Some children will also find the use of puppets helpful – they will feel more confident manipulating an inanimate object who tells the story first. See Gibson and Campbell (2013) for many valuable suggestions for working with puppets.

Vivian Gussin Paley (1990), an American early childhood educator, has extensively researched the importance of young children's storying in early childhood contexts and recognises that storying needs to be one of the 'primary realities in the preschool and kindergarten' (p. 6). Paley's *storytelling curriculum* places the child at the centre of learning, and powerfully shapes the context in which language develops (Cooper, 2005). This approach is based on listening to children's stories, and encourages parents, educators and caregivers to be curious about what children have to say, or are trying to express, and then assist them in this process. In her essay on listening to what the children say, Paley (1986) reflects:

> the goal is the same, no matter what the age . . . someone must be there to listen, respond and add a dab of glue to the important words that burst forth . . . the key is curiosity, and it is curiosity, not answers . . . as we seek to learn more about a child, we demonstrate the acts of observing, listening, questioning, and wondering. (p. 127)

Paley's approach places the child at the centre of the learning experience and recognises the crucial role storying has in the lives of young children.

Furthermore, as children develop their storying skills they draw on narrative models around them. Exposure to quality talking and listening experiences are essential for children's ability to story. If teachers are modelling explicit forms of storying, as previously described, then children will draw on these models as they create oral narratives of their own. The nature of young children being able to orally tell stories as observed by Fox (1993) is directly related to the concept of storying. In her study, Fox found that early exposure to quality literature is a defining feature of children's ability to tell their own stories. Fox collected, recorded and analysed numerous oral stories told by five preschool children, focusing on elements such as children's choice of words, phrases, story structure and personal styles of narration. Fox found that the children used multiple frames of reference to bring their stories to life, such as personal experiences, other oral stories, children's books, rhymes and verse, radio and television. Fox observes that children get themselves into a 'syntactic muddle' by attempting to use 'grammatically complex sentences' to make their story sound like 'story language', but importantly enjoy 'their freedom from the constraints of more mundane language interactions' (p. 28). She concluded that children exhibited a form of imaginative play as they drew on different story forms in their attempt to story.

Engel (1995) comments on children's storytelling development in the following way:

> By the time children are 3 years old . . . many of their stories will have a beginning, middle and an end . . . by the time they are 5 they will have distinctive personal styles of storytelling. They will also know the story custom of their particular community . . . by the age of 8, most children can tell several different types of stories upon request and can accurately relate complex events. (pp. 16–17)

One of the most powerful means to assist children in this learning is for the teacher or caregiver to orally tell stories and to listen to the stories of those in their care. When teachers engage in imaginative learning experiences, such as storying with children, they provide environments that build language, literacy and deeper understandings about the world.

REFLECTION

Consider the following three stories as told by young children:

Once there was a person in town who wanted money. He needed some food to eat. And he wanted a glass of milk. So he ran to the post office to get some money. But he didn't know where to go and he ended up in the forest. He ran 'til he found a cottage. And there was a witch inside so he didn't go in. He went to another cottage. And then he ran 'til he was trapped. And that's all. (Joshua, three years, eight months old)

Once upon a time there were three pirates. They sailed out to sea and when they got to shore they buried the treasure. (Scott, four years old).

One day when the emperor was getting out of bed he saw the nightingale out of his window. He called it in and it came in and it sang to him and then it went into the forest and talked to his friends. And then it came back to the emperor and sat on a little shelf and sang another song to the emperor. (Cathie, five years old).

As the teacher or caregiver, how might you honour and respond to these stories? Could you help the child extend the sequence of events, develop the characters further? How?

Some children choose to place themselves at the centre of a story. As Meek (2004) suggests, they fictionalise themselves in play creating a world 'where the fiction allows them to explore both the world they know and the one they "make up"'. Others will use a favourite piece of literature as a starting point. Karen Gallas (1992) claims that children's fictional stories expand 'the children's ability to speak about the more subterranean issues of the community: about belonging and inclusion, about unspoken wishes to overcome barriers.' (p 181)

Oral storying and the emergent creative writer

While this chapter emphasises the importance of the oral, this final section takes one further step and suggests that when children are exposed to quality talking and listening experiences including oral storytelling, it also helps them write stories (Wells 1986; Fox, 1993). For many children, confidence with sharing a story and then being able to listen actively to those told by others will facilitate their development of narrative writing. If children see the opportunity to write creatively as an extension from storytelling into a related art form and enjoy the writing process because they can choose what they write for themselves, they will see it as a meaningful tool for continued development of self and learning. Perhaps this may be because these opportunities have helped develop an understanding of the conventions including location in time and space, character development, a structuring of events, and the authorial voice. Once familiar with such conventions, the teller or writer can play with these conventions and experiment to make them their own.

There are many ways to facilitate the transition from story*teller* to emergent writer, moving from what is known to what is new. For example, the storytelling can be recorded or the teacher may scribe the story for the teller. Alternatively, the key moments in the story can be depicted as frozen images and then these images can be represented visually. Mackenzie and Veresov (2013) demonstrated that children whose teachers encouraged them to draw their stories in the first few months of school alongside learning to write, enabled them to create more complex stories than just using writing alone. Story maps can also be valuable at this point in learning to write.

Drawing it all together

Story is universal to all cultures. Children begin to story soon after they learn to talk. Some western cultures ignore the importance of story. This chapter has focused on the importance of fostering storying, both telling and retelling, and from the perspective of teachers, parents and children. Given that we use narrative to dream and talk to ourselves, there is obviously an important relationship between narrative and thought (Rosen, 1986; Bruner, 1990). It is important to work with a range of stories that will engage listeners and allow children to see themselves in the story. Receiving a story enables a listener to respond in their own individual way, making sense of it using their own experiences and understandings. As Rosen (1972) suggests, we all comprise many stories, including our own.

Questions for further discussion

- Are there storytelling competencies you can identify? If so, do you feel you are developing them? What could you do to further gain skills in storying?
- How can young children begin to develop digital storytelling skills?

Further reading

Campbell, V. (2012). Playing with storytelling. In R. Ewing (ed.), *The Creative Arts in the Lives of Young children: Play, Imagination, Learning*. Melbourne: ACER.

Collins, R. & Cooper, P. J. (2005). *The Power of Story: Teaching Through Storytelling* (2nd ed.) Long Grove: Waveland Press.

Mackenzie, N. & Veresov, N. (2013) How drawing can support writing acquisition: Text construction in early writing from a Vygotskian perspective. *Australasian Journal of Early Childhood* 38(4) December.

Useful websites

These websites enable you to listen to professional storytellers.

Story Bee: www.storybee.org

The Story Museum: www.storymuseum.org.uk/1001stories

References

Agard, J. (2014). *Book.* London: Walker Books.

Australian Government Department of Education, Employment and
    Workplace Relations for the Council of Australian Governments (2009).
    *Belonging, Being and Becoming. The Early Years Learning Framework for
    Australia (EYLF).* Canberra: Commonwealth of Australia.

Birch, C. L. (2000). *The Whole Story Handbook: Using Imagery to Complete the Story
    Experience.* Arkansas: August House Publishers.

Bruner, J. (1990). *Acts of Meaning: Four Lectures on Mind and Culture.* Cambridge,
    MA: Harvard University Press.

Campbell, V. (2008). Tales from the liminal classroom: Preservice teachers and
    oral storytelling. Unpublished Master of Education thesis, University of
    Sydney, NSW, Australia.

Cooper, P. M. (2005). Literacy learning and pedagogical purpose in Vivian
    Paley's storytelling curriculum. *Journal of Early Childhood Literacy,* 5(3),
    pp. 229–51.

Daniel, A. K. (2007). From folktales to algorithms: Developing the teacher's
    role as principal storyteller in the classroom. *Early Child Development
    and Care,* 177(6 & 7), pp. 735–50.

Egan, K. (1986). *Teaching as Storytelling: An Alternative Approach to Teaching
    and Curriculum in the Elementary School.* Chicago: University of
    Chicago Press.

—— (1997). *The Educated Mind: How Cognitive Tools Shape Our Understanding.*
    Chicago: University of Chicago Press.

Engel, S. (1995). *The Stories Children Tell: Making Sense of the Narratives of
    Childhood.* New York: W. H. Freeman & Co.

—— (1997). Storytelling in the first three years. Retrieved at: www.zerotothree
    .org/child-development/early-language-literacy/the-emergence-of-
    storytelling.html, viewed 2 June 2011.

—— (2000). Peeking through the curtain: Narratives as the boundary between
    secret and known. *Michigan Quarterly Review,* 39(2), pp. 195–208.

EYLF (2009)—see Australian Government Department of Education,
    Employment and Workplace Relations for the Council of Australian
    Governments, (2009).

Fox, C. (1983). Talking like a book: Young children's opening monologues.
    In M. Meek (ed.), *Opening Moves.* Bedford Way Papers No. 17.
    London: University of London Institute of Education.

—— (1993). *At the Very Edge of the Forest: The Influence of Literature on Story-telling
    by Children.* London: Cassell.

Gallas, K. (1992). When the children take the chair: A study of sharing time in a primary classroom. *Language Arts*, 69, March: pp. 172–182.

Gibson, R. & Campbell, V. (2013) Playing with Puppetry. In R. Ewing (ed.), *The Creative Arts in the lives of young children: Play, imagination, learning.* Melbourne: ACER.

Johnstone, K. (1989). *Impro: Improvisation and the Theatre.* London: Methuen Drama.

Hale D. J. (2006). *The Novel: An Anthology of Criticism and Theory 1900–2000.* Malden, MA: Blackwell Publishing.

Kuyvehoven, J. (2009). *In The Presence of Each Other.* Toronto: University of Toronto Press.

Livo, N. J. & Rietz, S. A. (1986). *Storytelling: Process and Practice.* Colorado: Libraries Unlimited.

Lowe, K. (2002). *What's the Story? Making Meaning in Primary Classrooms.* Sydney: Primary English Teaching Association.

McAdams, D. P. (2006). The problem of narrative coherence. *Journal of Constructivist Psychology,* 19, pp. 109–25.

Meek, M. (2004). Introductions, definitions, changes, attitudes. In P. Hunt (ed.), *International Companion of Children's Literature.* London: Routledge, pp. 1–12.

Minns, H. (1997). *Read It to me Now: Learning at Home and School.* (2nd edn). London: Open University Press.

Paley, V. G. (1986). On listening to what the children say. *Harvard Educational Review,* 56(2), pp. 122–31.

—— (1990). *The Boy Who Would Be a Helicopter: The Uses of Storytelling in the Classroom.* Cambridge, MA: Harvard University Press.

Palmer, P. J. (1998). *The Courage to Teach: Exploring the Inner Landscape of a Teacher's Life.* San Francisco: Jossey-Bass.

Rosen, H. (1972). Language and Class: A Critical Look at the Language of Basil Bernstein. *History Workshop No. 6,* Oxford: Ruskin College, 5 May 1972.

—— (1986). The importance of story. *Language Arts,* 63 (3) March, pp. 226–37.

Solis, S. (2006). *Storytime Yoga: Teaching Yoga to Children Through Story.* Boulder: The Mythic Yoga Studio, LLC.

Wells, G. (1986). *The Meaning Makers: Children Learning Language and Using Language to Learn.* Portsmouth, NH: Heinemann.

CHAPTER 10

Making meaning with image and text in picture books

Picture books have a rich history, from well-loved classics to postmodern, interactive stories and digital texts. This chapter explores the form and features of picture books and the concept of a metalanguage, which allows us to describe how words and pictures work together as part of the reading process. It concludes with strategies and activities for teaching visual literacy.

Anticipated outcomes for the chapter

After working through this chapter, you should be able to:

- appreciate the historical development of picture books
- identify the key features of picture books
- develop a metalanguage for analysing images within picture books
- consider appropriate pedagogies and strategies for teaching young children about the relationship between the visual and verbal modes in picture books.

SCENARIO: MONKEY AND ME

Monkey and me, monkey and me, monkey and me

We went to see, we went to see some . . .

Reading this story together for the first time, the children in the small group immediately take Emily Gravett's visual invitation to join in with predicting and making the story come alive. She invites readers to guess each new animal by setting up the visual design and image choice on each page. The engaging activity of repeating the lines invites reading along together, even though some children in the group are only beginning to decode print. Each page finishes with the promise of a new animal, but for the clever reader, the clues are everywhere. Six penguins and three chicks parade across the first page.

'Look, that baby penguin is scared of the fish,' says Sam, who has carefully noticed this visual detail.

As the story continues, the children notice that the shape of the little girl and her toy monkey mirrors the forthcoming animal, creating that wonderful feeling of being an 'insider' in the reading process. It is not only the shape of the girl bouncing like a kangaroo or swinging like a monkey; it is the typeface and lines that curve to mirror the next animal's behaviour.

'What might the next animal be?' enquires the teacher.

'Octopuses!', shouts Mia, 'because the monkey's arms and legs look like an octopus.'

The children are not only reading along with the written text and identifying the animals once they see them, but they have understood that the visual aspects of the pictures and the words also hold meanings and possibilities.

Introduction

Picture book (or picturebook)
A book where the pictures and words interdependently tell a story, and are often complemented by the cover, physical form and layout.

Picture books not only offer opportunities for shared and meaningful learning experiences for young children as they become readers, writers and literate individuals, but are also objects of art, design and literary study in their own right. Young children take delight in repeated re-readings. As our scenario shows, they can also notice the smallest details, which often escape adults. Given time to explore the layers of meaning, children begin to develop some intuitive knowledge about how pictures and text work, where texts teach what readers (and viewers) might learn. At the same time we know that knowledgeable teachers will extend and enhance this expertise, inviting readers 'down the rabbit hole' to not only explore the stories and characters, but also to give them insider knowledge about words and pictures.

In one sense the children reading *Monkey and Me* join in with the traditions of children and adults across the past millennia, who read pictures on temple walls, in scrolls, on stained glass windows, in illustrated manuscripts and on theatre and puppet show backdrops. Today's picture books can trace their heritage back more recently to the 20th century, where each **genre** and convention of various books have been established and shared. Picture books have a special place in the lives of children, not only because of their cultural and social value but because they begin to formalise and nurture the visual literacy skills that are so important across many other types of texts in our everyday lives.

> **Genre** Categorising different types of texts and literature, according to styles and conventions such as narrative and factual genres, as well as types of narratives such as realistic, fantasy and historical fiction.

A short history of picture books

The range of picture books from Australian, New Zealand, UK and US authors, as well as many other English-speaking countries, provides an astonishing selection of texts, both past and present. This is not even considering the variety of children's books from non-English speaking countries. Pat Pinsent notes the reluctance of English speakers to engage with texts in other languages, arguing that this pattern only developed over the past 400 years, while during the Renaissance period, English readers would not only have been familiar with Chaucer, Shakespeare and Milton, but also with writers from Italy, France and Spain (Harding & Pinsent, 2008).

While picture books as we know them today did not exist before the late 1890s, their antecedents stretch back over centuries. Illustrated texts based on the Bible and other religious writings evolved over the centuries, with book illustrations and the script itself having detailed and colourful decoration. Barbara Kiefer (2011) argues that picture books or texts with pictures included those with decorative ornamentation, illustrated versions of poetry such as Chaucer's *Canterbury Tales* and Aesop's fables. It was not until the 17th century that books may have been produced for children, such as Comenius's *The Visible World in Pictures* (1658).

Advances in printing technology during the late 19th century developed alongside changing attitudes to children's education. Many illustrated books produced in the early part of the 20th century were moral guides. Authors such as Beatrix Potter (*The Tale of Peter Rabbit*, 1902) wrote her own cautionary tales, while others illustrated classic stories, such as Mabel Lucie Atwell's *Mother Goose* (1910) and *Hans Christian Anderson's Fairy Tales* (1914) (Atwell, 1910; Andersen & Atwell, 1914). What is termed as the first 'true' picture book, *Clever Bill* by William Nicholson where the text and image work together, was published in 1926. The genre of contemporary picture books evolved from this period. The number, styles and variations of picture books have developed significantly since the early 20th century, reflecting changes in technology as well as cultural and social beliefs and practices.

Many picture books from the early to mid-20th century are still part of children's lives and classroom libraries today, having stood the test of time.

Table 10.1 Popular picture books from the early and mid-20th century

1920s–1950s	1928 – *Millions of Cats* by Wanda Gag (Puffin, 2006)
	1934 – *The Story of Babar the Little Elephant* by Jean de Brunhoff (Random House, 2002)
	1934 – *Blinky Bill* by Dorothy Wall (Harper Collins, 2009)
	1933 – *The Story about Ping* by Kurt Weise, illustrated by Majorie Flack (Grosset & Dunlap, 2002)
	1940 – *Horton Hatches the Egg* by Dr Suess (Harper Collins, 2004)
	1942 – The Little Golden books series begins
	1942 – *Digit Dick on the Barrier Reef* by Leslie Rees, illustrated by Walter Cunningham (Lansdowne Press, 1982)
	1950 – *Petunia* by Roger Duvoisin (Dragonfly Books, 2015)
	1959 – *Little Blue and Little Yellow* by Leo Lionni (Alfred A. Knopf, 2009)
1960s–1970s	1962 – *The Snowy Day* by Ezra Jack Keats (Viking, 2011)
	1963 – *Where the Wild Things Are* by Maurice Sendak (Random House Children's books, 2015)
	1968 – *Rosie's Walk* by Pat Hutchins (Red Fox, 2010)
	1969 – *The Very Hungry Caterpillar* by Eric Carle (Puffin, 2010)
	1970 – *Mr Gumpy's Outing* by John Burningham (Red Fox, 2010)
	1973 – *Father Christmas* by Raymond Briggs (Puffin Books, 2004)
	1974 – *The Bunyip of Berkley's Creek* by Jenny Wagner (Penguin, 2005)
	1978 – *Come Away from the Water, Shirley* by John Burningham (Red Fox, 2000)
	1979 – *Freight Train* by Donald Crews (Phoenix Yard, 2012)

Postmodernism Questioning, critiquing or playfully challenging accepted beliefs or practices in a variety of disciplines. In terms of picture books, postmodern influences include playing with or parodying traditional story forms and structures, using a number of metafictive devices.

Metafictive devices Techniques that draw the reader's attention to the constructed nature of the story. Examples include multistranded narratives, multiple narrators, nonlinear plots, narrators who address the reader or comment on their own narrations, unusual visual and page designs as well as the mixing of genre and narrative types.

Picture books continue to represent what we might term traditional narrative archetypes, which may cover stories of everyday events in children's lives, traditional style folk tales and fairytales, as well as mainstream genres such as humorous stories (often using animals as main characters), fantasies, mysteries, dramas and historical narratives (McDonald, 2013). However, during the 1980s, even more significant changes began to appear in the nature, content and style of children's picture books. These changes began to be discussed in the 1990s, with many researchers defining these changes as part of **postmodernism**. This term, which is notoriously elusive, reflected as well as influenced the changes in cultural understandings over the past 40 years, including the areas of architecture, philosophy, fashion, economics and literature. In terms of picture books, a number of techniques have become common, interrupting the traditional expectations of a story. For example, in Jon Scieszka and Lane Smith's *The Stinky Cheese Man and Other Fairly Stupid Tales* (Scieszka & Smith, 1993), Jack, the narrator, not only addresses the reader directly but argues with other characters, interrupts the story and has elements of the book itself come crashing down on him in the pictures. These techniques, which draw the reader's attention to the constructed nature of the story itself, are termed **metafictive devices**. Some examples of picture books that use these techniques are noted in Table 10.2.

Table 10.2 Examples of metafictive devices in picture books

Multiple narratives	*Come away from the water, Shirley* by John Burningham
Multiple voices and views	*Voices in the Park* by Anthony Browne
Narrators who address the reader or comment on their own narrations	*Don't Let the Pigeon Drive the Bus* by Mo Willems *Chester* by Melanie Watt *Interrupting Chicken* by David Ezra Stein
Layered meanings	*Wolves* by Emily Gravett *Drac and the Gremlin* by Alan Baillie and Jane Tanner
Unusual page design	*Flotsam; The Three Pigs* by David Weisner
Playful visual elements	*Journey* by Aaron Becker *Zoom* by Istvan Banyai
Intertextuality, parody and self-reference	*Who's Afraid of the Big Bad Book?* by Lauren Child *Willy the Dreamer* by Anthony Browne *The Red Book* by Barbara Lehman
Interactive formats	*The Jolly Postman or Other People's Stories* by Janet and Allan Ahlberg
Varied point of view	*Diary of a Wombat* by Jackie French
Contrasting or divergent image and written text	*Rosie's Walk* by Pat Hutchins *Good Dog Hank* by Jackie French/Nina Rycroft *No Bears* by Meg McKinlay and Leila Rudge

There are a great many books that provide a very thorough and detailed overview of the history, evolution and key ideas associated with children's literature including picture books (Salisbury, 2004; Mallett, 2010). In the Australian context, the seminal work of Maurice Saxby plays a critical role in outlining the development of children's literature (Saxby & Winch, 1991; Saxby, 1997), while more recent work by Anstey and Bull (2000) and McDonald (2013) provide commentary on current aspects of children's literature and picture books.

REFLECTION

Can you name a number of stories that you remember from your own childhood? You may have some particular books that were special, such as fairytales, traditional legends or religious stories. As we move into reading adult fiction and poetry, a rich childhood experience with books serves us well. They help us make connections between stories, understand literary allusions in canonical works from Shakespeare to Chaucer, as well as see archetypal narratives play out in contemporary novels and media. Many recent children's films either retell famous fairytales, or play with their ideas and characters, such as the Shrek films. Knowing the original stories allows children to be 'insiders' when they read and view such texts.

In this chapter and other chapters in this book, there are many suggested authors and titles to share with young children. Rather than being a set list, they are meant to introduce classic texts and well-known authors as well as pave the way to explore newer books and encourage children to do likewise. The *Australian Curriculum*: English suggests children have experiences with classic and contemporary authors and texts. They should also be exposed to texts that reflect Aboriginal and Torres Strait Islander histories and cultures, as well as Asia and Australia's engagement with Asia (Australian Curriculum Assessment and Reporting Authority, ACARA, 2015).

The parts of a picture book

Young children who have had experience with books will know how to find the cover and turn the pages from left to right in a picture book. However, there are many other features and terms which are important to understand and use correctly.

> Peritext Textual and visual features beyond the main story and pictures, such as the cover, endpages, dust jacket and dedication page.

Picture books are generally 32 pages in length, and come in hardback or paperback bindings. There are many features that extend beyond the pictures and written text. These are known as **peritext** which can include the cover, endpapers, title page, etc. Observant readers will often have noted how some features such as the endpapers (sometimes termed endpages, which are the first pages seen on opening and closing a picture book) are sometimes used by illustrators to give clues or set the mood for a story.

Often key features about the cover and binding are shared before reading a story aloud to children. Pointing out the title, author and illustrator are common practice, but teachers can also show how to carefully spread the spine of a book as it is opened, investigate the dust jacket and endpapers, which often give clues about the story and consider any dedication information before the title page.

There are a number of books for children *about* picture books and their features, including *It's a Book* by Lane Smith (2010). *Parsley Rabbit's Book about Books* (Watts & Legge, 2007) provides a simple and entertaining introduction to the various features of a book, including the technical information on the title page.

This book also presents features that are actually part of the story itself, such as the use of *flaps* to extend a page or hide objects, the various *shapes* and *sizes* that books come in as well as how books may have *stories* as well as *information*.

Making a class book provides opportunities to explore the features of a picture book. Oliver Jeffer's *The Incredible Book Eating Boy* (2006) follows Henry's exploits as he literally eats books. This book, with illustrations made up of collaged pieces of paper as well as pen and ink drawings, has a scrapbook feel to it. Figure 10.1 shows some of the features of a book which can become part of the reading and book-making discussion. The concept of the double-page spread (where illustrations

Figure 10.1 The cover of *Parsley Rabbit's Book about Books* (Watts & Legge, 2007)

Figure 10.2 A book-eating boy made using acrylic, aged pages and collaged materials.

are spread across the two pages) can be explained to children. The use of smaller frames containing different images that are spread across the page and the concept of a full bleed illustration where it extends to the page's edge can also be explained.

Children can create their own book-eating boy page by using old newsprint or copied pages from favourite novels, which have been aged using cold tea or paints (Lennox, 2011). Characters can be drawn using crayon or acrylic paints, as well as collaging other shapes and objects using various coloured paper and objects (see Figure 10.2). Each page can then be bound into a class book, complete with title pages and author/illustrator listings. For younger students, a helper might scribe a simple description of each child's work onto the page. For older students, the class can innovate on the story, jointly writing new events, where their pictures and words tell a new story.

Engaging with picture books using a visual metalanguage

Pictures have always been understood as integral to the unfolding narrative in picture books. They work together with the written text as part of the story. However, it has only been more recently that educators have acknowledged the need to make explicit to young readers how visual texts work, in a similar way to teaching about how print and reading works (Callow, 2013).

Metalanguage A vocabulary to talk about language (narration, genre, nouns, verbs etc.) as well as other communication modes, such as a visual metalanguage to talk about colour, line, movement, layout, design etc.

When we use technical terms to describe features about language or other media, we are using a **metalanguage**. This is a language to talk about language or other communication modes, whether we are describing the features of a story, the physical features of books or specific features about images, music and movement. The development of a metalanguage can enrich young learners' experience with picture books; however 'knowing what to say, in part, requires knowing what to look for' (Eisner, 2002 p. 87) so the role of the teacher as expert guide plays an important role here (Pantaleo, 2014).

Mode Communicative resources, which can include the written and visual mode, as well as spoken, gestural, spatial, video and audio resources.

When reading a picture book, readers use both the written mode and the visual mode in order to create meaning. A **mode** is a set of meaning-making resources that authors and illustrators draw from when creating a text (Jewitt, 2008). The written mode includes the use of various story genres, narrative structures, poetic and figurative language, as well as using language to describe events, settings and characters. The visual mode includes resources such as line, shape and colour to represent realistic or abstract images, suggest movement, gesture and emotion, as well as the use of point of view, page design and layout. When interpreting a picture book, readers and viewers also draw on their own skills and knowledge about each mode as they read. The concept of **multimodality** acknowledges that different texts will use a number of modes to create meaning, and these can include word, image, sound, music, movement, video and interactive elements (Kress, 2010). While this chapter focuses on picture books, children also need to engage with all types of multimodal texts including performance and drama, information books and websites as well as media, film and television. Chapter 11 explores in more detail the use of digital texts in the early childhood setting.

> Multimodality Texts that use two or more modes of communication, such as writing and visual materials in picture books, or video, audio and gesture in animated stories or interactive screen-based games.

Exploring the different levels of picture books

Talking about the various features of picture books before, during and after reading allows us to teach children about their various features. The joy of entering into a story world is not lessened when teachers, at suitable moments, point out the story genre, where it is set and who the main characters are, moving to then discuss how the author shapes our thinking about themes, such as friendship, sadness, courage and fear. Other features such as the narrative structure and the style of narration can also be explained when particular aspects of the story are revisited (Pantaleo, 2015). Examples of these types of story features are summarised in Table 10.3.

Focusing on the visual mode

Wordless texts are an excellent way of exploring the visual mode. Wordless (or nearly wordless) texts range from simple object books for babies and toddlers through to complex graphic novels for older children. Evelyn Arizpe's work (2013) provides some sound principles for enjoying and exploring a wordless story. When sharing a wordless book with children, do not expect an immediate verbalising of the story. Explore the images together, point out details and use think alouds to wonder about possible meanings, thus allowing children to go back and forward between the pages as they begin to make connections and offer opinions about the unfolding story. Give children time to read the text by themselves or with a friend. This initial engagement not only provides time for reflection but also supports children's aesthetic experience, by valuing picture books with time to explore and wonder (Pantaleo, 2015).

Having given time to read and enjoy a wordless text, children's knowledge about one or two specific visual features can be explored. The book *Fossil* by Bill Thomson (2013) is a wordless story, rendered in acrylic paint and pencil, about a young boy who discovers fossils in rocks, only to be very surprised when they come to life. After taking time to read and explore the story, a guiding adult

Table 10.3 Story-level features of picture books

Story level	Various story genres include:
	• realism, example *How to Heal a Broken Wing* by Bob Graham; or preparing for a Korean family meal in *Bee-bim Bop!* by Linda Sue Park and Ho Baek Lee
	• fantasy (magic, animal characters), example *Lullabyhullaballoo!* by Mick Inkpen; *Farmer Duck* by Martin Waddell and Helen Oxenbury
	• folktales and fairytales, example classic fairytales retold by Paul Galdone; *A Dark Dark Tale* by Ruth Brown
	• history, myths and fables, example Dreamtime stories such as *Turtle Dreaming* by Thompson and Recht; *Malu Kangaroo* by Judith Morecroft and Bronwyn Bancroft; *Aesop's fables*; Bible stories like *Noah's Ark* or *The First Christmas*
Narrative form and structures	• Setting – time and place of the story, example *Big Rain Coming* by Katrina Germein and Bronwyn Bancroft is set in outback Australia while *The Two Bullies* by Junko Morimoto is set in Japan many centuries ago.
	• Characters – people, animals or things, often with one or two main characters, example *Charlie and Lola* from the Lauren Child series; Olivia, the celebrated pig from the books by Ian Falconer; or the modern-day fable *Magpie Learns a Lesson* by Sally Morgan and Ezekiel Kwaymullina, illustrated by Tania Erzinger.
	• Theme – the central meanings or message of the story, example *Dingo's Tree* by Gladys Milroy and Jill Milroy explores care of the environment; *Amy and Louis* by Libby Gleeson and Freya Blackwood deals with friendship and loneliness.
	• Style – authors may develop particular styles using figurative language, colloquial language, humour and irony, while illustrators may also develop particular visual styles.
	• Plot structure – the narrative as a sequence of events, often with one or more problems which are resolved, example fairytales such as *Little Red Riding Hood* have the classic orientation, problem and resolution narrative structure. *Something from Nothing* by Phoebe Gilman has two different stories running parallel in visual and written form.
Voice/s	• Narrators – these are generally written in first or third person, and tell the story from their perspective, for example Pamela Allen's *Mr McGee* series has a third-person narrator while Anthony Browne's *Voices in the Park* has the one story told by four different voices and character viewpoints. Some narrators actually address the reader, such as *Don't Let the Pigeon Drive the Bus* by Mo Willems.
	• Focalising character – the story is told through the eyes and experiences of a particular character, example *Beware of the Storybook Wolves* by Lauren Child has a little boy called Herb as the focal character, while *Diary of a Wombat* by Jackie French is told through the voice and eyes of the wombat.

might focus on some specific visual feature, such as opening page 1 (Figure 10.3) which leads to the first complication in the narrative. Here the call-out boxes are used to focus the reader's attention on the actions and thoughts of the young boy. A combination of think alouds and questions will support young learners in understanding how visual images create the story we see. We might comment

Figure 10.3 Opening page of *Fossil* (Thomson, 2010)

on the call-out boxes – *Those small frames really make me look closely at what is happening.* We could predict what the boy is thinking and feeling and then note the unusual focus on the boy's foot – *I think that Bill Thomson wants us to notice that he might trip – what is it that happens next that is so important?* Other significant visual features throughout the book include use of close up shots as well as high and low angles.

There are a growing number of wordless texts that will appeal to all ages and interests, with a suggested list of titles in the reference list for this chapter.

Working with the visual and written modes

Rich teaching and learning experiences with literature, as outlined in Chapters 7 and 8, provide the setting for further exploration about how texts make meaning using words and pictures. As with wordless texts, time to talk, wonder and revisit stories together immerses children in literature, providing the foundation for more detailed learning about written and visual features.

Let us take an example to show how we can use a metalanguage to explore both words and pictures, using a picture book that is suitable for five to six year olds. The picture book *Pearl Barley and Charlie Parsley* is a delightful story about friendship between two very different children (Blabey, 2007). While the two friends do all the types of things that young children could choose to do, the qualities of each character are quite different, which promotes themes of friendship, self-esteem and kindness. Blabey's narration uses contrast and comparison to show each character's unique personality. His **mixed media** illustrations use a variety of colour and texture as well as playful layout and typography. The differences between Pearl and Charlie are highlighted on each page, both visually as well as in the

Mixed media Illustrations can be produced using paint, pencil, charcoal, watercolour or even collaged elements such as tissue, cardboard and other objects.

writing. In terms of written language, there is a repeated sentence structure that compares the personalities of each character:

> When Pearl Barley forgets her mittens on cold winter days
> Charlie Parsley holds her hand and makes them warm as toast.
> When Charlie Parsley feels scared of things
> Pearl Barley makes him feel brave.

Sensing verbs like 'feel' and 'forgets' describe feelings and thoughts, while descriptions like 'warm as toast' introduce children to metaphor. Simple noun groups such as 'cold winter days' serve to build an image of where the actions take place. The use of the conjunction 'when' signals a comparison to readers, prompting them to look to the second part of the sentence to find out how the other friend's qualities can help. But as we can see, only some of the information in this story of friendship and trust are revealed in the written text (see Figure 10.4).

(a)   (b)

Figure 10.4 Pages from *Pearl Barley and Charlie Parsley* (Blabey, 2007)

The pictures not only show Charlie feeling scared, with his sad mouth and pointed eyebrows, but we see a long, dark shadow in the background (which of course we know is Pearl). But it is not just Charlie's expression or the shadow that create a sense of anxiety. The close shot of Charlie in the foreground allows us to see his worry and feel empathy for him, compared to the mysterious stranger who is in long shot. The dark colours further emphasise fear, with a large block of black framing the page and almost overwhelming Charlie. As viewers we can follow Charlie's gaze upwards, which creates a strong vector, leading our eyes towards the dark stranger. Even the typography has jagged, uneven lines, further making the scene seem scary and unpredictable. Of course, the ellipsis in the written text leads us to the comparison page, where a brave Pearl, complete with paper pirate cap, sword and banana defends the smiling Charlie. We can see her solid stance, outstretched arms with Charlie happily riding on her back. Pearl's smile is exaggerated and the colours are bright and positive. They are both quite large figures, placed in the centre of the page, making them appear strong as Pearl cheekily gazes directly at us. She is definitely hero material!

As this example shows, we can move into more specific details about how words and images work together, using appropriate terms to help young readers understand what they are reading and viewing. The following section outlines key concepts and terms with a focus on the visual codes and elements in picture books.

Using a visual metalanguage when reading picture books

The specific **visual codes** used to describe the pages from *Pearl Barley and Charlie Parsley* draw on multimodal theory, as developed by Kress and van Leeuwen (2006). Other researchers in education have extended this work into classroom contexts, showing how teachers might choose key concepts and terms to integrate into literacy learning (Callow, 2013, 2015); Pantaleo, 2015; Unsworth & Macken-Horarik, 2015).

> **Visual codes (or grammar)** Specific features of the visual mode that describe how meaning is made including concepts such as gaze, high and low angles, close and long shots, salience and placement.

Teaching about the visual features of texts is part of teaching reading and literacy. The process of teaching reading, outlined in Chapters 7 and 8, emphasised the teacher's role in providing shared experiences of reading books with all children in the early years, moving to the more explicit practices of modelled, guided and independent reading in formal schooling. Drawing on the sociocultural model of reading from Chapter 8 (see Figure 8.1), we can assist young readers in developing various reader roles with both words and pictures. This includes explicit instruction as well as opportunities to predict, discuss, and create visual and multimodal texts in the classroom. Tables 10.4 and 10.5 summarise a number of features that can guide the planning of lessons and activities that teach about how image and text work together in a story.

Moving down from the story level features to the details of how visual texts make meaning further supports the development of the different reader roles (Freebody, 2007) discussed in Chapter 8. While the text user role links to the genre of narratives, the text participant role explores how meaning is made using words and pictures. A visual metalanguage is much like a *visual grammar* that helps children to develop code-breaking skills using the visual mode.

Table 10.5 lists a number of visual language terms and concepts including some examples of strategies and books to illustrate their use (Callow, 2013). As emphasised throughout this chapter, it is important to select a quality picture book first, and then choose the visual and written aspects that make it powerful, rather than teach a particular visual code by itself.

Table 10.4 Artistic and design features in *Pearl Barley and Charlie Parsley*

Artistic and design features	Examples from *Pearl Barley and Charlie Parsley*
• **Media** – illustrators may use drawings, paints, inks, pastels, washes, photographs or digital media	• Blabey uses acrylics and mixed media, where you can see the texture of the work if you look closely. When reading other books, discuss with children what type of paint or media that they think has been used. Experimenting with such media in visual arts further builds their knowledge.
• **Line** – different types of lines convey different meanings; vertical lines suggest height; diagonal or jagged lines create tension; curved lines suggest something more playful	• The strong vertical line of the shadow gives emphasis to the scary page, while on other pages curving lines suggest playfulness between Pearl and Charlie. Ask children to trace the lines on pages and discuss what is happening in the story. Do the lines play a part in suggesting movement or feelings?
• **Colour** – create a mood or reaction to a person, place or object, as well as cultural symbolic meanings such as red for danger; blue for sadness	• While simple, grey backgrounds set a sadder meaning on some pages with Charlie and Pearl, bright colour is used to highlight extravagant qualities, particularly Pearl's passion and energy. Comparing pages across a book allows the possible meanings of the colours used to be discussed.
• **Typography** – the choice of fonts can range from traditional to highly experimental in size, shape, colour and style	• While a simple font is used here, the shape of some lines of text are jagged or curved, again playing on how different each character is. Play with font choice on a projected screen or compare books that use different sized and coloured font, and then discuss how different choices change the feel of the story.

Table 10.5 Strategies to draw attention to visual language terms and concepts

Some visual language features (Callow, 2013)	Strategies to draw attention to these features in a picture book
What's happening? **Lines and vectors** – show action, expression, gestures, speech and thought	A vector is a line that suggests movement or action (Kress & Van Leeuwen, 2006). Discuss what is happening in a scene; trace the lines/vectors that show a character's actions and gaze. Compare the picture to the written text; are they similar or different? What is a character thinking or feeling? Mime a different expression to suggest a new or unexpected emotion. Eyebrows and mouths play an important role in showing a character's mood.

Some visual language features (Callow, 2013)	Strategies to draw attention to these features in a picture book
How do we interact and relate to the images? **Point of view** – the view of the front or back of character, over their shoulder or bird's eye view	Children can recreate a point of view from a page in the book and take a photo to discuss with the class, for example, the position of the boy from Thomson's *Fossil* or the high angle looking down on the two children in Gleeson's *Amy and Louis*. Think about how we feel as a viewer when we are placed in that viewing position. Set up a frozen tableau to represent characters interacting, and 'look' from different perspectives, such as over a character's shoulder, from a low angle or a worm's eye view.
Gaze to the viewer – direct gaze demands the viewer's attention	When a character looks directly at the viewer, they can really take our attention and draw our gaze. How does this make us feel? Find some examples when revisiting a story. Redraw a character, making the eyes look directly at or away from the viewer.
Shot distance – close, mid- or long shot suggests different levels of intimacy with the viewer	We feel differently depending on how close or far we may be positioned to a character. Anthony Browne's *Willy the Champ* and *Changes* both have effective use of close-up shots. Indigenous illustrator Dub Leffler's *Once There Was a Boy* uses a range of shot distances as well as points of view. Discuss why certain choices might have been used at those points in the story.
Angles – high-, low- or eye-level create various power relations with the viewer	Stand on a chair and look down on the class. Who looks or feels more powerful? Those who are up high or down low? Angles can suggest power. Gleeson and Blackwood's *Clancy and Millie and the Very Fine House* uses high and low angles, making a house appear very overwhelming to a small boy.
Salience – a key element that attracts a viewer's attention, such as colour, size, foregrounding or backgrounding	Looking at the example of the *Pearl Barley and Charlie Parsley* page, what takes your eye on each single page? The long shadow? Pearl's smile? With your class, glance away then look back at a page together. What elements are you immediately attracted to? Could the illustrator be using colour, size or placement to attract your attention? Why is it important in this part of the story?
Organisation – placement at the top or the bottom, at the left or the right or in the centre can emphasise an element	Whether there are two or twenty objects on a page, the illustrator decides where to place them. Objects or characters at the top of the page might suggest they are more important. Those in the centre may take our attention first. Oliver Jeffer's *The Incredible Book Eating Boy* places objects and characters of different sizes in a variety of positions around the page. Innovate on pages in drawing and art lessons to explore how the position can guide the viewer's gaze and focus.

REFLECTION

Choose a picture book that you wish to share with young children. Read it and then note down some of the visual features outlined in the previous section that stand out to you. Not all features should be explored; only the ones that play an important role in the story. Because we understand that it is the combination of words and images that make meaning, it is helpful to keep the following questions in mind as you plan comments, questions and activities for exploring your chosen text:

- How do the visual and written codes work together? Do the words say something different to the images? How do they complement each other?
- Are there examples where the images give extra or even contradictory meanings to the story?
- How do the words and images form our emotional response to the characters?

Do you react differently to the visuals than to the written text? What aspects are most powerful?

Creating visual and multimodal texts

Visual literacy involves talking about images and creating pictures. While young children begin the journey toward writing by drawing pictures, later on drawings are often treated as an added extra to accompany or decorate writing. However, as we have seen above, they in fact have their own meaning-making resources and grammar. Drawing and painting should be integrated as ways of making meaning when engaging and responding to stories. Children may create simple responses to a story, where they use bright colours and everyday objects (flowers, sunshine) to show happiness or, given time and guidance, they can develop more sophisticated images, such as kindergarten students who began to use some of Anthony Browne's designs in their response to his book Zoo (Styles & Arizpe, 2001). The subsequent talk about pictures also provides teachers with a way of assessing their students' literacy development.

Visual responses to picture books can include drawing and painting, as well as digital responses using photos, drawing and video creation (Bearne, 2009). A variety of digital applications for creating multimodal texts are discussed in Chapter 11. Other creative responses include collage, murals, models and puppet making (Gibson, 2013). While personal choice in pictures is important, teachers can also have children create specific character actions or emotions, playing with the different visual elements and designs.

Working with pictures and text provides opportunities for children to develop a range of interpretive skills and understandings. Engaging, rich texts provide the context for discussions that build on children's existing repertoires of knowledge when reading image and text. At the same time, teachers should scaffold concepts and metalanguage that further extend children's expertise in being able to read and enjoy multimodal texts.

Drawing it all together

By examining the picture book, we have seen the importance of its history and the visual design features which make contemporary picture books such a valuable part of children's literacy learning. Selecting a variety of classic and contemporary texts introduces children to the richness of English literature, and the various styles and techniques that authors and illustrators employ. By developing a metalanguage, teachers can draw children's attention to how words and pictures make meaning by modelling the reading process and using a range of activities as part of teaching literacy in early childhood and school settings.

Questions for further discussion

- Can you name a range of children's book authors and illustrators? Do you think you need to extend your own reading here?
- What activities in the visual arts might complement teaching children about how words and pictures work together?
- Compare a classic picture book with a more recent one. What are the similarities and differences both in the use of words as well as pictures?

Further reading

Roche, M. (2015). *Developing Children's Critical Thinking through Picturebooks: A Guide for Primary and Early Years Students and Teachers.* London: Routledge.

Schickedanz, J. A. & Collins, M. F. (2012). For Young Children, Pictures in Storybooks Are Rarely Worth a Thousand Words. *The Reading Teacher,* 65(8), pp. 539–49, DOI: 10.1002/TRTR.01080.

Smith, V. (2009). Making and breaking frames – Crossing the borders of expectation in picturebooks. In J. Evans (ed.), *Talking Beyond the Page: Reading and Responding to Picturebooks.* London: New York: Routledge, pp. 81–96.

Picture books

Ahlberg, J. & Ahlberg, A. (1986). *The Jolly Postman or Other People's Letters.* London: Heinemann.

Allen, P. (1992). *Mr McGee Goes to Sea*. Ringwood, Vic.: Viking.

Baillie, A. & Tanner, J. (1991). *Drac and the Gremlin*. Ringwood, Vic.: Puffin.

Banyai, I. (1998). *Zoom*. New York: Puffin Books.

Becker, A. (2014). *Journey*. London: Walker Books.

Blabey, A. (2007). *Pearl Barley and Charlie Parsley*. Melbourne: Penguin.

Brown, R. (1983). *A Dark Dark Tale*. London: Scholastic.

Browne, A. (1985). *Willy the Champ*. London: Julia MacRae Books.

—— (1994). *Zoo*. London: Red Fox.

—— (1998). *Willy the Dreamer* (US edn). Cambridge, MA: Candlewick Press.

—— (1999). *Voices in the Park*. London: Picture Corgi.

Briggs, R. (2004). *Father Christmas*. London: Puffin Books.

Brunhoff, J. D. & Haas, M. (2002). *The Story of Babar, the Little Elephant*. Sydney: Random House.

Burningham, J. (2000). *Come Away From the Water, Shirley*. London: Red Fox.

—— (2010). *Mr Gumpy's Outing*. London: Red Fox.

Carle, E. (2014). *The Very Hungry Caterpillar*. London: Puffin.

Child, L. (2001a). *Beware of the Storybook Wolves*. London: Hodder Children's.

—— (2001b). *I Am Not Sleepy and I Will Not Go to Bed: Featuring Charlie and Lola*. London: Orchard.

—— (2002). *Who's Afraid of the Big Bad Book*. London: Hodder Children's.

Cousins, L. (2006). *Noah's Ark*. London: Walker.

Crews, D. (2012). *Freight Train*. London: Phoenix Yard.

Davidson, S., Ferri, G. & Aesop. (2015). *Illustrated Stories from Aesop*. London: Usborne.

Duvoisin, R. (2015). *Petunia*. New York: Dragonfly Books.

Falconer, I. (2000). *Olivia*. London: Simon & Schuster.

Flack, M. & Wiese, K. (2000). *The Story about Ping*. New York: Grosset & Dunlap.

French, J. & Rycroft, N. (2014). *Good Dog Hank*. Sydney: HarperCollins.

French, J. & Whatley, B. (2007). *Diary of a Wombat*. Pymble, NSW: Angus & Robertson.

Gag, W. (2006). *Millions of Cats*. New York: Puffin.

Germein, K. & Bancroft, B. (2002). *Big Rain Coming*. Melbourne: Puffin Books.

Gilman, P. (2008). *Something From Nothing: Adapted from a Jewish Folktale*. Sydney: Scholastic.

Gleeson, L. & Blackwood, F. (2006). *Amy and Louis*. Sydney: Scholastic.

—— (2009). *Clancy and Millie and the Very Fine House*. Sydney: Little Hare Books.

Graham, B. (2008). *How to Heal a Broken Wing*. London: Walker Books.

Gravett, E. (2005). *Wolves*. London: Macmillan Children's Books.

Hutchins, P. (2010). *Rosie's Walk*. London: Red Fox.

Inkpen, M. (1995). *Lullabyhullaballoo!* London: Hodder Children's Books.

Jeffers, O. (2006). *The Incredible Book Eating Boy*. London: Harper Collins Children's Books.

Keats, E. J. (2011). *The Snowy Day*. New York: Viking.

Leffler, D. (2011). *Once There Was A Boy*. Broome, WA: Magabala Books.

Lehman, B. (2004). *The Red Book*. Boston, MA: Houghton Mifflin Co.

Lionni, L. (2009). *Little Blue and Little Yellow: A Story for Pippo and Ann and Other Children*. New York: Alfred A. Knopf.

McKinlay, M. & Rudge, L. (2011). *No Bears*. London: Walker Books.

Milroy, G. & Milroy, J. (2011). *Dingo's tree*. Broome, WA: Magabala Books.

Morecroft, J. & Bancroft, B. (2008). *Malu Kangaroo: How The First Children Learnt To Surf*. Sydney: Little Hare Books.

Morgan, S., Erzinger, T. & Kwaymullina, E. (2015). *Magpie Learns a Lesson*. Gosford: Scholastic Australia.

Morimoto, J. (1998). *The Two Bullies*. Sydney: Random House Australia.

Park, L. S. & Lee, H. B. (2008). *Bee-Bim Bop!* Boston, MA: Houghton Mifflin Harcourt.

Rees, L. & Hutchings, T. (1982). *Digit Dick on the Great Barrier Reef*. Sydney: Lansdowne Press.

Sendak, M. (2015). *Where The Wild Things Are*. London: Random House Children's Books.

Seuss, D. (2004). *Horton Hatches the Egg*. London: HarperCollins.

Smith, L. (2010). *It's a Book*. Sydney: Walker Book.

Stein, D. E. (2010). *Interrupting Chicken*. Somerville MA: Candlewick Press.

Thompson, L. & Recht, E. (2008). *Sharing Our Stories: Turtle Dreaming*. Melbourne: Pearson Rigby.

Waddell, M. & Oxenbury, H. (1996). *Farmer Duck*. London: Walker Books.

Wagner, J. & Brooks, R. (2005). *The Bunyip of Berkeley's Creek*. Melbourne: Penguin.

Wall, D. (2009). *The Complete Adventures of Blinky Bill*: Sydney: HarperCollins.

Watt, M. (2008). *Chester*. London: HarperCollins.

Watts, F. & Legge, D. (2007). *Parsley Rabbit's Book about Books*. Sydney: ABC Books.

Wiesner, D. (2001). *The Three Pigs*. New York: Clarion Books.

—— (2006). *Flotsam*. New York: Clarion Books.

Willems, M. (2003). *Don't Let the Pigeon Drive The Bus!* New York: Hyperion Books for Children.

Williams, M. (1994). *Greek Myths for Young Children*. London: Walker.

—— (2010). *Noah's Ark and Other Bible Stories*. London: Walker.

Wordless books

Baker, J. (2010). *Mirror*. London: Walker.

Lee, S. (2008). *Wave*. San Francisco, CA: Chronicle Books.

Pinkney, J. & Aesop. (2009). *The Lion and the Mouse*. New York: Little, Brown and Co. Books for Young Readers.

Raschka, C. (2011). *A Ball for Daisy*. New York: Schwartz & Wade Books.

Wiesner, D. (1991). *Tuesday*. New York: Clarion Books.

—— (2006). *Flotsam*. New York: Clarion Books.

References

Andersen, H. C. & Atwell, M. L. (1914). *Hans Christian Andersen's Fairy Tales*. London: Raphael Tuck and Sons.

Anstey, M. & Bull, G. (2000). *Reading the Visual: Written and Illustrated Children's Literature*. Sydney: Harcourt.

Arizpe, E. (2013). Meaning-making from wordless (or nearly wordless) picturebooks: What educational research expects and what readers have to say. *Cambridge Journal of Education,* 43(2), pp. 163–76. Retrieved at: http://eprints.gla.ac.uk/76005/.

Atwell, M. L. (1910). *Mother Goose*. London: Raphael Tuck and Sons.

Australian Curriculum Assessment and Reporting Authority (ACARA). (2015). *The Australian Curriculum: English* (Version 8.0). Retrieved at: www .australiancurriculum.edu.au.

Bearne, E. (2009). Exploring visual and digital texts creatively. In T. Cremin with H. Dombey, M. Lewis & E. Bearne (eds), *Teaching English Creatively*. Abingdon, Oxon: Routledge, pp. 142–54.

Blabey, A. (2007). *Pearl Barley and Charlie Parsley*. Melbourne: Penguin.

Callow, J. (2013). *The Shape of Text to Come: How Image And Text Work*. Sydney: Primary English Teaching Association Australia (PETAA).

—— (2015). Using Picture Books to assess multimodal knowledge and visual grammar. Paper presented at the 19th European Conference on Reading, Klagenfurt, Austria.

Cormenius, J. A. (1887). *Orbis Pictus*. [The Visible World in Pictures]. Originally published in 1658. Syracuse, New York: C.W. Bardeen.

Eisner, E. W. (2002). *The Arts and the Creation of Mind*. New Haven: Yale University Press.

Freebody, P. (2007). *Literacy Education in School: Research Perspectives from the Past, for the Future*. Melbourne: ACER.

Gibson, R. (2013). Playing with paint, clay and other media. In R. Ewing (ed.), *Creative Arts in the Lives of Young Children: Play, Imagination and Learning* Melbourne ACER, pp. 96–113.

Gravett, E. (2007). *Monkey and Me*. London: Macmillan Children's Books.

Harding, J. & Pinsent, P. (2008). *What Do You See?: International Perspectives on Children's Book Illustration*. Newcastle: Cambridge Scholars.

Jewitt, C. (2008). Multimodality and Literacy in School Classrooms. *Review of Research in Education*, 32(1), pp. 241–67, DOI:10.3102/0091732x07310586.

Kiefer, B. (2011). What is a Picturebook? Across The Borders of History. *New Review of Children's Literature and Librarianship*, 17(2), pp. 86–102, DOI:10.1080/13614541.2011.624898.

Kress, G. (2010). *Multimodality: A Social Semiotic Approach to Contemporary Communication*. London: Routledge.

Kress, G. & Van Leeuwen, T. (2006). *Reading Images: The Grammar of Visual Design* (2nd edn). London; New York: Routledge.

Lennox, C. (2011). The incredible book eating boy art activity for kids. Retrieved at: http://learningparade.typepad.co.uk/learning_parade/2011/03/the-incredible-book-eating-children.html, viewed 1 November 2015.

Mallett, M. (2010). *Choosing and Using Fiction and Non-Fiction 3–11: A Comprehensive Guide for Teachers and Student Teachers*. London; New York: Routledge.

McDonald, L. E. (2013). *A Literature Companion for Teachers*. Sydney: Primary English Teaching Association Australia (PETAA).

Nicholson, W. (1926). *Clever Bill*. London: Heinemann.

Pantaleo, S. (2014). Exploring the artwork in picturebooks with middle years students. *Journal of Children's Literature*, 40(1), pp. 15–26.

—— (2015). Primary students' understanding and appreciation of the artwork in picturebooks. *Journal of Early Childhood Literacy*, DOI:10.1177/1468798415569816.

Potter, B. (1902). *The Tale of Peter Rabbit*: London: Frederick Warne & Co.

Salisbury, M. (2004). *Illustrating Children's Books: Creating Pictures for Publication*. Sydney: Allen & Unwin.

Saxby, H. M. (1997). *Books in The Life of A Child: Bridges To Literature And Learning*. Melbourne: Macmillan.

Saxby, H. M. & Winch, G. (1991). *Give Them Wings: The Experience of Children's Literature* (2nd edn). Melbourne: Macmillan.

Scieszka, J. & Smith, L. (1993). *The Stinky Cheese Man and Other Fairly Stupid Tales*. London: Puffin Books.

Styles, M. & Arizpe, E. (2001). A gorilla with 'Grandpa's eyes': How children interpret visual texts – a case study of Anthony Browne's *Zoo*. *Children's Literature in Education,* 32(4), pp. 261.

Thomson, B. (2013). *Fossil*. Las Vegas, NV: Two Lions Amazon Publishing.

Unsworth, L. & Macken-Horarik, M. (2015). Interpretive responses to images in picture books by primary and secondary school students: Exploring curriculum expectations of a 'visual grammatics'. *English in Education,* 49(1), pp. 56–79, DOI:10.1111/eie.12047.

Watts, F. & Legge, D. (2007). *Parsley Rabbit's Book about Books*. Sydney: ABC Books.

CHAPTER 11

Digital literacies in the lives of young children

This chapter looks more closely at the types of digital resources that are integral to children's lives and their literacy landscape. Rather than seeing digital texts as additional to traditional literacy resources, they are in fact core texts, along with books and other media. Digital texts and experiences are intertwined with young children's lives, from popular culture to multimedia production.

Anticipated outcomes for the chapter

After working through this chapter, you should be able to:

- appreciate the role of digital texts in children's literacy lives
- understand key principles for integrating digital resources into literacy learning
- explore practical activities for teaching with digital resources.

SCENARIO: INTERACTIVE APP

Gathered around the iPad, a group of five-year-old children are exploring the interactive app *The Fantastic Flying Books of Morris Lessmore*, a story about the power of reading where Morris takes up residence in a library of living books. While a finger swipe across the screen will turn the screen pages of this book, it does not take long for the children to work out that exploring the content by touching, tapping and swiping the screen with their fingers yields other surprises. Wind storms are summoned, skies turn blue, music starts playing and books talk as the story unfolds. On some screens more traditional print literacy is explored – a bowl of milk allows letter-shaped cereal pieces to be dragged out to spell a word.

'I'm doing the alphabet,' explains Shafeef, while placing each letter in order.

'I'm going to write my name,' says May, while dragging out the letters, and Shafeef helpfully reminds her about which letters she needs. Some pages engage the children more closely than others, but the pull of the story is strong: 'Let's keep reading'. The story concludes with a very old Morris leaving his beloved books.

'Do books ever die?' asks Shafeef.

'They're not alive, silly!' Adina asserts. The conversation continues as to how stories might live in you until you are very old. Shafeef explains how you can even get lost in the book 'because you can't stop reading as it's so good'.

Introduction

The role of digital technology in children's lives begins even before birth, with parents often sharing pictures of scans; while after the birth, photos are emailed, uploaded and shared on various social media platforms. Many studies point out that 'childhood is highly technologized' (Burnett & Merchant, 2013 p. 575) where screens become part of children's lives very early and technology is embedded into their family's lives and into toys, videos, movies and entertainment (Marsh et al., 2005; Arthur et al., 2014). The rapid changes in technology, particularly **screen-based technology** over the past 15 years, have seen more complex technology in the hands of younger children (Verenikina & Kervin, 2011). The rate of technology change is a reality to be accepted but with a critical and selective eye. Educators need to develop their own technology skills and reflect on how to best nurture the related digital literacy skills that their young learners may already bring to school. This is aside from their requirement to be taught more traditional aspects of literacy.

Screen-based technology Any technology where users view or interact using an electronic screen; most commonly this involves computers, tablets, smartphones and handheld games.

In the opening scenario, a range of literacy skills were being exercised as the children engaged with *The Fantastic Flying Books of Morris Lessmore* (Moonbot

Studios, 2012). Both reading and listening to a narrative was complemented with a range of haptic learning (through the use of touch) and animated media, as well as interactive activities that reviewed print and letter–sound knowledge (see Chapter 8). The beauty of this particular interactive story was the way that the interactivity supported the story and the broader themes, where the children wanted to find out what happened and then discuss aspects of what they had learned. Engaging with a multimodal text like this was enjoyable and it enabled the children to use technology in purposeful and engaging ways as part of literacy learning.

The importance of technology in education is reflected in curriculum documents in many countries. In Australia, the *Early Years Learning Framework* (EYLF, 2009) and the *Australian Curriculum: English* (Australian Curriculum Assessment and Reporting Authority, ACARA, 2015a) both contain explicit statements about the inclusion of technologies in curriculum delivery, as does the *Australian Curriculum: The Arts* (ACARA, 2015b). With a curriculum-driven imperative to use technology, educators may need to refresh their attitudes and concepts of literacy in light of these new basics.

Literacy is already digital

Rather than seeing digital literacies as additional to traditional practices, it is helpful to see **digital texts** as existing resources in children's literacy repertoires. Chapter 3 presents a variety of ways that children use technology, from television viewing, playing with popular culture texts, engaging with interactive applications (**apps**) and creating multimodal experiences with augmented reality and digital resources. Each of these experiences has embedded literacy practices and knowledge, which children engage with and learn through. As with print texts, children engaging with digital texts can also develop the four reading roles, including code breaker, text participant and text user roles (outlined in Chapter 8) (Freebody, 2007) The media marketing and online nature of many digital literacy experiences also reminds us of the importance of developing the text analyst role in this area, as we seek to help young learners develop critical thinking about their world (Vasquez, 2004; Jones-Diaz et al., 2007).

Digital texts A term which includes electronic forms of print but which extends to any form of text (written, spoken or multimodal) which can be digitally presented.

App (shortened form of application) A generic term for any software program, often installed on hand-held and tablet devices.

Many academic textbooks over the years have prompted readers to reflect on the types of technology that a child experiences in a day, and the implications for literacy learning. While this activity in the 1980s might have flagged television as a key technology, and computer games during the 1990s, a current reflection will probably contain a mixture of old and new technologies. Children may begin the day by listening to the radio while parents read the news on a screen, followed by breakfast television programs, perhaps some shared videos and games on tablets.

Then there could be the possible scramble to use Mum or Dad's smartphone on the way to preschool and school. During the day they may engage with interactive whiteboard activities, read onscreen texts, create short videos, take photos and arrange them onscreen and sometimes print hard copies. Various apps and programs may be used to strengthen individual skills across subject areas. The whole class might view an educational television show or watch a film in order to enjoy it, then explore the visual and audio choices that have been used. On the way home children may video chat or text with a parent or grandparent, negotiate some more screen time for games or complete some online research, in between playing outside, soccer practice and family meal time. While each family will be different, a balanced day will often have a variety of screen and technology use, which embody a variety of literacy skills such as reading, writing, speaking and listening, as well as viewing and interacting.

Children's technology use in the home is usually shared, learnt through mentoring and active participation, as well as being purposeful and playful (Marsh, 2004). Understanding the collaborative and shared learning that happens in the home highlights the reality that young children will bring *existing* literacy skills and experiences, both digital and print, to the early childhood or school setting. Congruency between home and school is a particularly important aspect when supporting early learning, especially for children from low socioeconomic backgrounds (Marsh, 2013; Munns, Sawyer & Cole, 2013). Unfortunately the research suggests teachers are often reticent in using technology at school and early learning settings, a pattern that has been consistent for many years (Burnett & Merchant, 2013). The challenge for educators is how to acknowledge and build on existing digital skills. Then they can explore the many benefits that the use of technology offers in developing all areas of learning, particularly with digital literacy skills.

Media A variety of communication means, from more traditional forms such as newspapers, magazines, radio and television, to the evolving digital and multimedia forms, such as social media, online communities, digital video and other interactive forms.

The questions around technology use, young children and play (see Chapter 3) are also important considerations in this context. Recent research from the American Academy of Pediatrics has noted that **media**, like any other environment, can have positive and negative effects. They indicate that parents co-viewing television, using technology together and having media-free zones such as meal times are important. They also suggest considering 'daily screen time limits, discouraging screen use in children under age two, and informing and educating families about media rating systems' (Shifrin et al., 2015, p. 1).

If we consider all types of digital resources as literacy texts and practices, we can think more broadly about how we teach literacy in our early childhood and school settings. While more traditional literacy practices are still a core part of learning (see Figure 11.1), digital resources can be used to both enhance more traditional literacies, as well as explore the many new literacy practices that technology opens for learners, young and old (see Figure 11.2).

The division into separate facets of reading, writing, speaking and viewing is obviously problematic, even with traditional literacy practices. Watching television involves listening and viewing. Engaging with digital books and games often

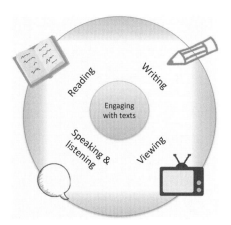

Figure 11.1 A traditional view of literacy practices

Figure 11.2 An expanded view of literacy practices that shows how digital resources complement and enhance the experience

combines reading, writing, speaking, listening and viewing, as well as the use of touch and movement.

Digital literacy practices should not just be considered as one large homogenous set that applies to all children and families. While much research has developed around understanding how **popular culture** and technology are part of all children's lives, there are still limited studies on more specific cultural groups and communities which require further research (Marsh, 2013, p. 219). Jackie Marsh's research shows that many bilingual children access a range of multilingual digital texts, and for many young children, their first encounters with English are through popular culture and the media.

> **Popular culture** A range of cultural practices, including gaming, television, music, movies, graphic novels, online resources and various media and performance texts.

Principles for planning digital literacy practices

Many early childhood settings and schools already integrate a number of digital literacy practices into daily activities. While teachers may share resources and reviews of helpful apps and websites, a number of useful principles and considerations emerge from research to help guide the choice of all types of digital learning activities (Burnett & Merchant, 2013; Flewitt, 2013; Larson & Marsh, 2013; Marsh, 2013; Dezuanni et al., 2015). These principles draw on technology and digital literacy studies that incorporate: desktop and laptop computer–based activities; iPad and tablet technologies; and gaming and popular culture resources, which may include television, video, and associated media and products. The principles include:

- play and creativity opportunities
- pedagogical choices
- relevant and engaging content and skills
- literacy enhanced by technology
- multimodal features
- access and technical considerations.

Play and creativity

A common theme throughout this book is the importance of play for young children. When considering digital literacy, play and playfulness can 'serve literacy by providing meaningful contexts that promote literacy activity, skills and strategies' (Flewitt, 2013, p. 305). Given the importance of extending our concept of what literacy entails, Kervin (2016) argues that playful interactions with carefully chosen digital apps and resources 'can help to enact expanded definitions of literacy as children use their developing repertoire of language resources for meaningful purposes' (p. 70).

Examples of using digital texts that encourage both play and creativity cover a range of literacy areas. Finding out from children and their families what popular culture texts are part of their lives might see the use of these audio or video clips in the classroom to stimulate play and discussion, as well as children creating their own photographs, videos and electronic books. This was exemplified in the scenario in Chapter 3 where young Anastasia drew on her love of the film *Frozen* to enhance her play and make-believe activities.

As part of free play, children can use digital cameras or tablets to record all sorts of images and video. They may be exploring the play area with its pets and toys, or use the technology to interview friends and then share the video with each other and their family. A number of tablet apps allow children to put their voices to puppets or objects they photograph (*Sock Puppets*, Smith Micro Software, 2015) and *Chatterpix*, Duck Duck Moose Inc, 2015, for example). These allow children to create puppet shows, talk to each other in character, take on roles and experiment with language and voice.

Playfulness and creativity can also be planned with more focused activities. iPad apps such as *Book Creator* (Red Jumper Limited, 2015) or *My Story* (Bright Bot, 2015) allow children to tell their own stories or innovate on known stories. By using a simple refrain from a story, such as 'I went walking, what did you see?' from Sue Machin and Julie Vivas *I Went Walking* (1989), young children can either take a photo of themselves or a friend, or use the picture choices in the app to create their own page, and add typed or handwritten text. *My Story* allows audio to be added and the final book can be saved as a video file or exported for printing.

Critical literacy Linked to the text analyst role (Chapter 8), critical literacy assists learners to question and discuss the ideas that a story, video or game might present, particularly in terms of attitudes to cultural representation, gender and belief.

Combining a thoughtful discussion of popular culture, media products and advertising through games and television also provides educators with **critical literacy** opportunities. There are many examples of how to assist young learners to

Figure 11.3 An image created with *My Story* app by Bright Bot

both enjoy and critique popular culture (Jones-Diaz et al., 2007; Vasquez & Felderman, 2012):

- Value children's home texts – view popular culture texts then discuss with children their ideas and preference for particular shows or characters.
- Analyse advertising choices – look at advertising for popular culture through the shows, toy merchandise tie-ins and in-app advertising – discuss how they persuade children. Talk about the activities, products and colours used to represent boys' and girls' interests.
- Observe the representation of diverse families and communities – compare characters from books, films and games where there is limited diversity compared to those with varied diversity. Ask 'Can you see your family here?' Discuss why seeing all types of people is important.
- Create digital innovations to stories, advertising and products – use technology to represent children's own families and friends using a variety of toys, colours and activities in their own versions of stories, advertising and video clips.

Pedagogical choices

Learning opportunities for digital literacy, based on constructivist approaches, supports many of the key learning principles for early childhood education. Planning activities that involve a clear learning purpose, collaborative use of digital resources, shared communication, discussion and active engagement are key to teaching with digital texts. Educators should also allow children to have agency (active control) and creative choices, depending on the task, so that exploration is supported, while necessary explicit teaching is also included to ensure success. These principles can be applied to the use of an interactive whiteboard (IWB) lesson as well as computer and iPad/tablet activities. The storytelling app *Puppet Pals* (Polished Play, 2013) allows children as young as four years old to animate onscreen puppet-like characters and record their voices, using various backdrops. The sound of much laughter always accompanies the use of this app. The screen puppets (which can be modified to show the children's faces on them) can grow, shrink or disappear from the screen. At the same time children can experiment using various voices to tell the stories that they are creating. The entire story can then be saved and shared as a movie file. While the affordances of the app allow development of verbal and storytelling skills as well as manipulation of multimodal elements, how the app is used in the classroom is a key consideration. Having read and discussed a variety of fairytales, a teacher might then work with the class or small groups to demonstrate the basic use of the software. The task to retell a known story with two or three characters means that the children will need to collaborate and discuss the story, choose the characters and then work out how they will rehearse then record their final movie. While the app lends itself to agency and creative choice, a teachers' pedagogical decisions need to allow children to 'take charge of content, design of the content and the way in which the content will be transmitted to their chosen audience' (Gattenhof & Dezuanni, 2015).

While some apps and software programs lend themselves to immediate interaction and collaboration, teachers need to consider how they use hardware like IWBs in ways that are collaborative, where control of the whiteboard is shared with students during the lesson. As with software like PowerPoint and Keynote, IWBs may have many 'bells and whistles' but they should be used with a clear learning purpose, where the children are doing the interacting. For example, a class might be reading the Mr McGee books by well-known author Pamela Allen. These books, which make use of rhyme and rhythm also have wonderful visual features. One technique that Allen uses is repeating the image of a character across a page to portray movement, as it creates a strong vector or action line across the page. Activities to teach about this visual feature might include those summarised in Table 11.1.

Providing relevant, engaging content in the classroom

All learning experiences should strive to have meaning and relevance for learners. In planning for the balanced use of screen time, Lisa Guernsey's 'three C's' of 'content, context and my child' reinforce the point that digital content should be relevant and of interest to young children (Guernsey, 2007).

The types of literacy activities that teachers plan should reflect the children's needs and interest, as well as the family and community. In response to a number of children talking about planes and their experiences at airports, one preschool integrated this topic of interest into a number of activities (Cotto, 2014). A pilot visited the classroom and the children turned their classroom into an airport, making tickets, signs and travel brochures. While they could not visit an airport, they used video technology to 'visit' and talk with an airport worker, seeing some of the activities live via Skype call (video phone call). Reading, writing, talking and listening are all embedded in activities like these, with technology playing an integrated and meaningful role. Similar activities can involve family and friends or experts visiting the class, using video technology, which also builds community connection and congruence between home and school.

Using technology across various learning areas and topics helps young children experience appropriate and relevant tools. A recent case study by Dooley and

Table 11.1 Using interactive whiteboards (IWBs) in teaching

Feature of text	Whiteboard tool	Literacy and pedagogical aspect
Show the sample page on the screen from the book. Discuss the actions in the image. The children think and discuss in pairs how they know the character is moving. Pairs then go to the front of the class and draw a line that traces the vector, and explain how they know this shows movement.	• Pen	• Learning focus: using visual metalanguage as part of retelling events • Collaborative discussion • Justification of reasoning
Discuss how the character is feeling as he or she flies or travels across the page. Children choose one of the repeated images and imagine what the character is thinking. They use the spotlighting tool to show their character and explain how the picture helped them decide what the character's feelings were. Scribe into a thought bubble the child's description or record audio where the child speaks the thoughts. Then attach this file to the image.	• Spotlight tool • Sound/audio tool • Thought bubble text box	• Learning focus: inferring character's feelings from images • Agency of child in highlighting image and creating/recording thoughts • Collaborative writing/ recording of thoughts
Apply other ways of using Pamela Allen's technique of repeating a character to show movement. Children sketch ideas on their own mini whiteboards, showing repetition of a figure. Invite some to come up and use the cloning tool to represent another line of movement for the onscreen character. Choose another child to explain where they see the vector onscreen and trace the line of movement themselves using the pen. Discuss how this new event might become part of the story.	• Cloning tool • Pen	• Learning focus: redesigning original page using visual resources and metalanguage • Agency of children – all sketch on whiteboards, individuals manipulate images and trace new vector • Creativity – redesign of character movement in the story

Dezuani (2015) detailed a preschool setting where iPads were used to find out scientific information, photograph and video hatching chickens and then create a poster about the events using the *Comic Life* app (Plasq, 2015). Supported by an adult helper, the children participated in all the various uses of technology, described by the researchers as a literacy event, where children's questions and interests were supported as they observed, discussed and captured their fascination with the growing chicks.

Figure 11.4 Interactive whiteboard (IWB) showing repeated character technique, drawn vectors, use of thought bubble and audio recording

REFLECTION

Many teachers feel that students know more about technology than they do. How can we differentiate between children's dexterity with technology and the way that a knowledgeable teacher might integrate children's technical agility to support higher order thinking and skills? In what ways could you use children's skills to encourage them as 'expert guides' as well as lead them to deeper engagement in their learning?

Literacy is enhanced by technology

It is very easy to be overwhelmed when browsing the extensive choice of programs and apps that are often categorised as 'educational' or as enhancing reading and writing for young children. Using the principles previously outlined, we need to ask ourselves if this use of technology enhances our literacy teaching in ways that are consistent with appropriate pedagogy and content.

Many educational apps bought by parents are likely to be drill and practice (Goodwin & Highfield, 2012; Highfield & Johnson, 2013), which Highfield and Goodwin argue lead to lower-level neural development and offer excessive reward-based learning. While short-term specific skills, such as letter–sound knowledge or handwriting can certainly be honed with an engaging interactive app, investing in digital resources that provide a variety of experiences and creative uses is a more appropriate approach to supporting literacy learning.

There are many interactive stories available, but as with print texts, some are well crafted and engaging while others lack style and depth. Book and app publisher Nosy Crow provides many high-quality ebooks and interactive stories, including classic fairytales such as *Snow White* (http://nosycrow.com/apps/snow-white) and *Little Red Riding Hood* (http://nosycrow.com/series/nosy-crow-fairy-tales). Author Chris Haughton's *Hat Monkey* app (Fox and Sheep GmbH, 2014) engages very young learners in helping monkey move around the house, sending him emoji text messages and talking to him on the phone. Three of Haughton's picture books are included as ebooks embedded into the app, featuring the delightful *Shh! We have a plan* (2014). The app is available in multiple languages including Japanese, Portuguese, Chinese and Spanish.

It is worth remembering that many well-known authors are releasing their picture books as Kindle or iBooks purchases. This means they can be used as big books projected onto a large screen, where modelled reading and discussion of pictures can be enjoyed by a large group or class. Current authors with electronic versions of their picture books include Emily Gravett, David Weisner, Anthony Browne, Aaron Blabey and Jackie French.

Multimodal features

The ease with which technology allows us to create and manipulate word, voice, sound and image means young children can become the photographer, the filmmaker, the digital artist and the radio host as they interact with their world. Chapter 10 explores the multimodal nature of picture books, providing a visual grammar that can also be adapted when making digital texts.

Apps such as iMovie (www.apple.com/au/ios/imovie) allow even very young children to create short stories and documentaries about their lives and experiences, experimenting with shot choices, movement and even special effects. Dezuanni and Gattenhoff (2015) argue that children should be using apps that include textual elements such as being able to write, draw, subtitle and record audio, experiences which 'allow for multi-sensory engagement' (p. 98). Having collected various photographs and videos, a simple plan or storyboard can be developed to organise a multimedia creation, where a mentor provides appropriate support and guidance for a recount, recipe, heartwarming story or swashbuckling adventure.

Multimodal elements also play a role in developing literacy skills across other learning areas. Apps like *Explain Everything* (2015) or *ShowMe* (2015) are similar to IWB software, where they allow students to draw, add images, create slide shows and record narration with their work. Art and drawing-based apps are plentiful, with a range of options and prices. While they cannot and should not replace paper-based media activities, they do offer a creative range of ways to make meaning visually as well as enabling children to experiment, reflect and then start a new piece if desired, without too much effort. Research into arts-based software suggests that having blank backgrounds, rather than templates is more helpful, as well as the facility for children to record their own thoughts about their work (Knight & Dooley, 2015). Saved commentaries also provide further insight into children's thinking and learning as part of assessment practices in the early years.

Access and technical considerations

While some schools or early learning centres may have limited technology at their disposal, resourceful teachers can often do many things with one or two shared tablets, digital cameras and a video projector. At the same time, teachers need to be aware of any significant issues around socioeconomic status for the community in which they work. While children from lower socioeconomic communities may have varied access to online resources and mobile devices, Burnett and Merchant (2013) note that 'young children in home and school contexts are differentiated by their access to "advantageous practice"'. The principles for technology use in this chapter reflect a number of features of engaging and inclusive pedagogies, particularly for students from low socioeconomic areas (Callow & Orlando, 2015).

All early childcare and school settings will have clear policies about the use of technology and appropriate online activities and behaviours. Always be sure to check the requirements for your setting, and ensure expectations for staff, parents/caregivers and children are clearly displayed. This aspect of technology can also be integrated when teaching about critical literacy and the text-analyst reader role (for more information, see Chapter 8).

Other technical considerations are ensuring students can easily access all types of technology in the classroom, ideally with routines where charging and updating of software is practical. The facility to share digital products and documents, particularly those created with iPad and tablet technologies, is important. Apps such as *My Story* allow children's books to be exported and printed, while other apps may have limited export facilities. Similarly, having ways to download and save movie and other digital files is essential for sharing and storage.

Drawing it all together

Digital texts are already part of children's worlds and literacy experiences, working in concert with more traditional practices. This chapter emphasises the importance of using technology that is informed by a number of key principles such as the significance of play and exploration, activities that foster creative and collaborative learning experiences and the use of technology which enhances engaging literacy learning. A selection of useful apps and software programs shows these principles in practice, and while future apps and technology will evolve, the same principles for using digital technology in the classroom should still prove a helpful guide for the near future.

Questions for further discussion

- Think of a favourite picture book – how could some of the digital resources in this chapter be used to enhance the enjoyment of your book?

- What criteria would you use to decide if an app or website would be useful to integrate into your learning context for literacy activities?
- How could you still use digital activities in your setting, even if you had only three or four tablets or hand-held devices and digital cameras?

Further reading

Arthur, L., Beecher, B. & Jones-Diaz, C. (2014). Utilising popular culture to extend children's literacy. *Diverse literacies in early childhood: A social justice approach*. Melbourne: ACER, pp. 65–85.

Kervin, L. (2015). PETAA Paper 201, Students writing with new technologies: The 2015 Donald Graves Address. Sydney: Primary English Teaching Association Australia (PETAA).

McLean, K. (2013). PETAA Paper 191, Towards a model for 21st century literacy learning in the early years classroom. Sydney: Primary English Teaching Association Australia (PETAA).

Apps and software

Book Creator: www.redjumper.net/bookcreator
Chatterpix: www.duckduckmoose.com
Comic Life: http://plasq.com
Explain Everything: http://explaineverything.com
Hat Monkey: www.foxandsheep.com
iMovie: www.apple.com/au/ios/imovie
Little Red Riding Hood: http://nosycrow.com/series/nosy-crow-fairy-tales/
My Story: http://mystoryapp.org
Puppet Pals: www.polishedplay.com
ShowMe: www.showme.com
Snow White: http://nosycrow.com/apps/snow-white
Sock Puppets: http://my.smithmicro.com
The Fantastic Flying Books of Morris Lessmore: http://morrislessmore.com

References

Arthur, L., Beecher, B., Death, E., Farmer, S. & Dockett, S. (2014). *Programming and Planning in Early Childhood Settings*: Melbourne: Cengage.

Australian Curriculum Assessment and Reporting Authority (ACARA) (2015a). *The Australian Curriculum: English* (Version 8.0). Retrieved at: www.australiancurriculum.edu.au.

—— (2015b). *Australian Curriculum: The Arts* (Foundation to Year 10, 7.5). Retrieved at: www.australiancurriculum.edu.au/download/f10.

Australian Department of Education, Employment and Workplace Relations for the Council of Australian Governments. (2009). *Belonging, Being & Becoming: The Early Years Learning Framework for Australia (EYLF)*. Canberra: Commonwealth of Australia. Retrieved at: www.mychild .gov.au.

Bright Bot. (2015). *My Story*. Retrieved at: http://mystoryapp.org.

Burnett, C. & Merchant, G. (2013). Learning, literacies and new technologies: The current context and future possibilities. In J. Larson & J. Marsh (eds), *The SAGE Handbook of Early Childhood Literacy* (2nd edn). London: SAGE, pp. 575–87.

Callow, J. & Orlando, J. (2015). Enabling exemplary teaching: A framework of student engagement for students from low socio-economic backgrounds with implications for technology and literacy practices. *Pedagogies: An International Journal*, 10(4), pp. 1–23, DOI:10.1080/ 1554480X.2015.1066678.

Cotto, L. M. (2014). Technology as a tool to strengthen the community. In C. Donohue (ed.), *Technology and Digital Media in the Early Years: Tools for Teaching and Learning*. London: Taylor & Francis, pp. 218–34.

Dezuanni, M., Dooley, K., Gattenhof, S. & Knight, L. (2015). *iPads in the Early Years: Developing Literacy and Creativity*. London: Routledge.

Dooley, K. & Dezuanni, M. (2015). Literacy and digital culture in the early years. In M. Dezuanni, K. Dooley, S. Gattenhof & L. Knight (eds), *IPads in the Early Years: Developing Literacy and Creativity*. London: Routledge, pp. 12–29.

Duck Duck Moose Inc. (2015). *Chatterpix*. Retrieved at: www.duckduckmoose .com.

Explain Everything. (2015). *Explain Everything*. Retrieved at: http:// explaineverything.com.

EYLF (2009)—see Australian Government Department of Education, Employment and Workplace Relations for the Council of Australian Governments (2009).

Flewitt, R. (2013). Multimodal perspectives on early childhood literacies. In J. Larson & J. Marsh (eds), *The SAGE Handbook of Early Childhood Literacy* (2nd edn). London: SAGE, pp. 295–311.

Fox and Sheep GmbH (2014). *Hat Monkey*. Retrieved at: www.foxandsheep .com.

Freebody, P. (2007). *Literacy Education In School: Research Perspectives from the Past, for the Future*. Melbourne: ACER.

Gattenhof, S. & Dezuanni, M. (2015). Drama, storymaking and iPads in the early years. In M. Dezuanni, K. Dooley, S. Gattenhof & L. Knight (eds), *iPads in the Early Years: Developing Literacy and Creativity*. London: Routledge, pp. 86–102.

Goodwin, K. & Highfield, K. (2012). iTouch and iLearn: An examination of 'educational' Apps. Paper presented at the Early Education and Technology for Children conference, Salt Lake City, Utah.

Guernsey, L. (2007). *Into the Minds of Babes: How Screen Time Affects Children from Birth to Age Five*: New York: Basic Books.

Haughton, C. (2014). *Shh! We Have a Plan*. London: Walker Books.

Highfield, K. & Johnson, K. (2013). Do Educational Apps Enhance Your Child's Learning? ABC Health and Wellbeing. Retrieved at: www.abc.net.au/health/talkinghealth/factbuster/stories/2013/10/24/3874488.htm, viewed 24 November 2015.

Jones-Diaz, C., Beecher, B. & Arthur, L. (2007). Children's worlds: globalisation and critical literacy. In L. Makin & C. Jones-Diaz (eds), *Literacies in Early Childhood: Changing Views, Challenging Practice*. Elsevier Australia, pp. 71–86.

Kervin, L. (February 2016). Powerful and playful literacy learning with digital technologies. *Australian Journal of Language and Literacy*, 39(1).

Knight, L. & Dooley, K. (2015). Visual arts learning with iPads. In M. Dezuanni, K. Dooley, S. Gattenhof & L. Knight (eds), *iPads in the Early Years: Developing Literacy and Creativity*. London: Routledge, pp. 103–22.

Larson, J. & Marsh, J. (2013). *The SAGE handbook of early childhood literacy* (2nd edn). London: Sage.

Machin, S. & Vivas, J. (1989). *I Went Walking*. Adelaide: Omnibus.

Marsh, J. (2004). The techno-literacy practices of young children. *Journal of Early Childhood Literacy*, 2(1), pp. 51–66, DOI:10.1177/1476718X0421003.

—— (2013). Early Childhood Literacy and Popular Culture. In J. Larson & J. Marsh (eds), *The SAGE Handbook of Early Childhood Literacy* (2nd edn). London: SAGE, pp. 207–23.

Marsh, J., Brooks, G., Hughes, J., Ritchie, L., Roberts, S. & Wright, K. (2005). Digital beginnings: Young people's use of popular culture, media and new technologies. Report. University of Sheffield: Sheffield.

Moonbot Studios (2012). *The Fantastic Flying Books of Morris Lessmore*. Retrieved at http://morrislessmore.com.

Munns, G., Sawyer, W. & Cole, B. (2013). *Exemplary Teachers of Students in Poverty*. Abingdon, Oxon; New York: Routledge.

Plasq (2015). *Comic Life*. Retrieved at: http://plasq.com.

Polished Play (2013). *Puppet Pals*. Retrieved at: www.polishedplay.com.

Red Jumper Limited (2015). *Book Creator*. Retrieved at: www.redjumper.net/bookcreator.

Shifrin, D., Brown, A., Hill, D., Jana, L. & Flinn, S. K. (2015). Growing up digital: Media Research Symposium. American Academy of Pediatrics. Retrieved at: www.aap.org/en-us/Documents/digital_media _symposium_proceedings.pdf, viewed 25 November 2015.

ShowMe (2015). *ShowMe*. Retrieved at www.showme.com.

Smith Micro Software, Inc. (2015). *Sock Puppets*. Retrieved at: http:// my.smithmicro.com.

Vasquez, V. M. (2004). *Negotiating Critical Literacies with Young Children*. Mahwah, NJ: Lawrence Erlbaum Associates.

Vasquez, V. M. & Felderman, C. B. (2012). *Technology and Critical Literacy in Early Childhood*: London: Routledge.

Verenikina, I. & Kervin, L. (2011). iPads, digital play and pre-schoolers. *He Kupu*, 2(5), pp. 4–19.

CHAPTER 12

Language and literacy assessment in early childhood contexts and classrooms

Assessment strategies need to be authentic (Newmann & Archbald, 1992) or educative (Groundwater-Smith, Ewing & Le Cornu, 2014). In a context where the concept of literacy is being narrowed and where achievement is increasingly measured by testing, this chapter focuses on the central role that formative assessment should play in early childhood contexts and classrooms. It draws on the *Early Years Learning Framework* (EYLF, 2009) to show how observing what a child already knows and understands will help plan for future learning in early childhood contexts and classrooms.

Anticipated outcomes for the chapter

After working through this chapter, you should be able to:

- define what is meant by authentic and educative literacy assessment, assessing for learning and assessment of learning in early childhood settings
- reflect on what it means to use inclusive and educative literacy assessment strategies and principles in your early childhood context/classroom
- acknowledge that no judgement that we make can be value-free or 'objective'
- understand how the *Early Years Learning Framework* outcomes can help us focus on appropriate assessment strategies for early childhood contexts
- Develop a portfolio which authentically records a child's literacy progress.

SCENARIO: 'READING TOGETHER IS JUST AN ORDEAL FOR BOTH OF US'

I don't know what to do. I have a great relationship with my five year old EXCEPT when I ask him to read to me. We used to have so much fun together sharing books but since he's been at school, it's all changed. When I remind him about his reading homework we can get quite heated with each other. He's supposed to read for 15 minutes every night but he finds all kinds of excuses to procrastinate. I'm worried because reading is just so important and I don't want him to fall behind his classmates. He's not at the same level as his best friend. And he refuses to spend time with me at home learning his sight words. I just don't understand why he is behaving like this. (Eleni, mother of Mohammed)

Like many parents, Eleni is keen for her son to learn to read as quickly and effortlessly as possible. It is not unusual for parents like Eleni to conflate learning to read with doing well at school. Her own anxiety about Mohammed learning to read may be inadvertently contributing to her son's attitude to reading. How could Eleni change these dynamics being played out in regards to home reading? What assumptions is she making about her son's literacy learning? Do you think there is a reasonable basis for her assumptions?

Introduction

From the beginning of this book we have suggested that learning is socially constructed and it follows that assessment tasks at any age should also reflect the constructivist nature of learning; that is, assessment is contextual and should be flexible. We have also discussed the variations in language development as well as the diverse cultures that children bring to learning to be literate. They will develop different orientations to and expectations about what literacy is in their first five years and will bring this to school.

Many western countries currently focus on achievement gauged through a child's performance against benchmarks or in tests (Ewing, 2014). Babies and toddlers are measured against benchmarks – the mother of one young baby we know was informed her newborn baby was not sleeping enough and another was told that her two-month-old baby was not 'talking' enough. While it is always important to identify children's learning needs and especially identify those children in need of extra support, there is a perception that continual screening procedures and testing of literacy achievement will contribute to the raising of educational standards and improved economic productivity. Sometimes this kind of auditing begins very early in the life of a child, but we know there are huge differences in the way young children develop so these results can often be questionable. It is important not to lose sight of the main purpose of educational evaluation, assessment and measurement.

We believe making judgements about children's literacy learning should primarily be about enabling educators and parents to make better informed decisions about how best to help children learn, improving the quality of early childhood centres, preschools and schools and ensuring effective educational resources are available for all. To make judgements about children's language development and literacy learning the teacher–child–parent relationship needs to be positive and trusting. An educator who always interacts meaningfully with the children in their care will be more likely to understand their individual learning needs. Therefore they will be able to tailor language-and-literacy teaching and learning experiences, and implement strategies to meet these needs. Constant comparisons of same-age children with other children in the early learning setting or school context are not always helpful. National and international comparisons are also costly and time consuming and should never be the main purpose of **educative assessment**.

Educative assessment Assessment strategies and experiences that are designed to improve children's learning rather than audit their learning.

This chapter begins by defining the key concepts of evaluation, assessment and measurement. It emphasises the importance of **assessment for learning** and uses the principles in the *Early Years Learning Framework* (2009) to discuss **authentic literacy assessment** practices, and those that are as educative and inclusive. Examples of authentic diagnostic and formative assessment tasks, and the use of learning stories and portfolios in early childhood settings are discussed. In these examples we have particularly focused on Timothy's learning journey over several years of preschool and during his first six months of school. We have used his portfolios to provide a more detailed understanding of how his learning journey in literacy has been documented and how helpful that this been for both his parents and his teachers.

Assessment for learning Assessment practices designed to assist students to be more effective learners and practices used to shape future learning activities for students.

Authentic literacy assessment Assessment that is designed to be meaningful, worthwhile and related as much as possible to real-world literacy activities.

Key concepts: Evaluation, assessment and measurement

The terms evaluation, assessment and measurement are often conflated and used synonymously in the educational assessment literature. For the purposes of this chapter we have provided some definitions.

Evaluation

Making value-based judgements are central to any kind of evaluation process and educators make many hundreds of these each day, often unconsciously. The concept of *evaluation* includes the word 'value' and can be understood as an overarching concept that refers to making a judgement or estimate about the worth of some information that has been collected to use in decision making.

All evaluative processes are subjective and are always affected by context. Educators must think carefully about unexamined assumptions they make and, whether these assumptions are informal or formal, they should be aware that their judgements are underpinned by their own values, beliefs and experience. Parents, students, community members and government audiences also have their own sets of values and beliefs (Groundwater-Smith & Nicoll, 1980) even if they are not made explicit. In the scenario described earlier Mohammed's mother believes it is important for him to learn to read as early as possible, that his reading to her of readers pitched at certain reading levels will help the process and that he is in danger of falling behind his peers because he is not reading at the same level. There is little research evidence that suggests that early reading leads to better academic outcomes. In fact many European countries do not begin the formal teaching of reading until a child is seven.

Assessment

In education, assessment is another inclusive term that refers to all informal and formal methods used by teachers, students and others to interpret information about student progress or teacher effectiveness. Yet Stefanakis (2002) traces the word 'assess' to the Latin word, 'assidere' meaning 'to sit beside' (p. 9) and therefore suggests the word means sitting beside the learner. Assessment conceived in this way will focus on what will enhance a child's learning. As Davies and Edwards (2001) assert:

> The principal purpose of education should be helping young people acquire the dispositions, skills, understandings and values that will enable them to live their lives intelligently, meaningfully, constructively and cooperatively in the midst of the complexity, uncertainty and instability they will increasingly encounter. (p. 105)

Assessment for learning: Formative assessment

Assessment *for* learning, formative assessment, denotes evidence or information that the teacher gathers during a child's learning journey to monitor their learning and adapt teaching and learning strategies to progressively meet individual needs. According to Anne Davies (2000) ongoing assessment for learning requires the deep involvement of both the teacher and the learner. Outcomes must be clear, monitoring must be systematic and evidence of learning must be provided and shared. Teachers are constantly gathering such information through observing, listening, questioning, and reflecting.

Diagnostic assessment Benchmarking prior to learning taking place: pre 'test'. 'What do they know before we start?'

During the beginning weeks of a year at a centre, preschool or school, and before beginning a particular unit or theme, they will gather information for **diagnostic assessment** to develop understandings about what the children know and understand about a particular area or concept. This may be through some kind of benchmarking activity. Collecting diagnostic information about what a toddler, preschooler or six year old understands represents one kind of formative assessment. Formative assessment is crucial in improving student learning (Black & Wiliam, 1998). Teachers need to know where to start the learning process (diagnostic, assessment *for* learning), how it is going (formative assessment, assessment *for* learning) as well as what learning has actually taken place (**assessment *of* learning**) at a particular point in time. Making judgements about learning achievements is a complex process in relation to planning and implementing play-based learning activities and curriculum experiences. Many of these judgements are informal or sometimes they are almost unconscious, such as observations of a baby learning to crawl or a toddler listening to a story being read aloud or a group of children at play or talking together.

> **Assessment of learning**
> Assessment practices that are designed to ascertain what students have learned after a series of learning experiences or a unit.

Authentic assessment

In 1994 the Australian Curriculum Studies Association (ACSA) suggested that authentic assessment should be recognised as a highly complex and often inexact process that, as far as possible, identifies children's achievements and goals for further learning. Authentic assessment should:

- facilitate learning
- use explicit criteria
- identify student strengths
- include all aspects of the curriculum
- encourage multiple intended learning outcomes
- use a range of strategies to make judgements
- enable self-assessment where possible
- provide opportunities for collaboration and negotiation of tasks
- provide more than one opportunity to meet requirements
- be sensitive to culture, gender, ethnic and linguistic background socioeconomic status, physical disability and geographical location
- be authentic in terms of the 'real' world.

(Adapted from the original Australian Curriculum Studies Authentic Assessment Principles (ACSA), 1994. These principles are embedded in ACSA's guiding principles for student assessment accessed at www.acsa.edu.au/pages/page22.asp).

Assessing language and literacy development

Care must be taken with how we collect information and how useful it is. As Joan Mason (1991) commented nearly 25 years ago: 'it seems that just about any cognitive or motor skill can be found to relate positively to future reading achievement' (p. 1). If too much attention is focused on ticking off checklists of discrete skills, assigning marks or comparing one child with another, those who are less successful may begin to receive messages (often unintentionally) that they lack ability or are not able to learn. Then they sometimes react negatively to similar learning situations that they think might lead to more failure. However, an early childhood centre or classroom where there is a culture of success and the belief that every child can and will achieve, provides very powerful alternative messages about the learning process.

Examples of formative literacy assessment strategies frequently used in early childhood settings and classrooms relate to a child's understanding of books, pictures and electronic devices, and how the child is to engage with them. This can be easily observed as a child is absorbed in a book in the reading corner, playing a game on a hand-held device or as the teacher or a parent is sharing a book with one child or a small group of children. Judith Shikedanz (1999) suggested that over time, young children develop early literacy behaviours including what she termed:

- 'bookhandling' behaviours: a baby or young toddler may initially chew the pages of a book (or attempt to eat a hand-held device) but progresses quickly to know how to turn the pages and interact with the book
- 'storyreading' behaviours: three and four years olds will single out familiar objects and favourite pages, point out and imitate actions, and ultimately join in the reading of familiar words and refrains. Some will learn sections of a story by heart.

More formal observations in the first year of school often adapt Marie Clay's (2000) 'concepts about print' to:

- document a child's ability to orient the book
- follow the direction of the print on the page
- use appropriate book vocabulary like 'word', 'letter'
- monitor a child's engagement with the content as discussed in Chapter 6.

Running record A diagnostic strategy used to determine a child's use of a range of cues when reading an unknown text.

Another example of diagnostic assessment often used in the early school years is a **running record** of a child's oral reading of an unknown text. Running records developed from the miscue-analysis work related to Ken and Yetta Goodman's psycholinguistic model of reading (1973). First published in 1973, miscue analysis was adapted by Marie Clay (1987) and Max Kemp for use with younger children but it is usually not used before a child is beginning to develop some confidence with their reading at about six or seven years old. A running record provides the teacher with information about the kinds of thinking strategies that a child who is emerging with their literacy skills uses when reading an unfamiliar text judged to be around the level they are currently reading. As the child reads this unfamiliar book, the teacher notes how the child uses their reading cues (discussed in Chapter 8). If it is evident that a child consistently prioritises one kind of cue (semantic, syntactic or graphophonic) during their reading of this new text and neglects the others, then the teacher can use this information in planning to model other cues for the child. Many teachers record the child reading so they can listen to it again and annotate it using accepted conventions for later reference. There are now a number of YouTube demonstrations and helpful apps (for example: https://recordofreading.wordpress.com).

Alongside a running record, a teacher might also ask the child to retell that part of the story. Alternatively they may use some of Aidan Chambers *Tell Me* questions as discussed in Chapter 7 to gauge how well a child has understood the text that they have been reading aloud.

Formative assessment enables teachers to provide children and their parents with specific feedback about an individual child's learning in, or understanding of, a particular area. It then should be followed by some goal setting with the child. The use of explicit feedback along the way is an important strategy when building children's resilience and supporting a culture of successful learning in early childhood settings.

Assessment of learning: Summative assessment

Summative assessment happens at the end of a particular learning journey when the questions are more likely to be: Have the children learnt what I planned for them? What do they understand in this area/about this topic? What else have they learnt? This kind of assessment is most often highlighted and care needs to be taken that such assessment tasks ensure they allow children to demonstrate what they do know rather than what they do not know. Evidence also needs to be gathered on more than one occasion and in a range of different ways to be more reflective of learning. Formative and summative assessments work best when they inform each other in meaningful ways.

Figure 12.1 demonstrates a summative assessment checklist for a preschool child. It summarises a range of areas from cognitive to fine and gross motor skills.

Measurement

Sometimes the information gathered formatively is measured. When a numerical score, grade or name is assigned against an established scale or ideal, measurement has occurred. As soon as a baby is born, they are assigned an Apgar score (out of ten) to measure general condition at birth based on their heart rate, breathing rate, muscle tone, reflex and colour. Children's level of reading or writing is often given a score (a reading age as opposed to a chronological age) and this is sometimes used to determine ability grouping in early childhood classrooms for particular tasks. Care needs to be taken about focusing too much on scores gathered early in a child's formal learning experience.

Tests

Standardised testing involves comparing student results with those of a group said to be similar (for example same age, nationality, gender or socioeconomic status). If test results are compared publicly or used for another purpose, they are referred to as high-stakes testing. Examples include the publication of results or linking teachers'

Standardised testing Tests administered and scored under standard conditions.

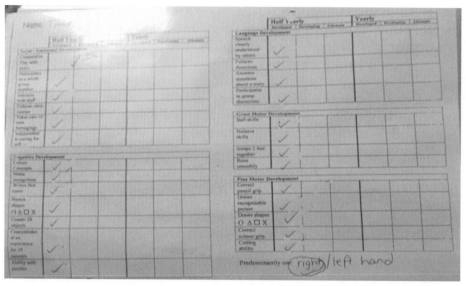

Figure 12.1 A checklist of cognitive and fine and gross motor skills for a preschooler

renumeration to improved test scores. For further reading about some of the dangers of high-stakes testing see, for example, Nichols and Berliner (2007).

The use of test results to rank children or schools is unproductive: test results can often be more of an indication of the economic realities in a particular community. Such tests are often poor predictors of what learners will achieve in other assessment contexts and can cause students a great deal of anxiety. Politicians and educational bureaucrats expect continual improvement in test results from one year to the next even though cohorts will differ dramatically. In Australia the Literacy Coalition has provided a critique of the National Assessment Program – Literacy and Numeracy (NAPLAN). Called *Say No to NAPLAN* it included twenty short papers that critique overuse of tests (Literacy Educators Coalition, n.d.).

In the next section we suggest that a child's progress in early childhood centres, preschools and classrooms can be linked productively with the *Early Years Learning Outcomes* (EYLF, 2009).

Linking language and literacy development with the Early Years Learning Outcomes (2009)

Many preschools now use the Early Years Learning Outcomes in their ongoing formative assessment of the children in their care. Table 12.1 shows examples from a child's preschool learning portfolio with the relevant outcomes referenced.

Table 12.1 Early Years Learning Outcomes

Outcome	Definition
1. Children have a strong sense of identity	They: • feel safe, secure and supported • develop their emerging autonomy, interdependence, resilience and sense of agency • develop knowledge and confident self identities • learn to interact in relation to others with care, empathy and respect.
2. Children are connected with and contribute to their world	They: • develop a sense of belonging to groups and communities and an understanding of the reciprocal rights and responsibilities necessary for active community participation • respond with diversity and respect • become aware of fairness • become socially responsible and show respect for the environment.
3. Children have a strong sense of wellbeing	They: • become strong in their social and emotional wellbeing • take responsibility for their own health and physical wellbeing.
4. Children are confident and involved learners	They: • develop dispositions for learning such as curiosity, cooperation, confidence, creativity, commitment, enthusiasm, persistence, imagination and reflexivity • develop a range of skills and processes such as problem solving, inquiry, experimentation, hypothesising, researching and investigating • transfer and adapt what they have learned from one context to another • resource their own learning through connecting with people, place, technologies, and natural and processed material.
5. Children are effective communicators	They: • interact verbally and non verbally with others for a range of purposes • engage with a range of texts and gain meaning from those texts • express ideas and make meaning using a range of media • begin to understand how symbols and pattern systems work • use information and communication technologies to access information, investigate ideas and represent their thinking.

Source: *Early Years Learning Framework*, (*EYLF*, 2009, p. 19)

Principles of assessment

The following assessment principles provide a starting point for authentic literacy assessment in early childhood contexts and help realise the *Early Years Learning Framework* Outcomes listed above.

Code	Outcome description	Developing	Celebrated
	Children have a strong sense of identity		
1	Separates easily from parents in familiar surroundings		✓
2	Shows interest in other children and being part of a group		✓
3	Engages in familiar pretend play		✓
4	Takes turns with minimal direction		✓
5	Follows classroom routine		✓
6	Responds to ideas and suggestions from others		✓
7	Takes pride in own achievements : resists help	✓	
8	Recognises their individual achievements and the achievements of others.		✓
9	Demonstrates an increasing capacity for self regulation		✓
Comments	Timothy separates from his parents well and quickly engages in an activity at preschool. He does often request educators help with a task even when it is not necessary but is learning to be more independent. He follows routines well.		
	Children are effective communicators		
1	Talks to other people about familiar objects and events		✓
2	Answers and asks simple questions		✓
3	Makes need known		✓
4	Follows two step direction		✓
5	Can retell a favourite story		✓
6	Speaks clearly enough to be understood by most people.		✓
7	Enjoys looking at and labels pictures in books		✓
8	Joins in singing familiar songs		✓
9	Uses a variety of things (pens, pencils, textas, paintbrushes) to draw, scribble or to write.		✓
Comments	Timothy has excellent verbal skills. He can comprehend and recount stories and explain drawings and constructions both to an individual and in front of a large group. He uses many forms of media to meaningfully express himself		
	Children are confident and involved learners		
1	Matches pictures which are the same		✓
2	Recognises that numbers can be used to count		✓
3	Counts 10 objects		✓

Figure 12.2 This excerpt from Timothy's portfolio in his first preschool year demonstrates how the *EYLF* outcomes have been used to record his progress

Establish a caring, supportive, risk-free learning community

A supportive and learning environment, where there is an 'ethic of care' (Noddings, 1992) in which children feel safe and encouraged to make mistakes and learn from them, invites risk taking. It enables teachers to set goals with children and provide them with feedback about how they are going. It also helps children think about the learning process.

Such a learning community aims for an appropriate balance of success and challenge in which children's linguistic and cultural diversity is taken into account at all times.

Focus on children's engagement in the task

Many educators consider that engaging children in meaningful tasks includes incorporating their interests and enabling them to see the relevance in what they are doing. Where possible, choice and negotiation over some of the decisions will foster this engagement.

Build positive relationships with students

The most effective teachers are warm, caring, supportive and enthusiastic. They strive to develop positive relationships with their students and respond to their affective and learning needs. They are sensitive and careful in their observations, and they listen carefully to ensure they document children's progress and achievements.

Use a range of different assessment strategies

There are many ways to collect evidence about a child's knowledge and understanding. In early childhood contexts it is important to frequently engage children in respectful and meaningful conversations (Chapters 2, 4, 7 and 9) about their imaginative play (Chapters 2 and 3), literacy understandings (Chapters 7 and 8) and learning processes. A range of potential assessment strategies can be used to assess children's literacy understandings and progress.

Potential assessment strategies

- Literacy games with a particular purpose
- Formal and informal observations and learning stories of play-based activities
- Retelling a story/storytelling
- Short oral presentations/performances
- Model building to a specific set of directions
- Mind, concept map or story maps
- Problem-solving tasks
- Interpretation of an image
- Photos/video recordings
- Collage, creative drawing, sculpting and writing in response to a story
- Freeze frames and sculptures
- Audio recording of open-ended discussions initiated by a teacher or children
- Cumulative portfolios
- Interviews or focus groups.

(Adapted from Ewing (2014))

Modify strategies to be culturally relevant and linguistically possible

The linguistic and cultural diversity of children must be acknowledged when designing assessment tasks. Culturally relevant pedagogy emphasises the importance of high academic expectations, continued development of children's competence in their first language and own culture, and the avoidance of the cultural norms and values in institutions that perpetuate inequities. Children's diverse ways of being, their strengths, interests, beliefs, feelings and values are embraced (Compton-Lilly, 2008).

Assessment tasks may sometimes be biased as some students may not have the background information to enable them to understand the task as well as others. For example, those students who have observed and cared for chickens as they hatch in their classroom are more likely to be able to discuss their needs and how to care for them than those who have not. Children living in regional or remote bush environments may not relate to stories about the beach until their understanding of such a different context is developed. Some young children in severely drought-afflicted areas may not understand the concept of 'rain' until it is carefully explained.

In addition, Tanner (2001) underlines that requiring a child to explain a decision or action can be linguistically demanding for those whose mother tongue is different to the dominant language in use.

Encourage children's identity development and autonomy

It is important to offer young children appropriate choices and decision-making opportunities whenever possible so they continue to develop their sense of voice and independence in their own learning. Identifying a learner's literacy strengths and providing specific feedback on areas needing further development helps build children's sense of who they are. Children can help collect, organise and communicate evidence of their learning and should be encouraged to share this with others.

Show consistent use of teacher judgement

Teachers and educators are the primary agents of assessment in early childhood settings and classrooms. When multiple assessment tasks are undertaken by a cohort of children across a range of different contexts, and for a number of different teachers, consistency of teachers' professional judgements may become an important issue. Teachers need systematic opportunities to discuss between each other work samples and expectations of the children in their care. When assessing children's work it is important to look carefully at what has been presented rather than just use a standard that was expected at a particular age or stage. It is also important that assessment tasks effectively engage the learner so that they will undertake the task with at least some degree of enthusiasm.

Avoid labelling or stereotyping

Many classrooms, preschools and centres will include children who are facing interpersonal, emotional, behavioural or academic challenges to their learning. Often these challenges are closely interrelated; sometimes they can be disruptive and lead to some negativity towards the child or their family. A teacher or caregiver who can provide caring, individualised attention, and culturally responsive teaching and learning experiences that are supported by other professionals can help avoid negative stereotyping and expectations. Van Manen (1995) used the concept of **pedagogical tact** to describe the teacher who seemed to intuitively sense the appropriate action based on their 'perceptive pedagogical understandings of children's individual nature and circumstances' (pp. 44–5). Worthy et al. (2012) describe a highly capable classroom literacy teacher who engages in **re-storying** to remove harmful stereotypes from several children who begin their year in the early childhood classroom with trouble-making labels.

Pedagogical tact A term used to describe a teacher's intuitive way of reading and responding to an individual child's needs.

Re-storying In this context, it refers to changing the response to a child's needs by reframing our language and approach while avoiding labels and stereotypes.

Involving children in self and peer assessment

Children should be encouraged to engage in peer assessment as well as assessing themselves. To assess self or peers effectively, children need to be part of a learning community in which trust has been developed so they are not afraid to take risks. They need to have a clear understanding of the purpose of a particular learning task. Often the only way to achieve this is through negotiating the purpose and teacher's expectations with the children. The teacher's meaning and expectations may not always be transparent so involving children in the development of explicit criteria and teacher expectations is also essential. Gathering a range of viewpoints from the child, parent, peers and teacher invariably leads to a far richer picture of any individual's skills and abilities in a particular area.

REFLECTION

What beliefs, assumptions, experiences, criteria might guide a teacher selecting picture books for her culturally diverse group of two- to three-year-old toddlers in a long daycare centre in a socioeconomically disadvantaged area? How will these choices differ if she is making decisions about books for the preschool reading corner in the same centre?

Towards meaningful assessment: Learning stories, rich tasks and portfolios

In the centre or classroom the teacher may gather information from a range of different activities on a number of occasions to make judgements about what students know, what they do not know, how they learn best, the effectiveness of their learning in a particular area and the appropriateness of the decisions that the teacher has made in responding to the students' learning needs and abilities. Ideally, it is always good to share these understandings with other teachers, parents and caregivers because people often respond differently in different contexts.

Learning stories are narratives that frequently include photos used to describe a child's or small group of children's learning process. They may include specific events and interactions, an analysis and a linking to the *Early Years Learning Framework* where appropriate. Learning stories focus on what the child can do.

Portfolios are a way of gathering, organising, presenting and sharing information from a rich variety of sources. These can demonstrate what a learner has achieved over a period of time and is capable of doing in a specific learning area or reflect what they have learnt more generally. They can include both formative (planning a project) and summative artefacts (the final project) as well as reflective statements about the learning process. Sometimes the learner can play a role in choosing the contents to be included, thus becoming an active agent in the process. Eportfolios are becoming more popular given that they enable a range of media to be used to demonstrate achievement by using the latest emerging technologies.

Cumulative portfolios reflect a child's learning over time and are an excellent way to demonstrate the learning journey. Bass and Walker (2015) remind us, however, not to be consumed by such documentation and quote statistics that suggest some early childhood teachers spend too much time and energy on the documentation aspect of their role. Documentation must not take over – its purpose must remain clear and it must be useful for all stakeholders. Some research demonstrates that teachers and educators spend far too much time on the documentation and this reduces their time to focus on intentional teaching.

Figure 12.3 shows an excerpt of a learning story from three-year-old Timothy's portfolio at the beginning of his first term of preschool.

he tapped them together repeating the same pattern he was making earlier.

Educator analysis and reflections:

Timothy spent most of his time in the sandpit playing independently, moving from one area to another, and engaging in a few different experiences with the sand. He demonstrates an enjoyment in using the sand, and also demonstrates the ability to speak up for himself to other children about what he is doing.

mplications for planning:

- Provide opportunities for Timothy to feel a sense of belonging in this new environment, and opportunities for connecting with other children through common interests. "In early childhood and throughout life, relationships are crucial to a sense of belonging" (EYLF, p7)

Figure 12.3 Excerpt from a learning story in a preschooler's portfolio

Rich tasks

Recently there has been a degree of interest in developing relevant assessment tasks that are clearly connected to real-life situations. Often termed **rich assessment tasks**, they draw on the writings of John Dewey (1916), and, more recently Paulo Freire (1985) to allow students to think beyond set boundaries to solve multidimensional problems, and demonstrate deeper learning and understanding about concepts, ideas and issues. Rich tasks are defined as 'culminating performances or demonstrations or products that are purposeful and model a life role' (Education Queensland, 2001, p. 5). For example, a child might be asked to make a robot using as many of the junk materials provided as possible, or build a garage where all the vehicles can be stored, or help design the playground space.

> **Rich assessment tasks** These are assessment tasks that have meaning/purpose and are related to real life activities.

There is no playing the 'guess what's in the teacher's head' game or the typical teacher initiates – students *respond* – teacher provides *evaluation* or *feedback* (IRE/F) cycle that can lead children away from building on each others' ideas and suggestions to think more imaginatively.

Performance-based assessment tasks

Similarly **performance assessment** tasks ask children to combine prior knowledge with recent learning, skills and understanding to demonstrate what they can do. Examples could include an oral presentation about someone who is special to me as discussed in the opening of Chapter 5.

> **Performance assessment** A focus on what students can do with their knowledge and understandings.

Figure 12.4 shows excerpt from five-year-old Timothy's version of Tullet's (2010) highly interactive book *Press Here*. In this book Tullet instructs the reader to press different coloured dots and to shake them. When the reader turns the page their action has led to consequences. For example, pressing the yellow dot firmly might make it larger. Shaking the page might mean the dots have moved on the next page. While Timothy has used Tullet's concepts and modelled the imperative tone used by Tullet, it is his own adaptation. Apart from some help he sought with some spelling Timothy completed the task unassisted.

Both rich tasks and performance assessment tasks help learners develop their understanding and refinement of processes involved with assessment including:

- analysing what is expected in an assessment task to identify critical elements
- understanding the key words (describe, compare, explain and make)
- planning, often visualising, what is involved in responding to the task
- managing time effectively
- reflecting on and processing learning.

Such metacognitive skills certainly relate to Bloom's taxonomy (1956). DeBono's thinking skills (1970) and Gardner's multiple intelligences (1983, Gardner, Kornhaber & Wake, 1996).

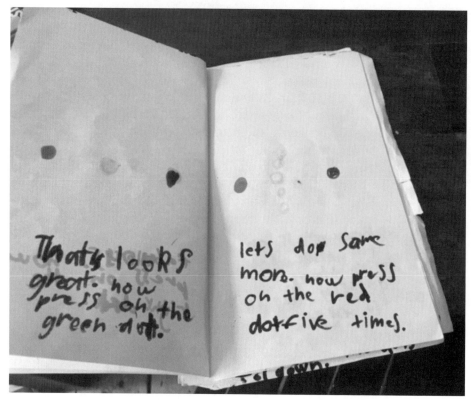

Figure 12.4 Five-year-old Timothy's version of Tullet's book *Press Here*

What skills and understanding do you think Timothy's version of the book might demonstrate? What other examples of Timothy's writing might be useful for the teacher in assessing his writing?

Drawing it all together

Smith and Lovat (2003, p. 169) suggest that evaluation is at the heart of any teaching and curriculum process. Teachers gather evidence to work out where each learner is up to and to make judgements about which learning experiences will help them take the next steps in the learning process. At the same time they need to evaluate the effectiveness of strategies and activities that they are using in facilitating learning processes. It is often a temptation to gather information about those learning behaviours or outcomes that are easy to measure or check off a list. At all times we must remember that just because some things can be measured more easily does not mean they are the only things that should be assessed.

Some teachers feel that mandated national targets and reporting schemes can undermine teachers' decision making in early childhood centres, preschools and school contexts, and therefore these schemes sometimes reduce the role of the teacher to merely one of a technician ticking boxes. It is certainly possible that some teachers feel that their professional decision making has been compromised. One early years learning teacher told us that she did not feel she had time to teach any more: she was so busy checking her children's sight words. Bass and Walker (2015) remind us not to over-document but to stay in the moment with the children we are working with and focus explicitly on our observation, scaffolding, modelling and communicating. William et al. warn us not to allow children to be 'deprived of opportunities to maximise and demonstrate their individual potential' (1999, p. 146).

In making evaluative judgements about learners' literacy development we must not emphasise one kind of assessment approach over another – it must not be an either-or proposition. Teachers must embed a balance of diagnostic, formative and summative assessment approaches and include both assessment *of* and *for* learning. Assessment tasks must produce reliable information based on a range of strategies and ensure multiple opportunities to demonstrate learning. They should allow us to celebrate the child's achievements and set goals for future learning. Learning experiences should be regularly adjusted in response to information gained from assessment tasks. Learners can be involved in ongoing assessment, develop a shared understanding of its purposes and contribute to the collection of the information.

Recent policy documents like *Early Years Learning Framework* (2009) and *The Melbourne Declaration* (MCEETYA, 2008) emphasise the need for creative problem solvers who can engage in collaborative behaviour and work in a sustained way. It is important to further develop quality teaching and learning frameworks that link with the ever-increasing research that points to the importance of imaginative approaches to learning and assessment – even though attributes like creativity, imagination, collaboration, perseverance, resilience can be difficult to measure.

Questions for further discussion

- Choose two examples of assessment strategies that you are not familiar with. Explore these in some detail. What kinds of learning outcomes could be assessed using each one?
- Do you think young children can assess their learning and the work of their peers? How would you introduce these opportunities?
- If the teacher/educator is the main assessor in the early childhood centre or classroom, how can we best foster teacher professional learning in effective assessment?
- The NSW Department of Education and Training has introduced a program called *Best Start*. This assessment program is designed for teachers to assess children at the beginning of their first year of school. The materials include a literacy analysis guide and recording sheet and can be accessed at:

www.curriculumsupport.education.nsw.gov.au/literacy/publications/index
.htm. After examining the materials, do you think the program aligns with the
principles in this chapter?

• How can attributes like creativity, critical thinking, resilience, motivation,
persistence, curiosity, empathy, self-awareness and self-discipline be assessed
in early childhood settings?

Further reading

Bass, S. & Walker, K. (2015). Planning, documentation and assessment. *Early
Childhood Play Matters: Intentional Teaching through Play: Birth to Six Years.*
Melbourne: ACER, pp. 75–90.

Clay, M. (2000). *Concepts About Print: What Have Children Learned about Printed
Language?* Portsmouth, NH: Heinemann.

EYLF (2009)—see Australian Government Department of Education,
Employment and Workplace Relations for the Council of Australian
Governments (2009).

Tullet, H. (2010). *Press Here.* Sydney: Allen and Unwin.

Worthy, J., Conslavo, A., Bogard, T. & Russell, K. (2012) Fostering academic and
social growth in a primary literacy workshop classroom. 'Restorying'
students with negative reputations. *The Elementary School Journal* 112 (4),
pp. 568–89.

References

Australian Government Department of Education, Employment and
Workplace Relations for the Council of Australian Governments (2009).
*Belonging, Being and Becoming. The Early Years Learning Framework for
Australia (EYLF).* Canberra: Commonwealth of Australia. Retrieved at:
www.mychild.gov.au/agenda/early-years-framework.

Black, P. & William, D. (1998). Inside the black box: Raising standards through
classroom assessment. *Phi Delta Kappan*, October, pp. 139–48.

Bloom, B. (1956). *Taxonomy of Educational Objectives: Cognitive Domain.*
Longman: London.

Clay, M. (1987). *The Early Detection of Reading Difficulties* (3rd edn). New
Zealand: Heinemann.

Compton-Lilly, C. (2008). Teaching struggling readers: Capitalizing on diversity
for effective learning. Struggling Readers Column, *The Reading Teacher.*
61(8), pp. 668–72.

Davies, A. (2000). *Making Classroom Assessment Work*. Merville, BC: Connections Publishing.

Davies, M. & Edwards, G. (2001). Will the Curriculum Caterpillar Ever Fly? In M. Fielding (ed.), *Taking Education Really Seriously: Four Years Hard Labour*. London: Routledge Falmer.

De Bono, E. (1970). *Lateral Thinking*. London: Penguin.

Dewey, J. (1916). *Democracy and Education: An Introduction to the Philosophy of Education*. New York: Macmillan.

Education Queensland (2001). *New Basics—The Why, What, How and When of Rich Tasks*. Queensland State Education. Retrieved at: http://education. qld.gov.au/corporate/newbasics/html/richtasks/richtasks.html.

Ewing, R. (2014). *Curriculum and Assessment: Storylines*. Melbourne: Oxford University Press. [Chapters 1 and 4 are key references for this chapter.]

EYLF (2009)—see Australian Government Department of Education, Employment and Workplace Relations for the Council of Australian Governments, (2009)

Freire, P. (1985). *The Politics of Education: Culture, Power and Liberation*. South Hadley, MA: Bergin & Garvey.

Gardner, H. (1983). *Frames of Mind: The Theory of Multiple Intelligences*, New York: Basic Books.

Gardner, H., Kornhaber, M. & Wake, W. (eds) (1996). *Intelligence: Multiple Perspectives*. New York: Harcourt Brace.

Goodman, K. (1973). Miscues: Windows on the reading process. In K. Goodman (ed.), *Miscue Analysis: Applications to Reading Instruction*. Urbana, Il: NCTE, pp. 3–14.

Groundwater-Smith, S. & Nicoll, V. (1980). *Evaluation in the Primary School*. Sydney: Novak.

Groundwater-Smith, S., Ewing, R. & Le Cornu, R. (2014). *Teaching. Challenges and Dilemmas* (5th edn). Melbourne: Cengage, ch. 11.

Kemp, M. (1987). *Watching Children Read and Write*. Melbourne: Nelson Australia.

Literacy Educators Coalition (n.d.). Say No to NAPLAN Sets 1 and 2. Retrieved at: www.literacyeducators.com.au/naplan/naplan-articles, viewed 25 November 2015.

Mason, J. (1991). *When Is Your Child Ready To Read? Primary English Note*. Sydney: Primary English Teaching Association Australia (PETAA).

MCEETYA (2008)—see Ministerial Council on Education, Employment, Trading and Youth Affairs.

Ministerial Council on Education, Employment, Trading and Youth Affairs (MCEETYA) (2008). *Melbourne Declaration on Educational Goals for Young Australians*. Canberra: MCEETYA.

Newmann, F. & Archbald, D. (1992). The nature of authentic academic achievement. In H. Berlak, F. Newmann, E. Adams, D. Archbald, T. Burgess, J. Raven and T. Romberg, *Toward a New Science of Educational Testing and Assessment*. New York: State University of New York Press, pp. 1–21.

Nichols, S. & Berliner, D. (2007). High stakes testing and the corruption of America's Schools. *Harvard Education Letter*, 23(2), pp. 1–2.

Noddings, N. (1992). *The Challenge to Care In Schools : An Alternative Approach to Education*. New York: Teachers College Press.

Schickedanz, J. (1999). *Much More Than The ABCs: The Early Stages of Reading and Writing*. Washington, DC: NAEYC.

Smith, D. & Lovat, D. (2003). *Curriculum. Action on Reflection* (4th edn). Melbourne: Thomson, ch. 12.

Stefanakis, E. (2002). *Multiple Intelligences and Portfolios*. Portsmouth, NH: Heinemann.

Tanner, D. (2001). *Authentic Assessment: A Solution, or Part of the Problem?* Chapel Hill, NC: University of North Carolina Press.

Van Manen, M. (1995). On the epistemology of reflective practice. *Teachers and Teaching: Theory and Practice* 1(1), pp. 33–50.

Williams, D., Johnson, B, Peters, J. with Cormack, P. (1999). Assessment: From standardised to authentic approaches. In B. Johnson and A. Reid (eds). *Contesting the Curriculum*. Katoomba: Social Science Press.

Index